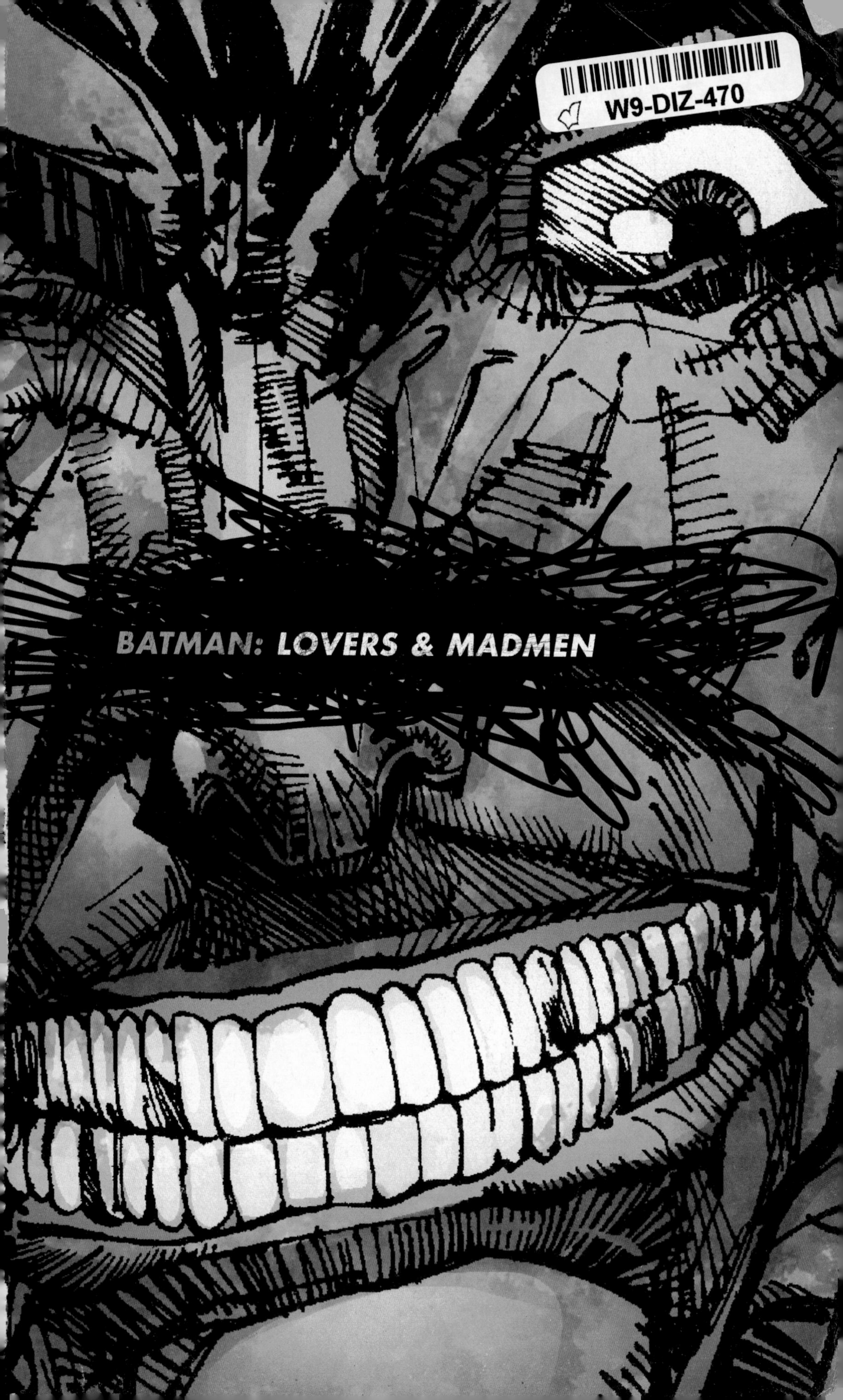
BATMAN: LOVERS & MADMEN

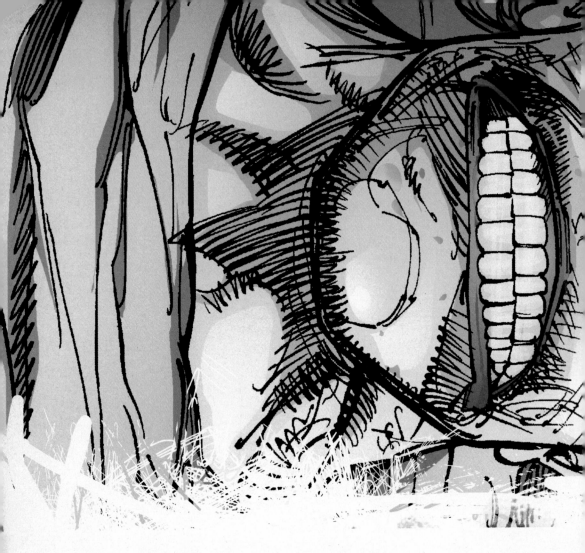

BATMAN: LOV

MICHAEL GREEN writer   **DENYS COWAN** penciller

I.L.L. colorist

BATMAN created by **BOB KANE**

DAN DIDIO Senior VP-Executive Editor | **MIKE CARLIN** Editor-original series | **TOM PALMER, JR.** Associate Editor-original series
PETER HAMBOUSSI Editor-collected edition | **ROBBIN BROSTERMAN** Senior Art Director | **PAUL LEVITZ** President & Publisher
GEORG BREWER VP-Design & DC Direct Creative | **RICHARD BRUNING** Senior VP-Creative Director | **PATRICK CALDON**
Executive VP-Finance & Operations | **CHRIS CARAMALIS** VP-Finance | **JOHN CUNNINGHAM** VP-Marketing | **TERRI CUNNINGHAM**
VP-Managing Editor | **ALISON GILL** VP-Manufacturing | **DAVID HYDE** VP-Publicity | **HANK KANALZ** VP-General Manager, WildStorm
JIM LEE Editorial Director-WildStorm | **PAULA LOWITT** Senior VP-Business & Legal Affairs | **MARYELLEN MCLAUGHLIN**
VP-Advertising & Custom Publishing | **JOHN NEE** Senior VP-Business Development | **GREGORY NOVECK** Senior VP-Creative Affairs
SUE POHJA VP-Book Trade Sales | **STEVE ROTTERDAM** Senior VP-Sales & Marketing | **CHERYL RUBIN** Senior VP-Brand
Management | **JEFF TROJAN** VP-Business Development, DC Direct | **BOB WAYNE** VP-Sales

RS & MADMEN

JOHN FLOYD inker

TRAVIS LANHAM   **KEN LOPEZ** letterers

Cover art by Denys Cowan and John Floyd | Publication design by Amelia Grohman | Thanks to Craig "Rex" Perry

BATMAN: LOVERS AND MADMEN
Published by DC Comics. Cover, introduction and compilation Copyright © 2008 DC Comics. All Rights Reserved.
Originally published in single magazine form in BATMAN CONFIDENTIAL #7-12. Copyright © 2007, 2008 DC Comics.
All Rights Reserved. All characters, their distinctive likenesses and related elements featured in this publication are
trademarks of DC Comics. The stories, characters and incidents featured in this publication are entirely fictional.
DC Comics does not read or accept unsolicited submissions of ideas, stories or artwork.

DC COMICS | 1700 Broadway, New York, NY 10019 | A Warner Bros. Entertainment Company.
Printed in Canada.   First Printing.   HC ISBN: 978-1-4012-1683-2   SC ISBN: 978-1-4012-1742-6

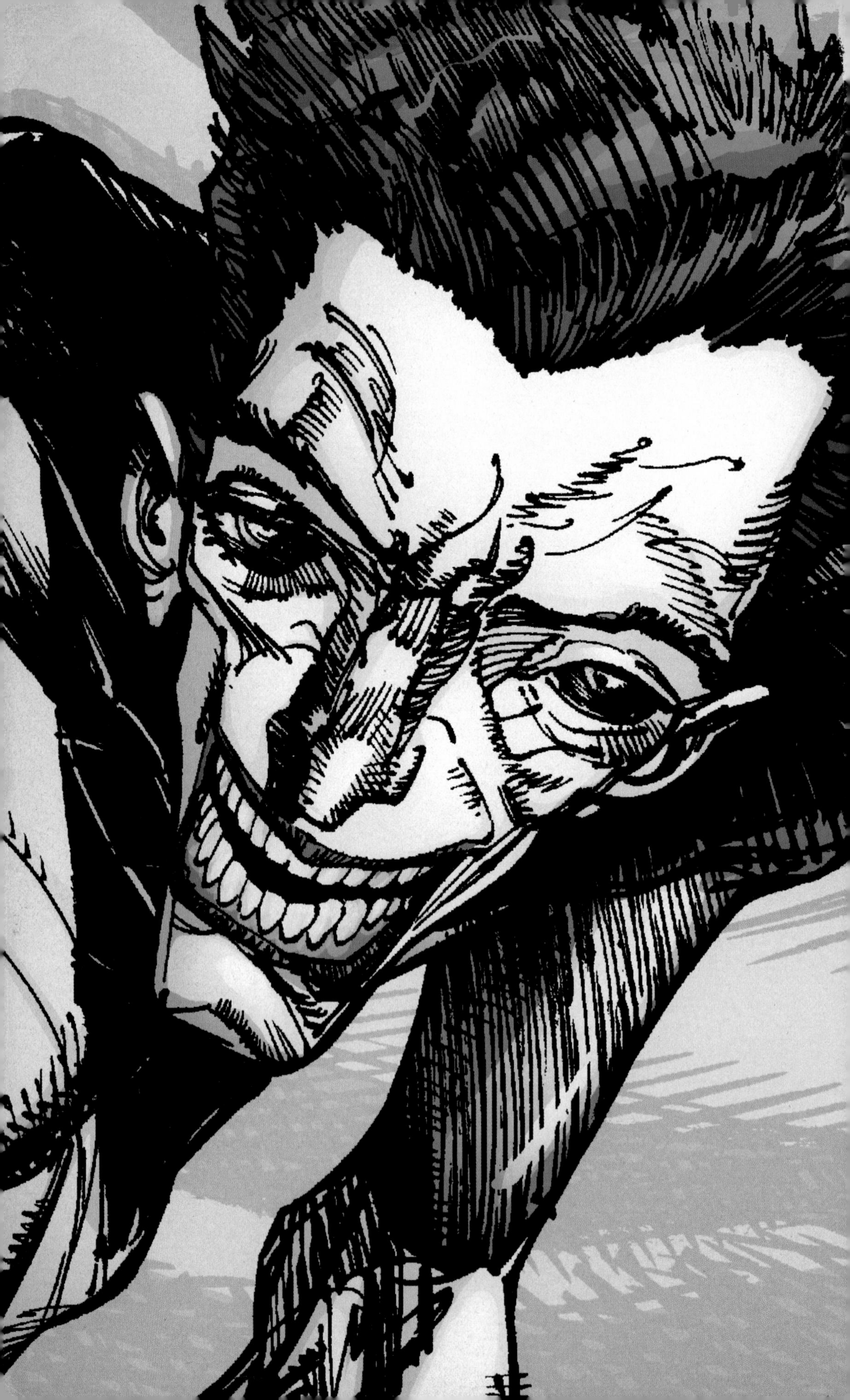

EVERYONE
WANTS TO
WRITE THE JOKER.

Imagine the moment: DC Comics gives you the chance to write your first Batman story. Now who do you want him to fight?

Exactly.

The Joker.

But it's hard to write the Joker.

Not because he's a tough character to understand. He's easy to understand. He's insane. And for nearly sixty years, writers and artists have filled comic book after comic book with literally thousands of examples of that insanity in action.

The problem is, over the years, far too many people have taken "insane" to mean "funny." And so they give us stories of the Joker being "funny." He laughs, he squirts the lapel flower, he electrocutes people with the hand buzzer. Oh, ho, ho. That's our Joker.

And that's fine.

But the best Joker stories, the ones we put up on the pedestal, come from the people who understand that "insane" can also mean "scary." Insanity isn't just a dumb one-liner and some oversized HAHAHAHA dialogue. Insanity is madness. Madness is darkness. And darkness is the Batman.

That's what Michael Green understands in LOVERS & MADMEN. See the title? Get it? Not Madman. Madmen. Two exceptionally angry, haunted, obsessed and gifted men aimed straight at each other. That's not just a good fight. It's a terrifying fight.

You can see it on nearly every page. Look at the scene with Dr. Crane (nice touch): Batman calls the Joker a criminal, and Crane replies, "He's not a criminal. This isn't crime. This is evil." Look at the calm, haunting moment—rendered so eerily by the masterful Denys Cowan—at the end of Chapter One where the Joker says that Batman looks…ridiculous. Or when he asks the little girl at the circus who he should spray first—which turns into one of the few Joker killings that actually bothered me after.

That is madness. It's at the core of both characters. It's why an examination of one must include an examination of the other. As the story says, "I owe it all to you. I didn't know what to do with myself till a man put on a mask and called himself Bat."

And that's why Michael Green is so good.

Sure, there are other reasons. Read it. You'll see. But by the end, you'll realize one truth that can't be ignored: a truly great Joker story can't help but explore Batman as well. And it's why everyone who writes Batman wants to write the Joker.

Plus, Joker calls Batman "bunny," which makes me laugh every time.

Brad Meltzer Fort Lauderdale, Florida 2008

Brad Meltzer is the best-selling author of The Book of Fate, The Tenth Justice, The Millionaires and The Zero Game. He is also the author of the critically acclaimed comic books IDENTITY CRISIS, GREEN ARROW: ARCHER'S QUEST and JUSTICE LEAGUE OF AMERICA: THE TORNADO'S PATH.

chapter one IT'S FUNNY

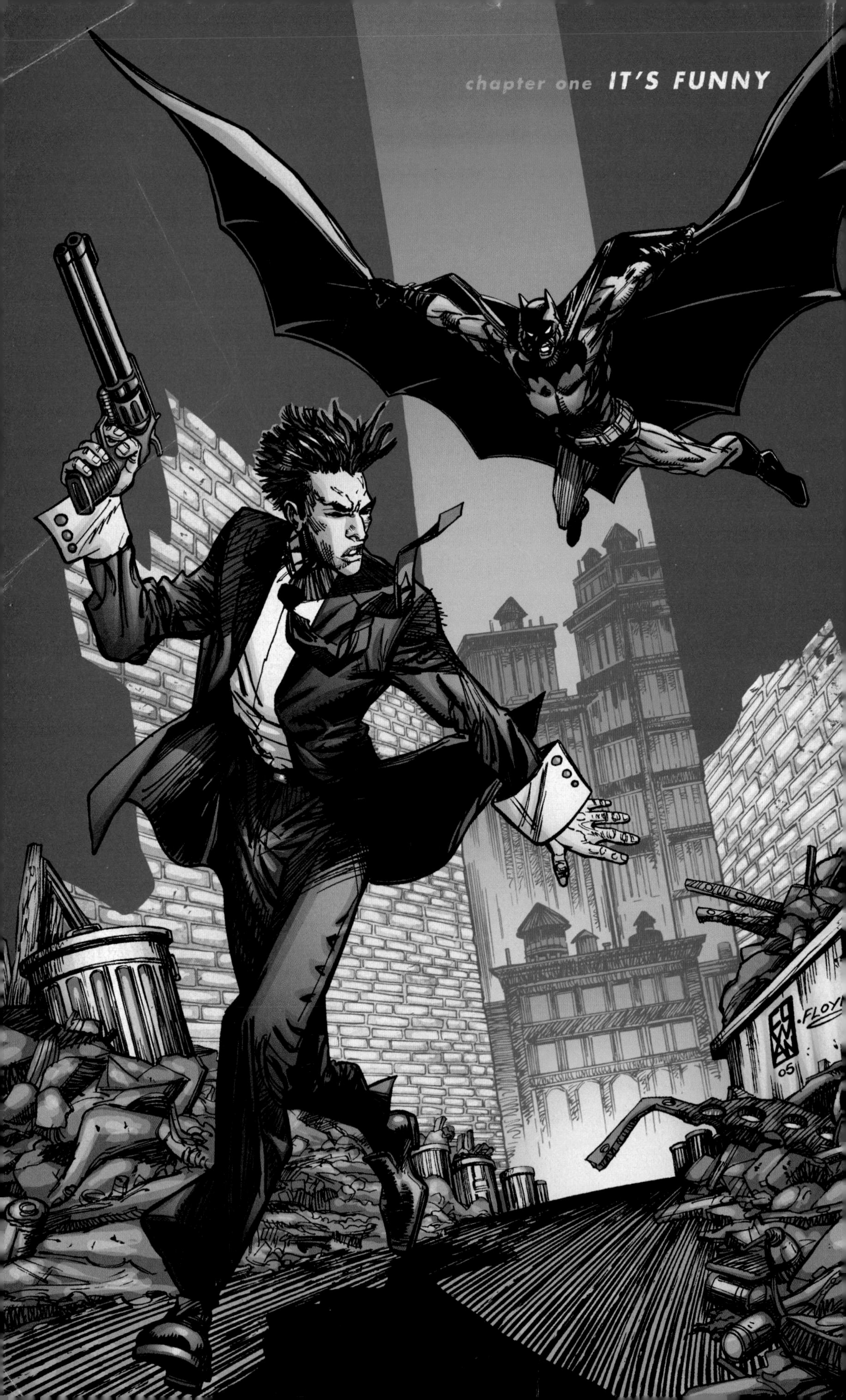

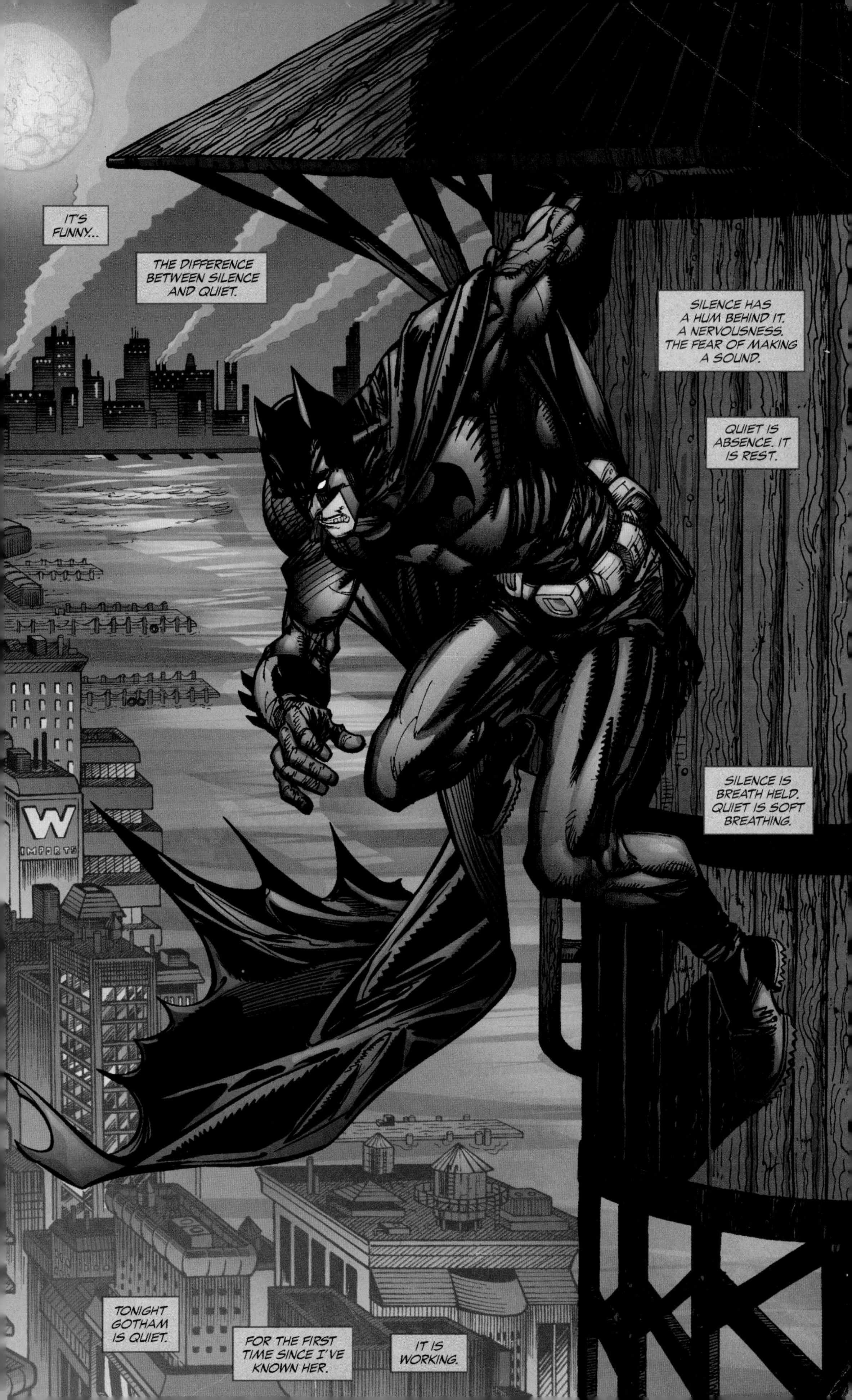
IT'S FUNNY...
THE DIFFERENCE BETWEEN SILENCE AND QUIET.
SILENCE HAS A HUM BEHIND IT. A NERVOUSNESS. THE FEAR OF MAKING A SOUND.
QUIET IS ABSENCE. IT IS REST.
SILENCE IS BREATH HELD. QUIET IS SOFT BREATHING.
TONIGHT GOTHAM IS QUIET.
FOR THE FIRST TIME SINCE I'VE KNOWN HER.
IT IS WORKING.
W
IMPORTS

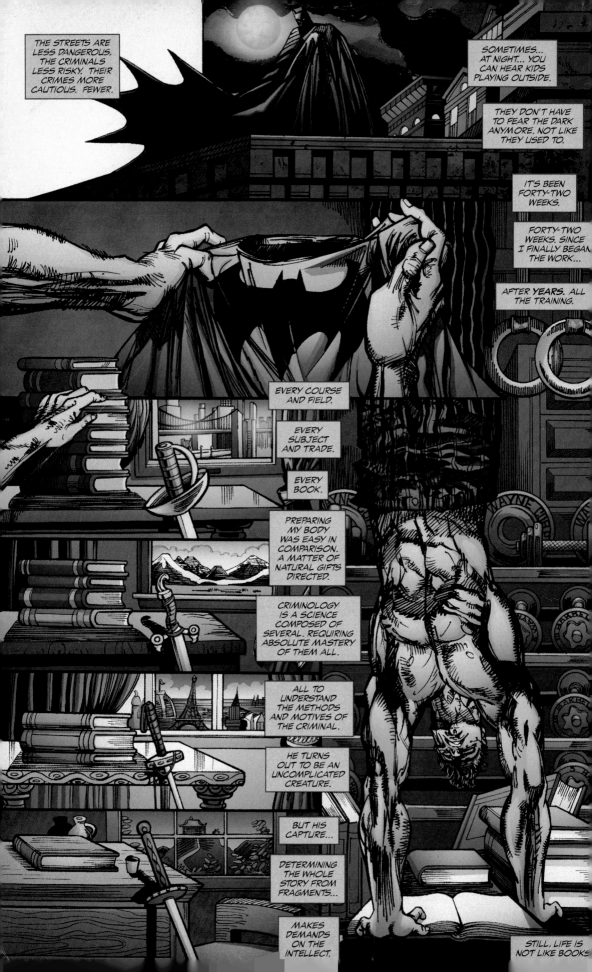

THE STREETS ARE LESS DANGEROUS. THE CRIMINALS LESS RISKY. THEIR CRIMES MORE CAUTIOUS. FEWER.

SOMETIMES... AT NIGHT... YOU CAN HEAR KIDS PLAYING OUTSIDE.

THEY DON'T HAVE TO FEAR THE DARK ANYMORE. NOT LIKE THEY USED TO.

IT'S BEEN FORTY-TWO WEEKS.

FORTY-TWO WEEKS. SINCE I FINALLY BEGAN THE WORK...

AFTER YEARS. ALL THE TRAINING.

EVERY COURSE AND FIELD.

EVERY SUBJECT AND TRADE.

EVERY BOOK.

PREPARING MY BODY WAS EASY IN COMPARISON. A MATTER OF NATURAL GIFTS DIRECTED.

CRIMINOLOGY IS A SCIENCE COMPOSED OF SEVERAL. REQUIRING ABSOLUTE MASTERY OF THEM ALL.

ALL TO UNDERSTAND THE METHODS AND MOTIVES OF THE CRIMINAL.

HE TURNS OUT TO BE AN UNCOMPLICATED CREATURE.

BUT HIS CAPTURE...

DETERMINING THE WHOLE STORY FROM FRAGMENTS...

MAKES DEMANDS ON THE INTELLECT.

STILL, LIFE IS NOT LIKE BOOKS

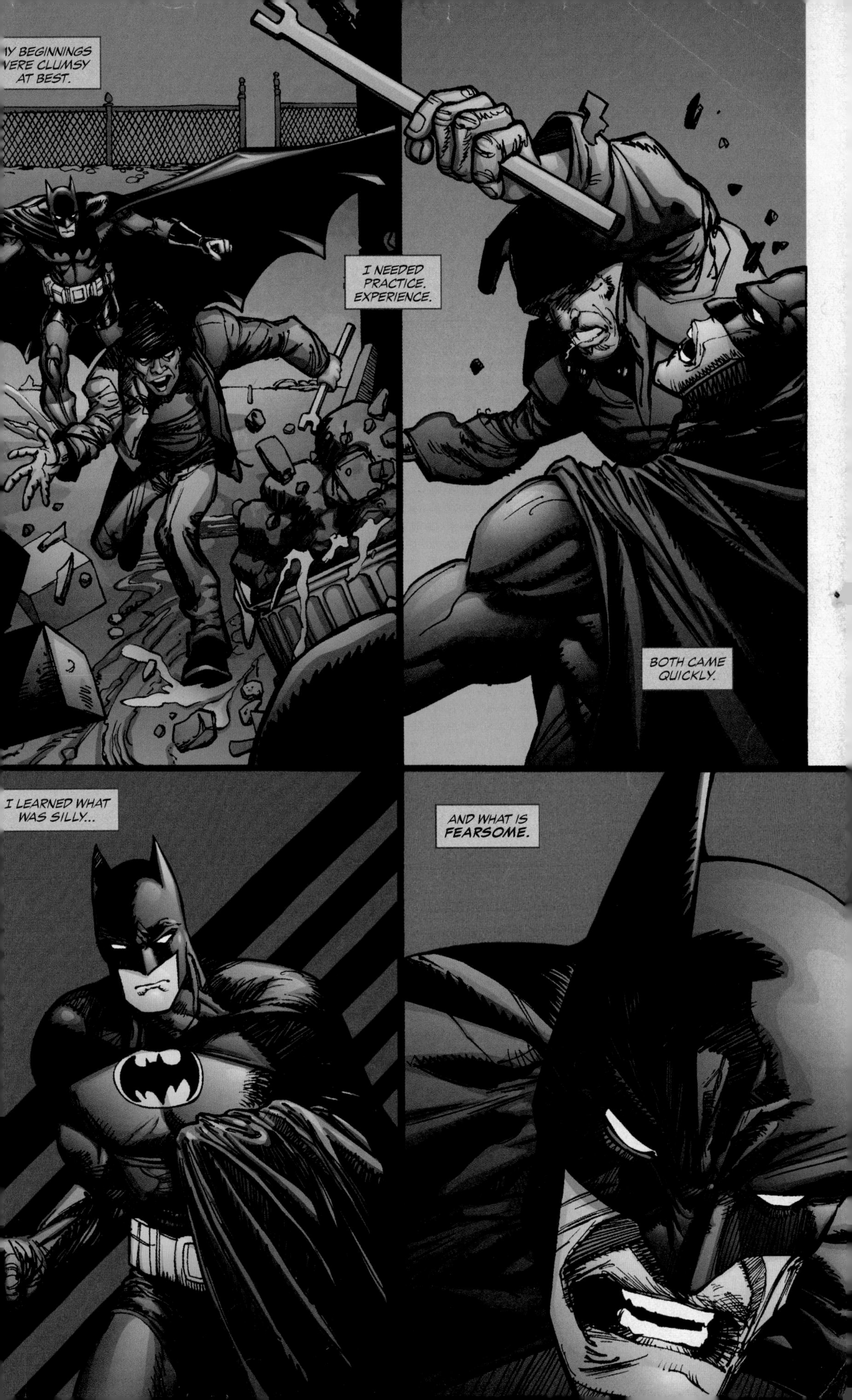
MY BEGINNINGS WERE CLUMSY AT BEST.
I NEEDED PRACTICE. EXPERIENCE.
BOTH CAME QUICKLY.
I LEARNED WHAT WAS SILLY...
AND WHAT IS FEARSOME.

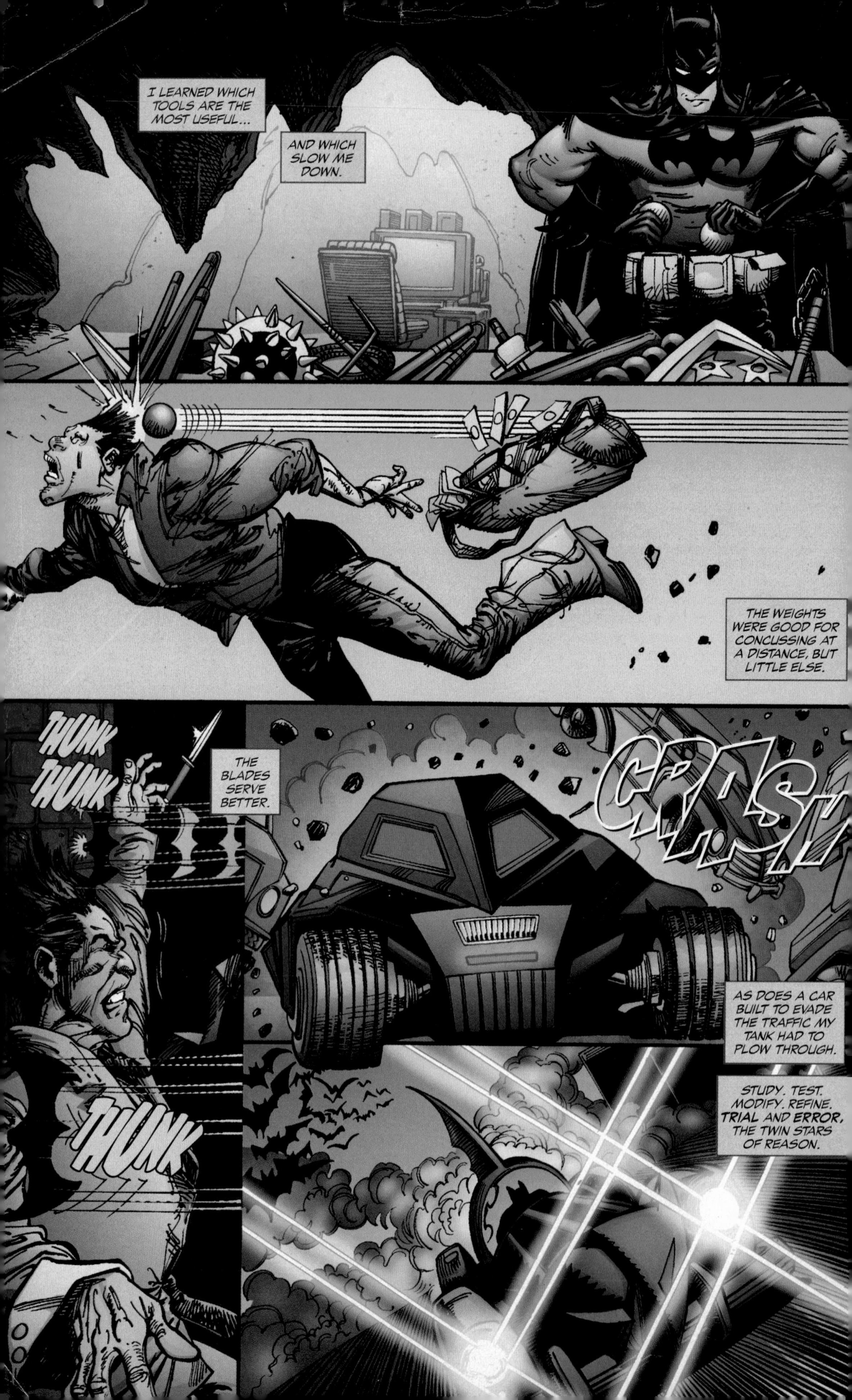
I LEARNED WHICH TOOLS ARE THE MOST USEFUL...
AND WHICH SLOW ME DOWN.
THE WEIGHTS WERE GOOD FOR CONCUSSING AT A DISTANCE, BUT LITTLE ELSE.
THUNK THUNK
THE BLADES SERVE BETTER.
THUNK
CRASH
AS DOES A CAR BUILT TO EVADE THE TRAFFIC MY TANK HAD TO PLOW THROUGH.
STUDY. TEST. MODIFY. REFINE. TRIAL AND ERROR, THE TWIN STARS OF REASON.

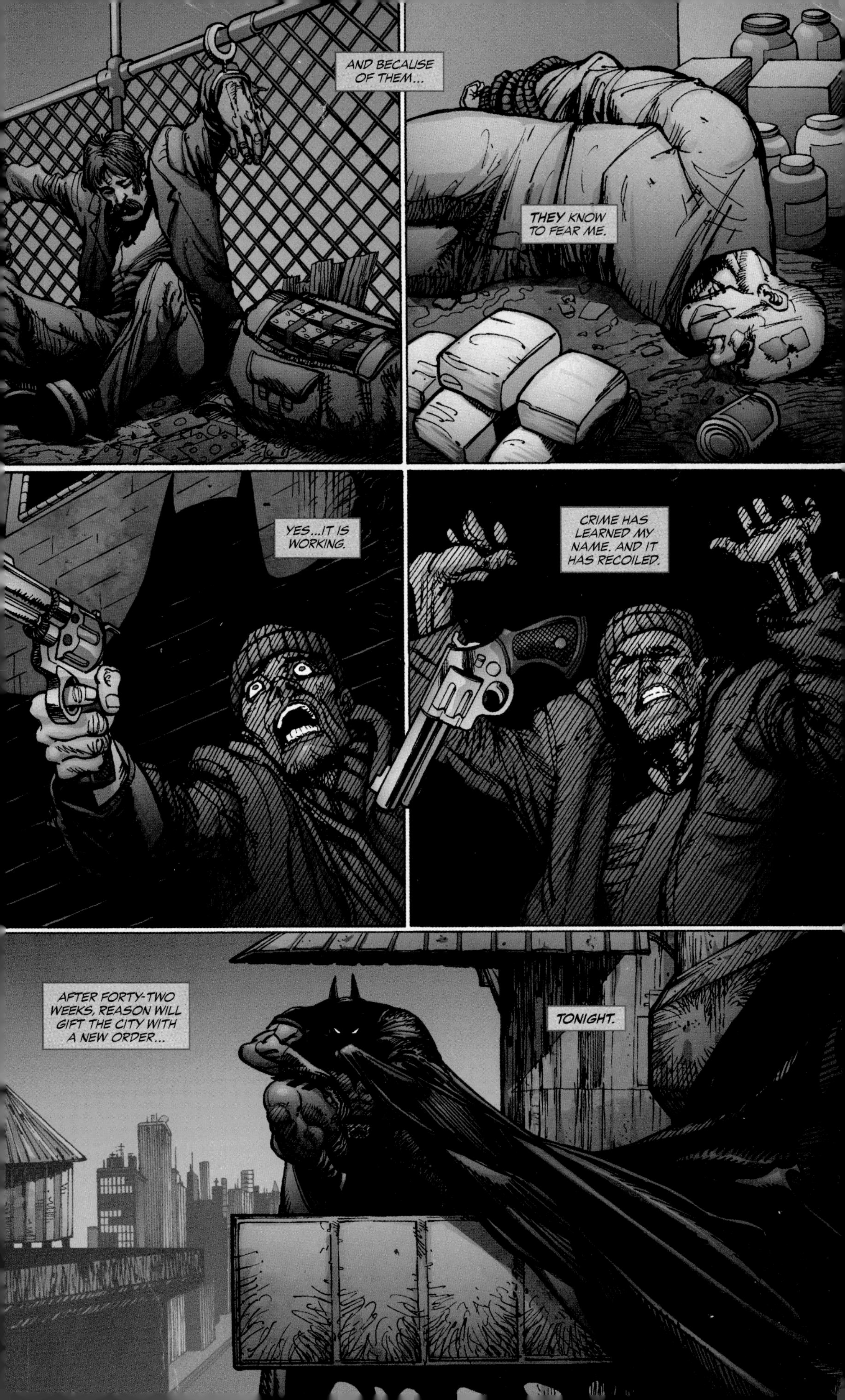
AND BECAUSE OF THEM...
THEY KNOW TO FEAR ME.
YES...IT IS WORKING.
CRIME HAS LEARNED MY NAME. AND IT HAS RECOILED.
AFTER FORTY-TWO WEEKS, REASON WILL GIFT THE CITY WITH A NEW ORDER...
TONIGHT.

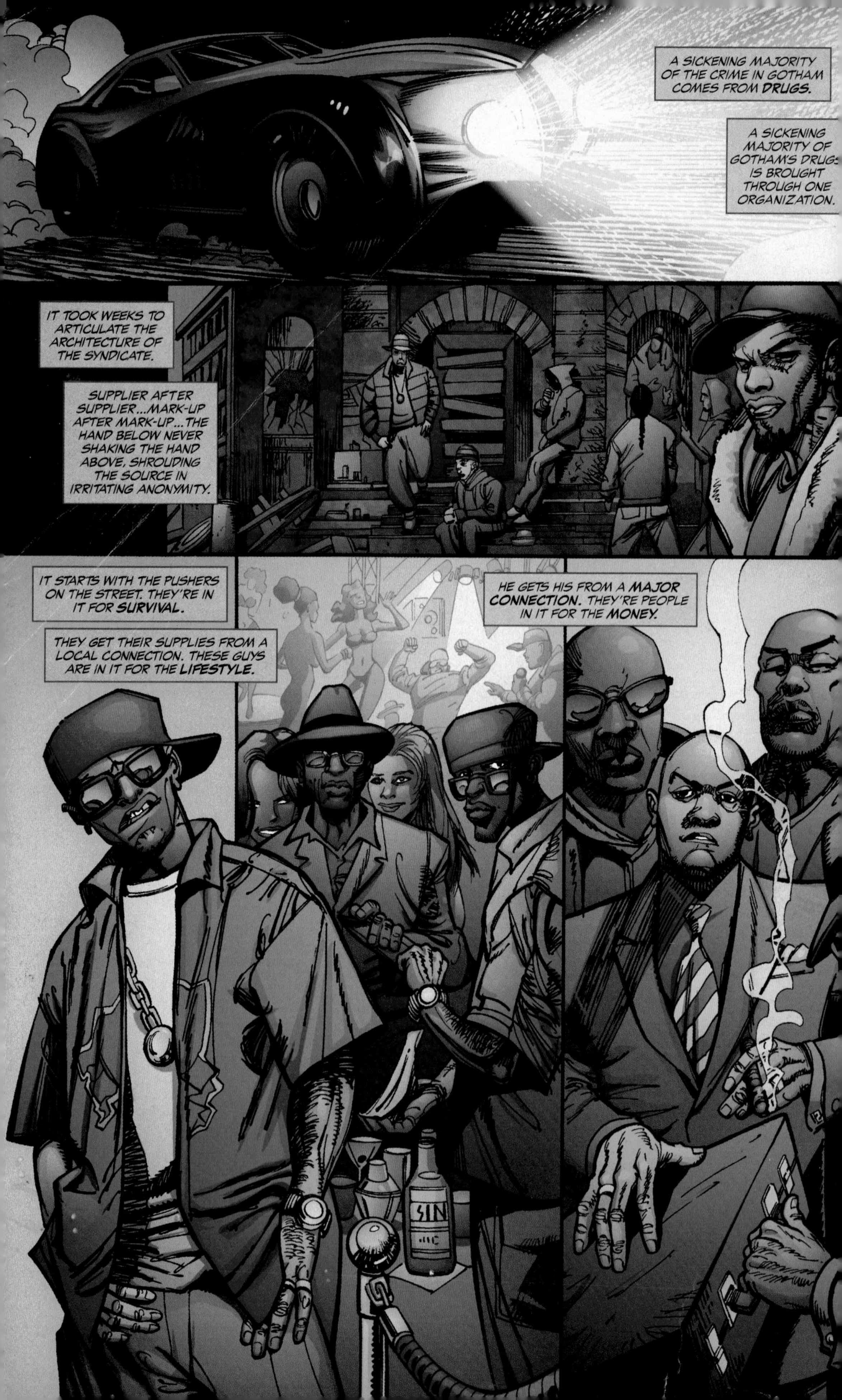

A SICKENING MAJORITY OF THE CRIME IN GOTHAM COMES FROM **DRUGS**.
A SICKENING MAJORITY OF GOTHAM'S DRUGS IS BROUGHT THROUGH ONE ORGANIZATION.
IT TOOK WEEKS TO ARTICULATE THE ARCHITECTURE OF THE SYNDICATE.
SUPPLIER AFTER SUPPLIER...MARK-UP AFTER MARK-UP...THE HAND BELOW NEVER SHAKING THE HAND ABOVE, SHROUDING THE SOURCE IN IRRITATING ANONYMITY.
IT STARTS WITH THE PUSHERS ON THE STREET. THEY'RE IN IT FOR **SURVIVAL**.
THEY GET THEIR SUPPLIES FROM A LOCAL CONNECTION. THESE GUYS ARE IN IT FOR THE **LIFESTYLE**.
HE GETS HIS FROM A **MAJOR CONNECTION**. THEY'RE PEOPLE IN IT FOR THE **MONEY**.

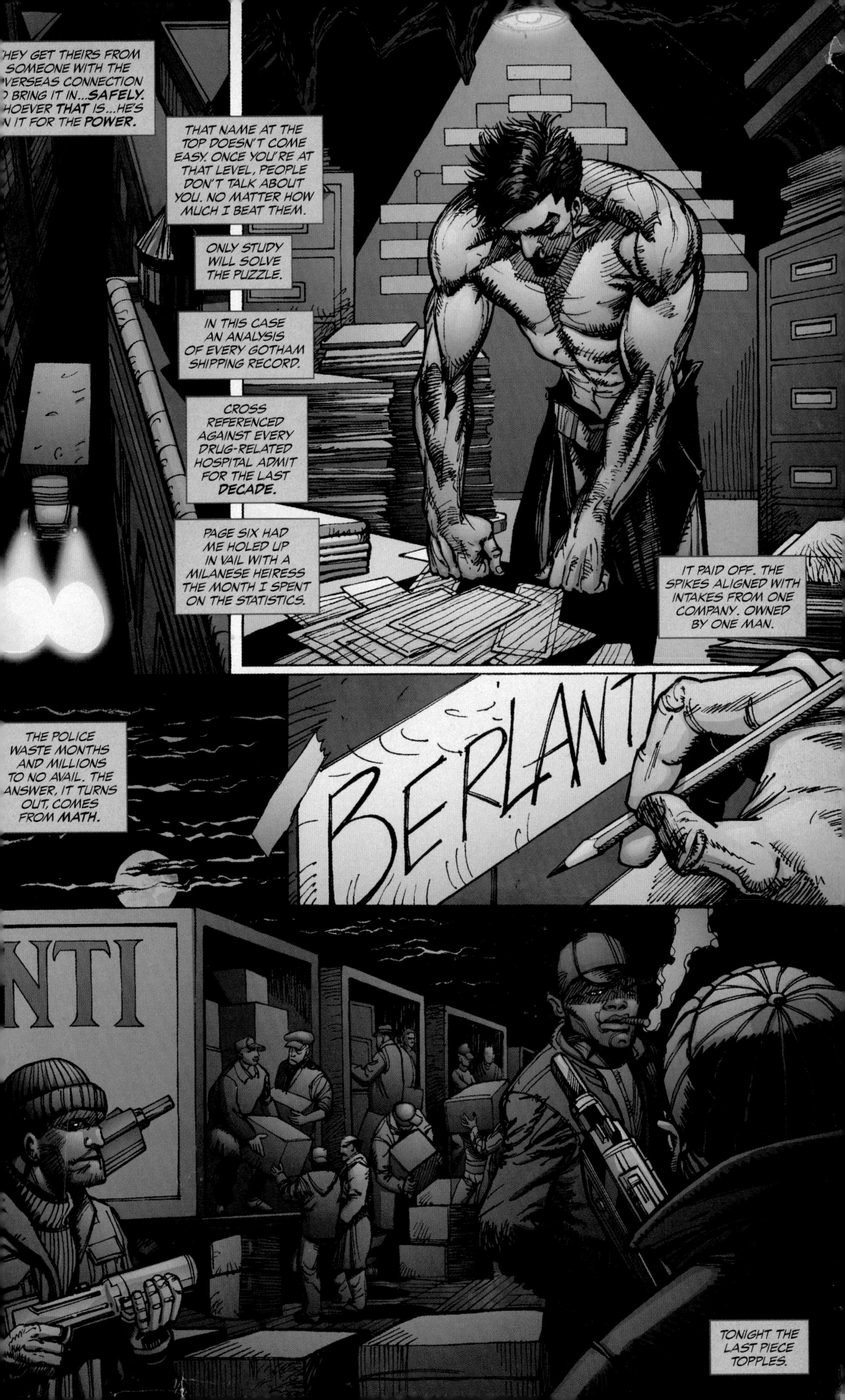

HEY GET THEIRS FROM SOMEONE WITH THE VERSEAS CONNECTION O BRING IT IN...SAFELY. HOEVER THAT IS...HE'S N IT FOR THE POWER.
THAT NAME AT THE TOP DOESN'T COME EASY. ONCE YOU'RE AT THAT LEVEL, PEOPLE DON'T TALK ABOUT YOU. NO MATTER HOW MUCH I BEAT THEM.
ONLY STUDY WILL SOLVE THE PUZZLE.
IN THIS CASE AN ANALYSIS OF EVERY GOTHAM SHIPPING RECORD.
CROSS REFERENCED AGAINST EVERY DRUG-RELATED HOSPITAL ADMIT FOR THE LAST DECADE.
PAGE SIX HAD ME HOLED UP IN VAIL WITH A MILANESE HEIRESS THE MONTH I SPENT ON THE STATISTICS.
IT PAID OFF. THE SPIKES ALIGNED WITH INTAKES FROM ONE COMPANY. OWNED BY ONE MAN.
THE POLICE WASTE MONTHS AND MILLIONS TO NO AVAIL. THE ANSWER, IT TURNS OUT, COMES FROM MATH.
BERLANTI
NTI
TONIGHT THE LAST PIECE TOPPLES.

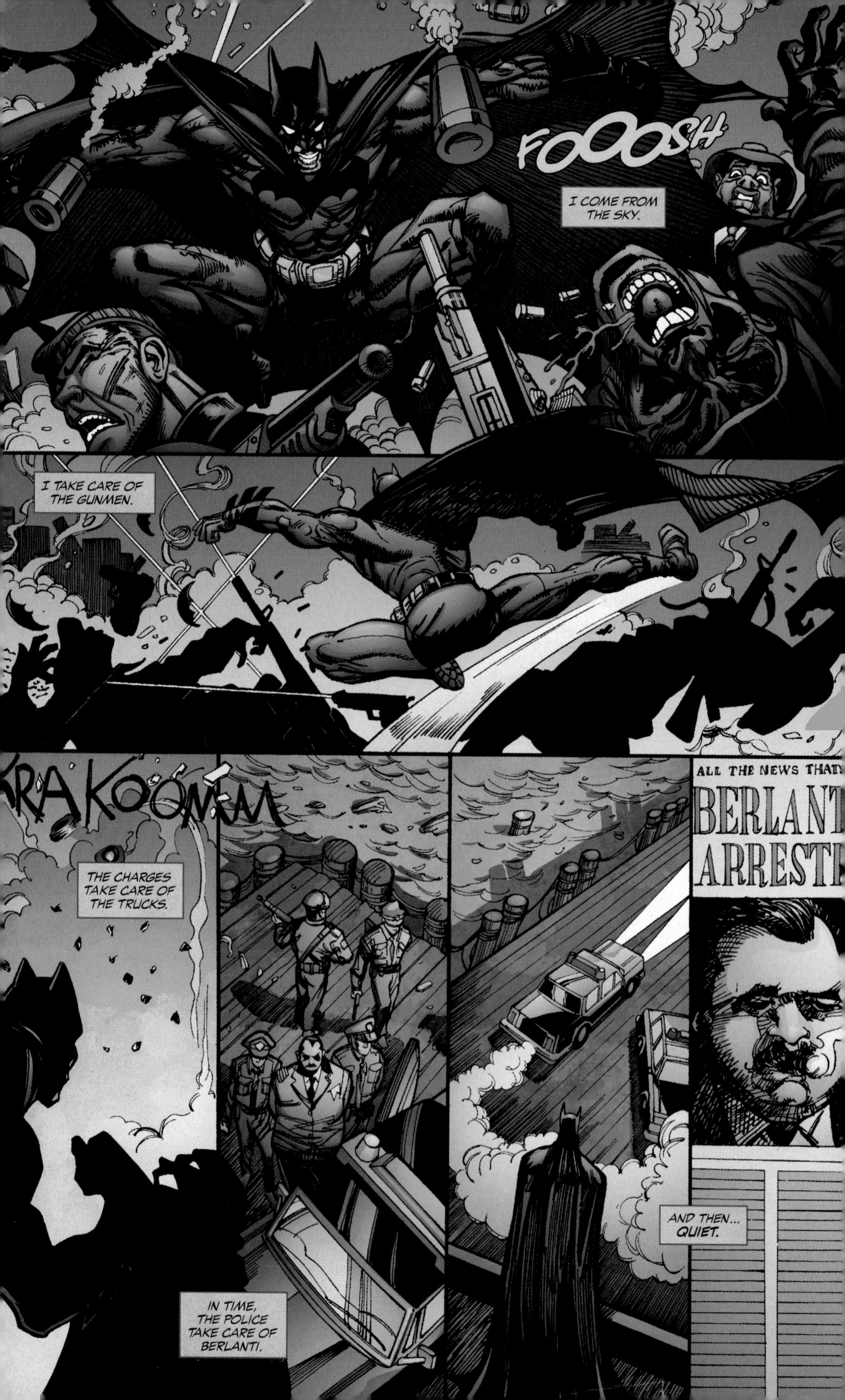
FOOOSH
I COME FROM THE SKY.
I TAKE CARE OF THE GUNMEN.
KRAKOOMM
THE CHARGES TAKE CARE OF THE TRUCKS.
IN TIME, THE POLICE TAKE CARE OF BERLANTI.
AND THEN... QUIET.
ALL THE NEWS THAT'S
BERLANT
ARREST

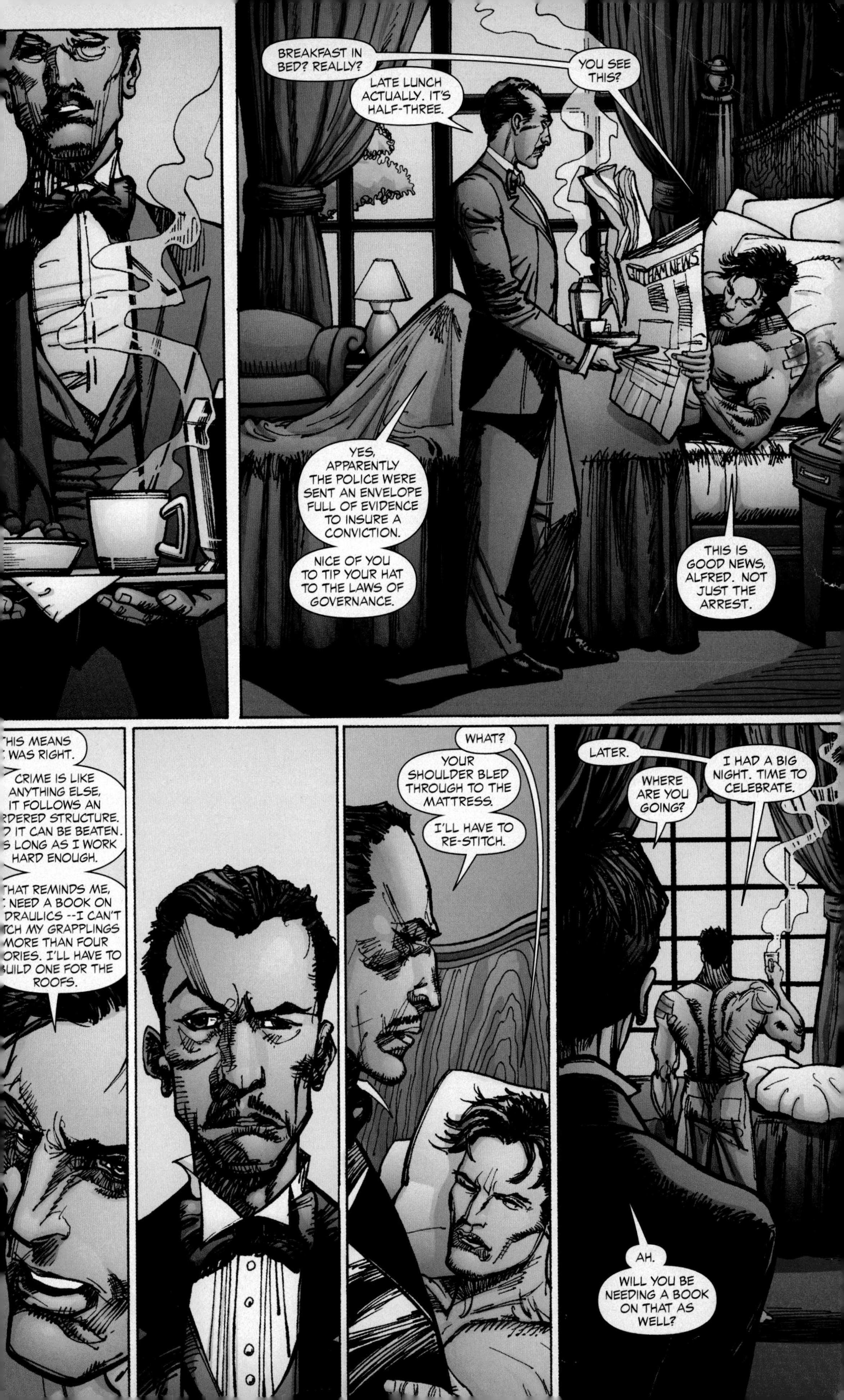

BREAKFAST IN BED? REALLY?
LATE LUNCH ACTUALLY. IT'S HALF-THREE.
YOU SEE THIS?
GOTHAM NEWS
YES, APPARENTLY THE POLICE WERE SENT AN ENVELOPE FULL OF EVIDENCE TO INSURE A CONVICTION.
NICE OF YOU TO TIP YOUR HAT TO THE LAWS OF GOVERNANCE.
THIS IS GOOD NEWS, ALFRED. NOT JUST THE ARREST.
THIS MEANS WAS RIGHT.
CRIME IS LIKE ANYTHING ELSE, IT FOLLOWS AN RDERED STRUCTURE. IT CAN BE BEATEN. S LONG AS I WORK HARD ENOUGH.
THAT REMINDS ME, NEED A BOOK ON DRAULICS --I CAN'T TCH MY GRAPPLINGS MORE THAN FOUR ORIES. I'LL HAVE TO UILD ONE FOR THE ROOFS.
WHAT?
YOUR SHOULDER BLED THROUGH TO THE MATTRESS.
I'LL HAVE TO RE-STITCH.
LATER.
WHERE ARE YOU GOING?
I HAD A BIG NIGHT. TIME TO CELEBRATE.
AH.
WILL YOU BE NEEDING A BOOK ON THAT AS WELL?

PICASSO'S HARLEQUINS

THE EXHIBIT WAS SUPPOSED TO CLOSE YESTERDAY. I MADE A CALL. CHEATING, I KNOW...BUT I'M CELEBRATING.

BUMP

OH.

SOR... ABOU... THAT

DO YOU KNOW WHICH WAY TO THE HARLEQUINS? I WAS HOPING TO CATCH THEM TODAY.

NORTH WING. YOU'RE IN LUCK, THEY EXTENDED THE EXHIBIT BY A DAY.

SOME VERY ENTITLED-FEELING DONORS ASKED TO SEE IT. MY BOSSES OBLIGED.

THEN YOU WORK HERE.

I'M *SUPPOSED* TO BE WORKING HERE--I JUST LEFT A MORISOT DRAWING IN THE MIDDLE OF A DELICATE RESTORATION SO I COULD GIVE A PRIVATE TOUR.

FOR THESE DONORS?

FOR THESE GIN-FUELED BLUEBLOODS WHO COULDN'T TELL A PICASSO'S HARLEQUIN FROM A PISSARRO'S HOARFROST FROM A RAY'S PIZZA.

I'M LORNA, BY THE WAY. LORNA SHORE.

FIGURE IF YOU'RE GETTING MY LIFE STORY YOU SHOULD PROBABLY KNOW MY NAME.

UM...WANNA TELL ME YOURS?

WHY ARE YOU SMILING? IT'S A COMMON QUESTION.

I DON'T GET ASKED THAT A LOT.

PEOPLE DON'T LIKE YOU?

PEOPLE USUALLY KNOW ME FIRST.

WHY? ARE YOU SOMEONE WORTH KNOWING?

I'M NOT SURE.

GOOD. I LIKE A GUY WITH SELF-ESTEEM.

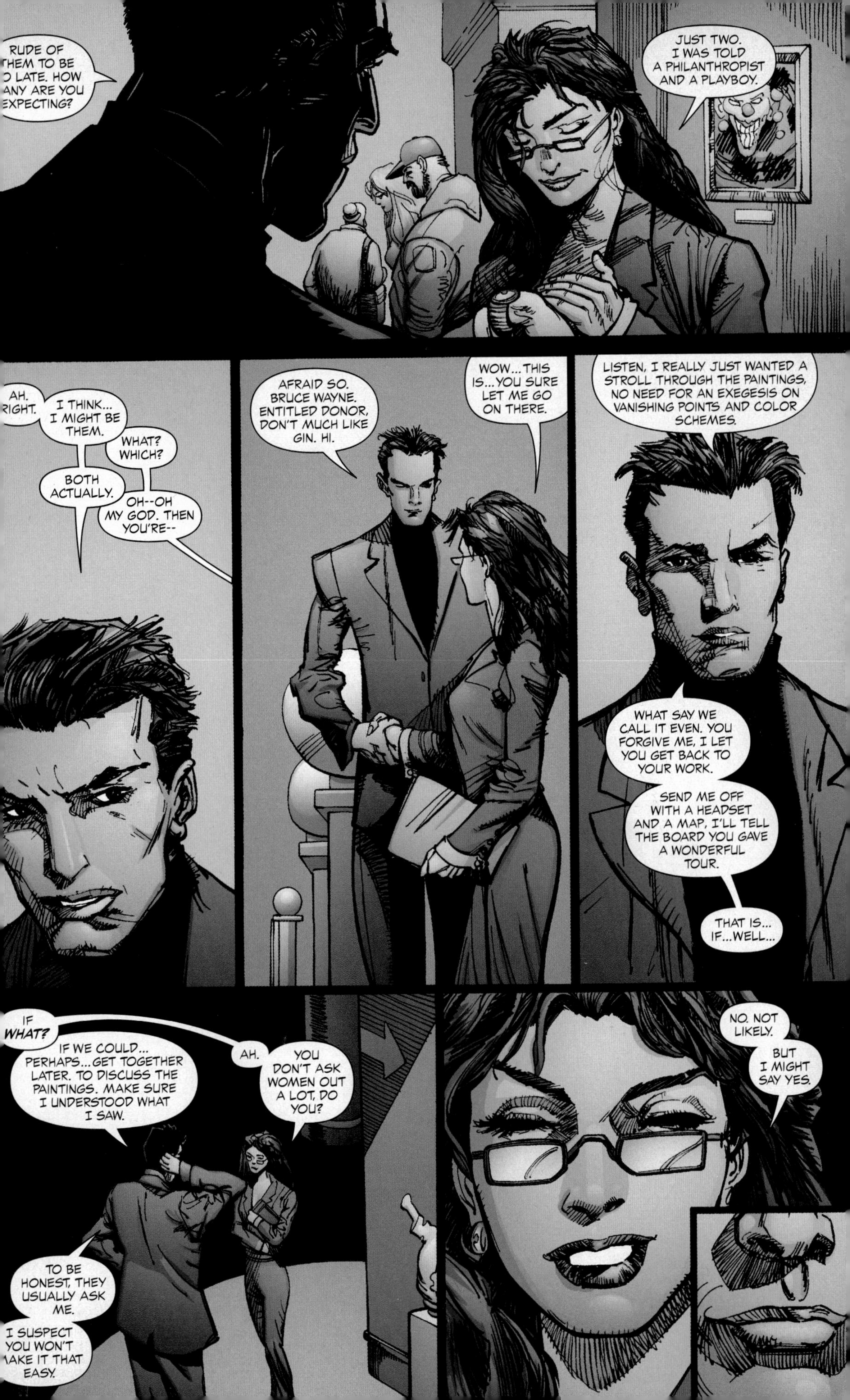
RUDE OF
THEM TO BE
O LATE. HOW
ANY ARE YOU
EXPECTING?
JUST TWO. I WAS TOLD A PHILANTHROPIST AND A PLAYBOY.
AH. RIGHT.
I THINK... I MIGHT BE THEM.
WHAT? WHICH?
BOTH ACTUALLY.
OH--OH MY GOD. THEN YOU'RE--
AFRAID SO. BRUCE WAYNE. ENTITLED DONOR, DON'T MUCH LIKE GIN. HI.
WOW...THIS IS...YOU SURE LET ME GO ON THERE.
LISTEN, I REALLY JUST WANTED A STROLL THROUGH THE PAINTINGS, NO NEED FOR AN EXEGESIS ON VANISHING POINTS AND COLOR SCHEMES.
WHAT SAY WE CALL IT EVEN. YOU FORGIVE ME, I LET YOU GET BACK TO YOUR WORK.
SEND ME OFF WITH A HEADSET AND A MAP, I'LL TELL THE BOARD YOU GAVE A WONDERFUL TOUR.
THAT IS... IF...WELL...
IF WHAT?
IF WE COULD... PERHAPS...GET TOGETHER LATER. TO DISCUSS THE PAINTINGS. MAKE SURE I UNDERSTOOD WHAT I SAW.
AH.
YOU DON'T ASK WOMEN OUT A LOT, DO YOU?
TO BE HONEST, THEY USUALLY ASK ME.
I SUSPECT YOU WON'T
AKE IT THAT EASY.
NO. NOT LIKELY.
BUT I MIGHT SAY YES.

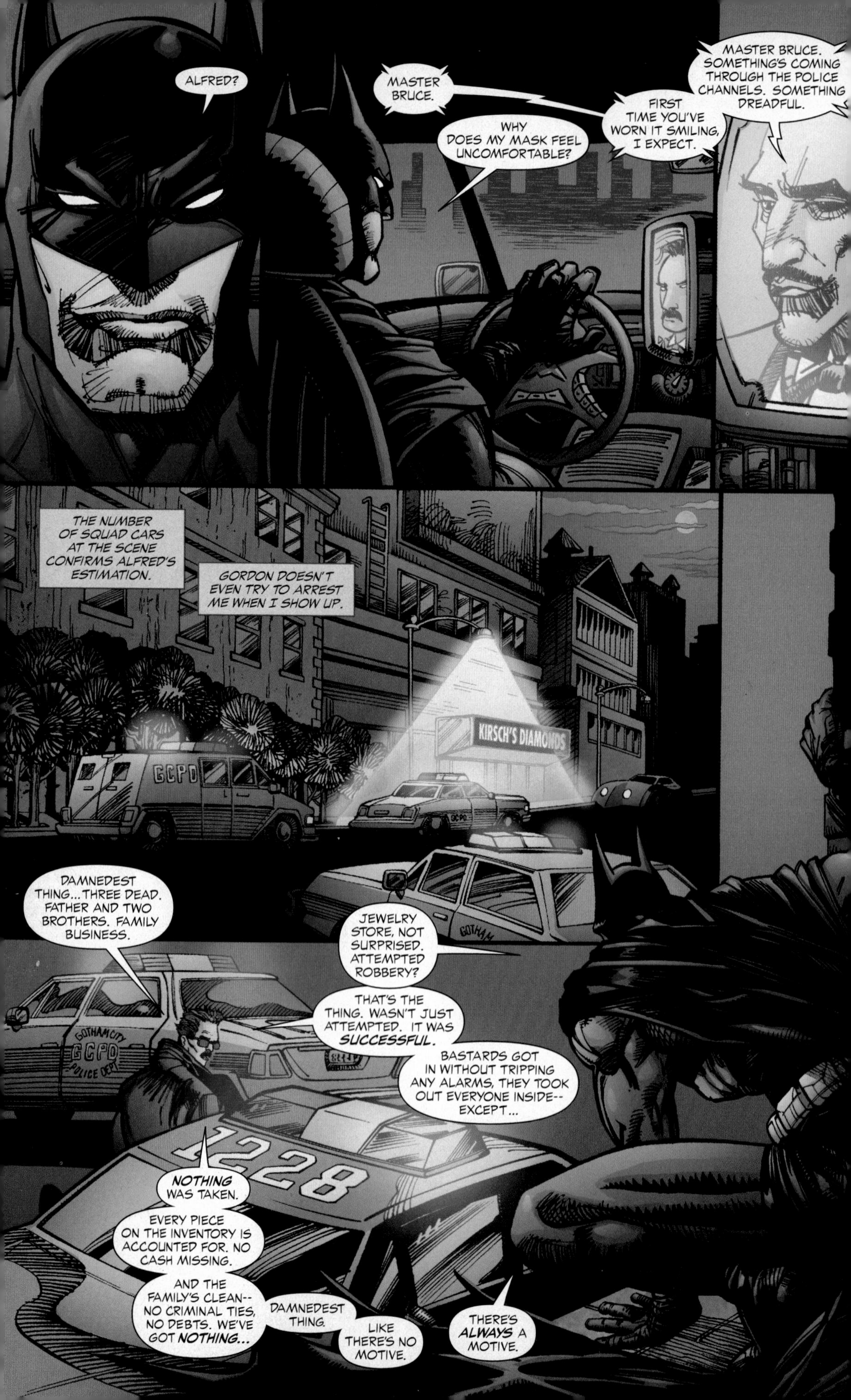
ALFRED?
MASTER BRUCE.
WHY DOES MY MASK FEEL UNCOMFORTABLE?
FIRST TIME YOU'VE WORN IT SMILING, I EXPECT.
MASTER BRUCE. SOMETHING'S COMING THROUGH THE POLICE CHANNELS. SOMETHING DREADFUL.
THE NUMBER OF SQUAD CARS AT THE SCENE CONFIRMS ALFRED'S ESTIMATION.
GORDON DOESN'T EVEN TRY TO ARREST ME WHEN I SHOW UP.
KIRSCH'S DIAMONDS
GCPD
DAMNEDEST THING... THREE DEAD. FATHER AND TWO BROTHERS. FAMILY BUSINESS.
JEWELRY STORE, NOT SURPRISED. ATTEMPTED ROBBERY?
THAT'S THE THING. WASN'T JUST ATTEMPTED. IT WAS SUCCESSFUL.
BASTARDS GOT IN WITHOUT TRIPPING ANY ALARMS, THEY TOOK OUT EVERYONE INSIDE-- EXCEPT...
NOTHING WAS TAKEN.
EVERY PIECE ON THE INVENTORY IS ACCOUNTED FOR. NO CASH MISSING.
AND THE FAMILY'S CLEAN-- NO CRIMINAL TIES, NO DEBTS. WE'VE GOT NOTHING...
DAMNEDEST THING.
LIKE THERE'S NO MOTIVE.
THERE'S ALWAYS A MOTIVE.

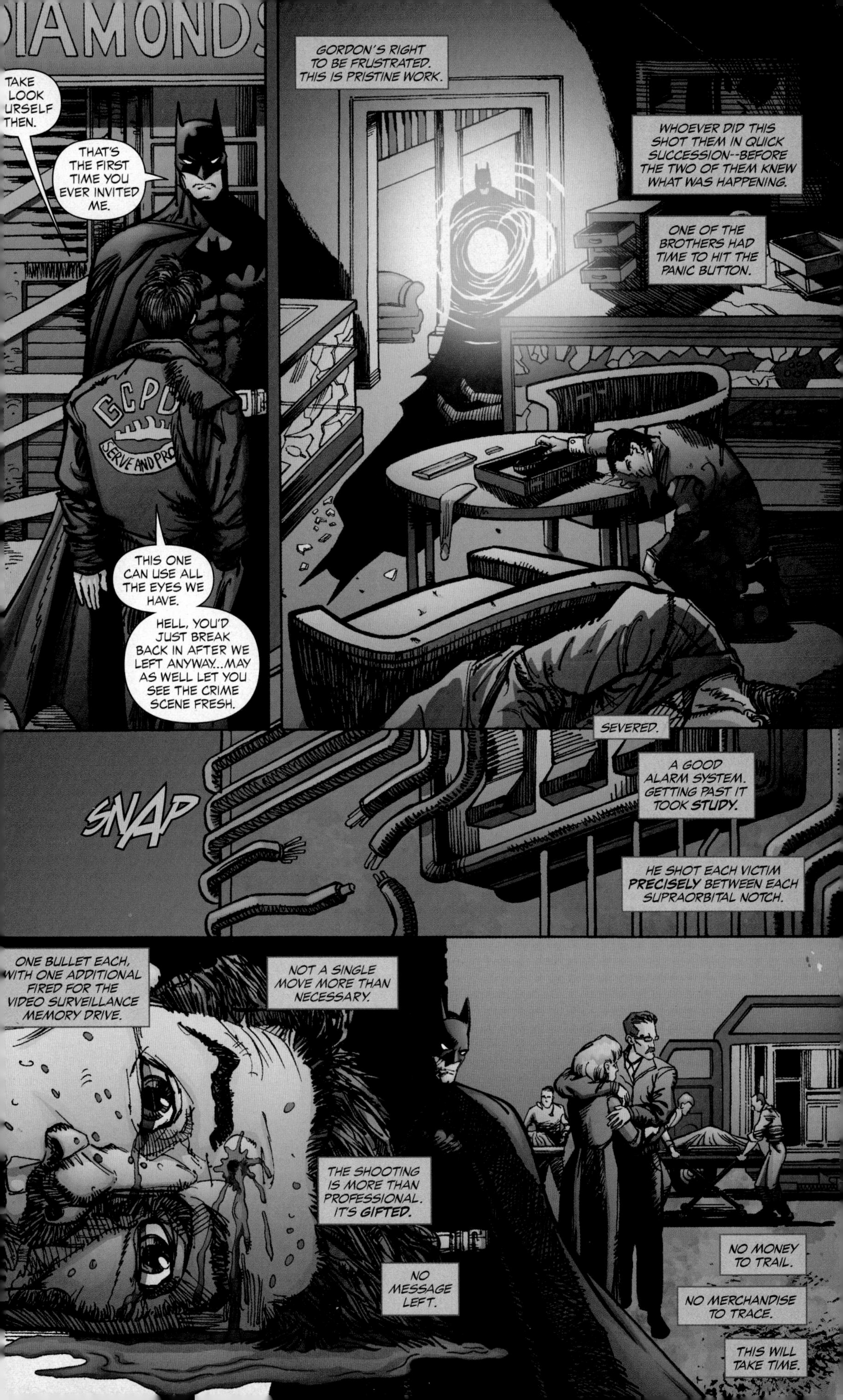
DIAMONDS
TAKE LOOK URSELF THEN.
THAT'S THE FIRST TIME YOU EVER INVITED ME.
GCPD
SERVE AND PRO
THIS ONE CAN USE ALL THE EYES WE HAVE.
HELL, YOU'D JUST BREAK BACK IN AFTER WE LEFT ANYWAY...MAY AS WELL LET YOU SEE THE CRIME SCENE FRESH.
GORDON'S RIGHT TO BE FRUSTRATED. THIS IS PRISTINE WORK.
WHOEVER DID THIS SHOT THEM IN QUICK SUCCESSION--BEFORE THE TWO OF THEM KNEW WHAT WAS HAPPENING.
ONE OF THE BROTHERS HAD TIME TO HIT THE PANIC BUTTON.
SEVERED.
SNAP
A GOOD ALARM SYSTEM. GETTING PAST IT TOOK **STUDY.**
HE SHOT EACH VICTIM **PRECISELY** BETWEEN EACH SUPRAORBITAL NOTCH.
ONE BULLET EACH, WITH ONE ADDITIONAL FIRED FOR THE VIDEO SURVEILLANCE MEMORY DRIVE.
NOT A SINGLE MOVE MORE THAN NECESSARY.
THE SHOOTING IS MORE THAN PROFESSIONAL. IT'S **GIFTED.**
NO MESSAGE LEFT.
NO MONEY TO TRAIL.
NO MERCHANDISE TO TRACE.
THIS WILL TAKE TIME.

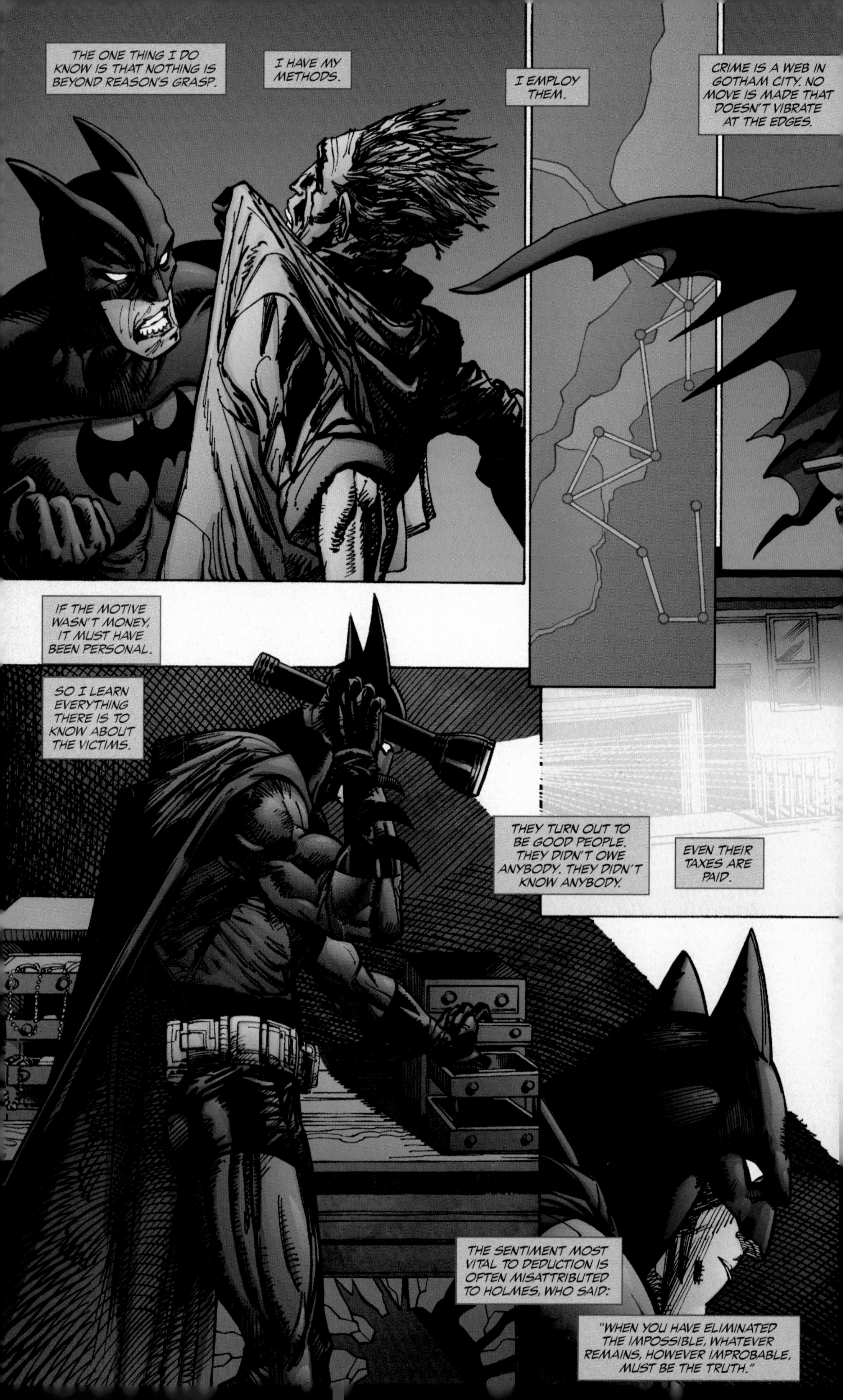
THE ONE THING I DO KNOW IS THAT NOTHING IS BEYOND REASON'S GRASP.
I HAVE MY METHODS.
I EMPLOY THEM.
CRIME IS A WEB IN GOTHAM CITY. NO MOVE IS MADE THAT DOESN'T VIBRATE AT THE EDGES.
IF THE MOTIVE WASN'T MONEY, IT MUST HAVE BEEN PERSONAL.
SO I LEARN EVERYTHING THERE IS TO KNOW ABOUT THE VICTIMS.
THEY TURN OUT TO BE GOOD PEOPLE. THEY DIDN'T OWE ANYBODY. THEY DIDN'T KNOW ANYBODY.
EVEN THEIR TAXES ARE PAID.
THE SENTIMENT MOST VITAL TO DEDUCTION IS OFTEN MISATTRIBUTED TO HOLMES, WHO SAID:
"WHEN YOU HAVE ELIMINATED THE IMPOSSIBLE, WHATEVER REMAINS, HOWEVER IMPROBABLE, MUST BE THE TRUTH."

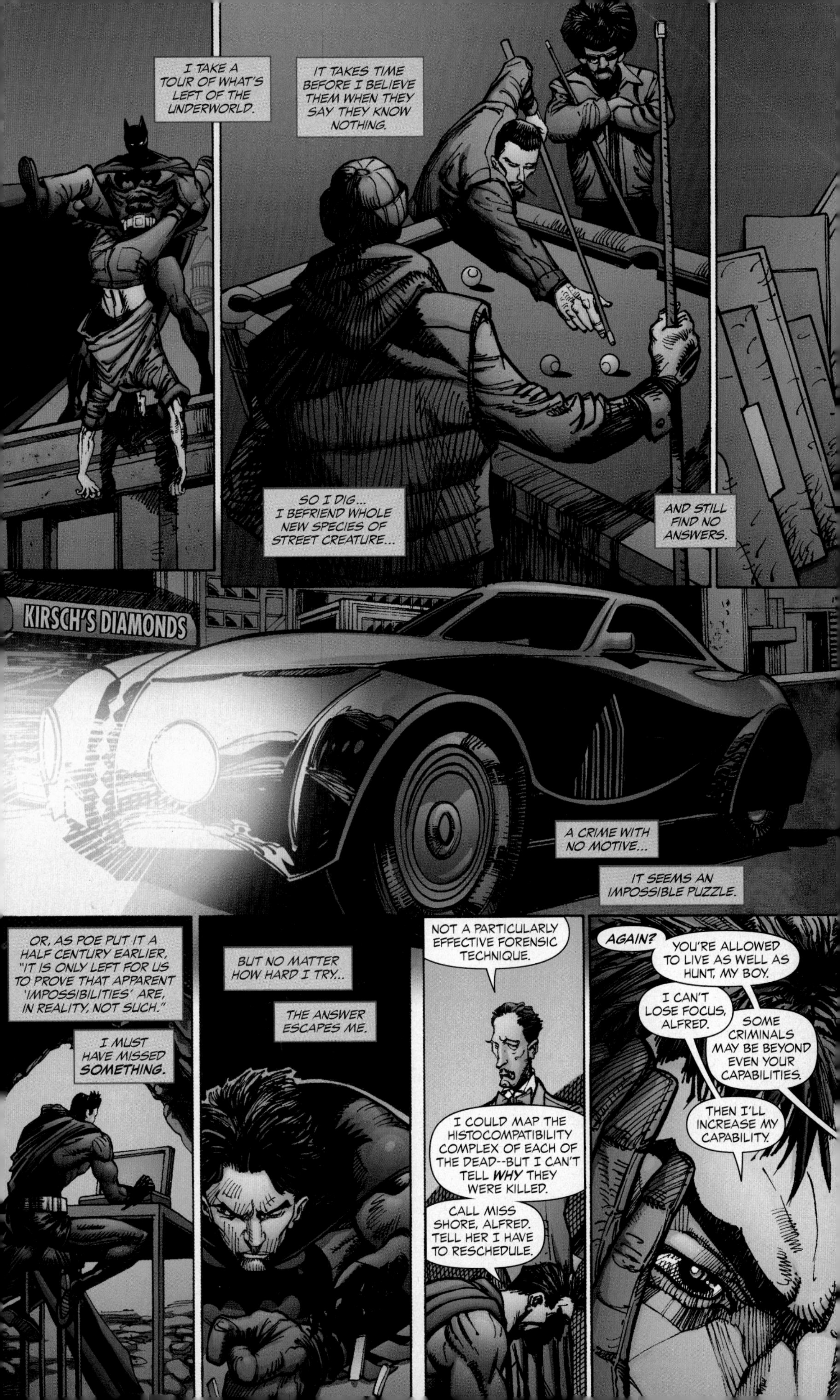
I TAKE A TOUR OF WHAT'S LEFT OF THE UNDERWORLD.
IT TAKES TIME BEFORE I BELIEVE THEM WHEN THEY SAY THEY KNOW NOTHING.
SO I DIG... I BEFRIEND WHOLE NEW SPECIES OF STREET CREATURE...
AND STILL FIND NO ANSWERS.
KIRSCH'S DIAMONDS
A CRIME WITH NO MOTIVE...
IT SEEMS AN IMPOSSIBLE PUZZLE.
OR, AS POE PUT IT A HALF CENTURY EARLIER, "IT IS ONLY LEFT FOR US TO PROVE THAT APPARENT 'IMPOSSIBILITIES' ARE, IN REALITY, NOT SUCH."
I MUST HAVE MISSED SOMETHING.
BUT NO MATTER HOW HARD I TRY...
THE ANSWER ESCAPES ME.
NOT A PARTICULARLY EFFECTIVE FORENSIC TECHNIQUE.
I COULD MAP THE HISTOCOMPATIBILITY COMPLEX OF EACH OF THE DEAD--BUT I CAN'T TELL WHY THEY WERE KILLED.
CALL MISS SHORE, ALFRED. TELL HER I HAVE TO RESCHEDULE.
AGAIN?
YOU'RE ALLOWED TO LIVE AS WELL AS HUNT, MY BOY.
I CAN'T LOSE FOCUS, ALFRED.
SOME CRIMINALS MAY BE BEYOND EVEN YOUR CAPABILITIES.
THEN I'LL INCREASE MY CAPABILITY.

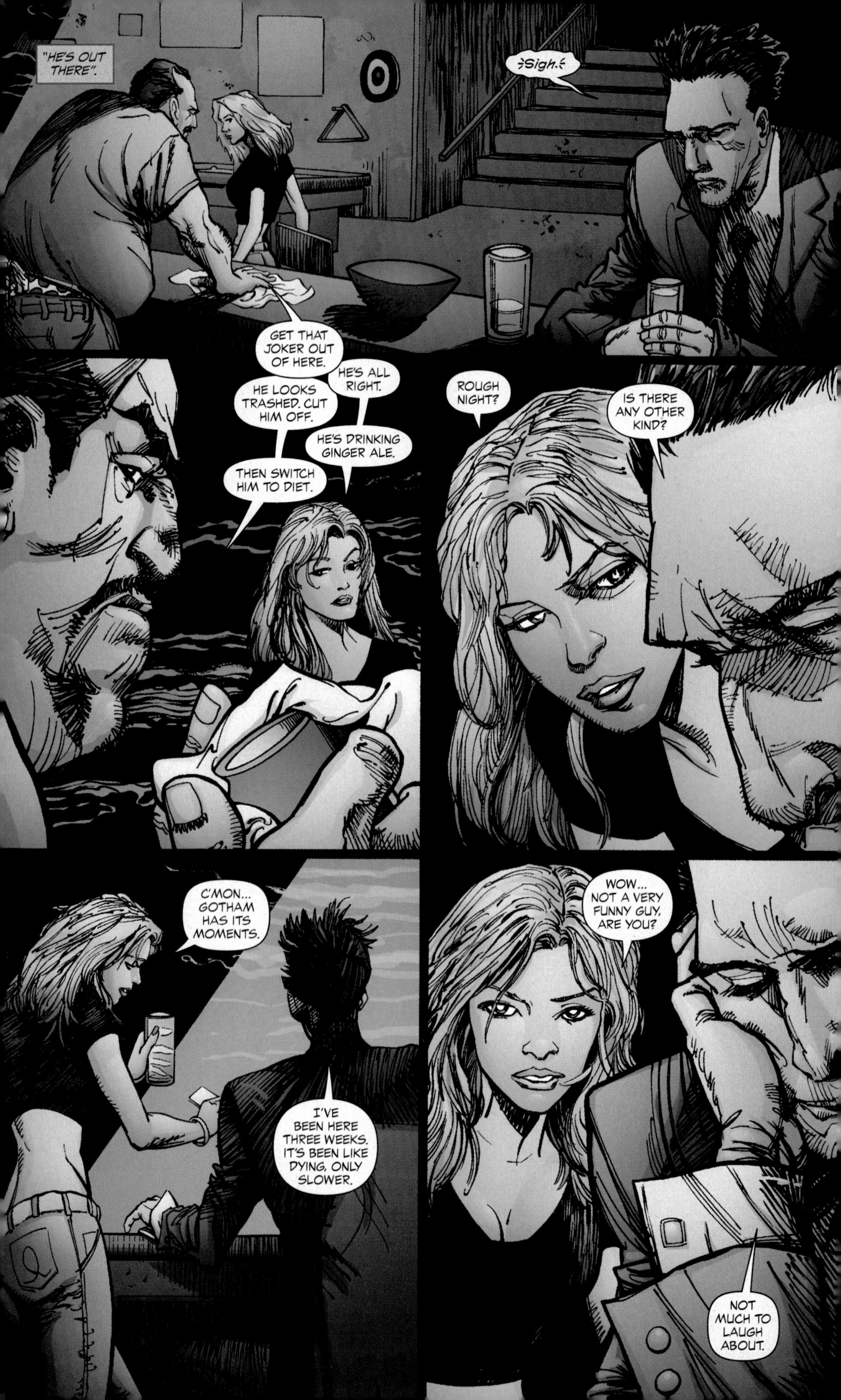
"HE'S OUT THERE".
Sigh.
GET THAT JOKER OUT OF HERE.
HE'S ALL RIGHT.
HE LOOKS TRASHED. CUT HIM OFF.
HE'S DRINKING GINGER ALE.
THEN SWITCH HIM TO DIET.
ROUGH NIGHT?
IS THERE ANY OTHER KIND?
C'MON... GOTHAM HAS ITS MOMENTS.
I'VE BEEN HERE THREE WEEKS. IT'S BEEN LIKE DYING, ONLY SLOWER.
WOW... NOT A VERY FUNNY GUY, ARE YOU?
NOT MUCH TO LAUGH ABOUT.

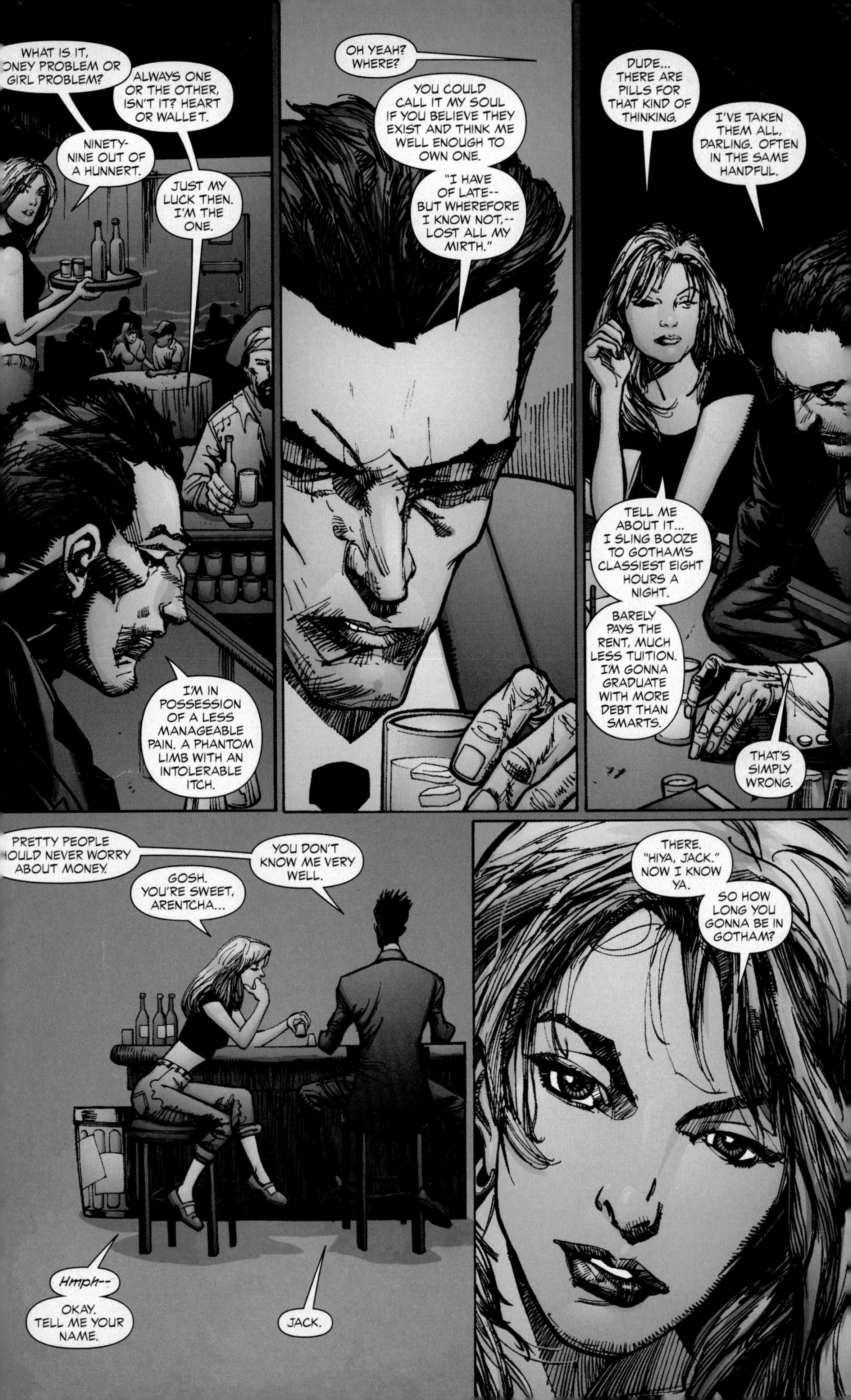
WHAT IS IT, ONEY PROBLEM OR GIRL PROBLEM?
ALWAYS ONE OR THE OTHER, ISN'T IT? HEART OR WALLET.
NINETY-NINE OUT OF A HUNNERT.
JUST MY LUCK THEN. I'M THE ONE.
I'M IN POSSESSION OF A LESS MANAGEABLE PAIN. A PHANTOM LIMB WITH AN INTOLERABLE ITCH.
OH YEAH? WHERE?
YOU COULD CALL IT MY SOUL IF YOU BELIEVE THEY EXIST AND THINK ME WELL ENOUGH TO OWN ONE.
"I HAVE OF LATE-- BUT WHEREFORE I KNOW NOT,-- LOST ALL MY MIRTH."
DUDE... THERE ARE PILLS FOR THAT KIND OF THINKING.
I'VE TAKEN THEM ALL, DARLING. OFTEN IN THE SAME HANDFUL.
TELL ME ABOUT IT... I SLING BOOZE TO GOTHAM'S CLASSIEST EIGHT HOURS A NIGHT.
BARELY PAYS THE RENT, MUCH LESS TUITION. I'M GONNA GRADUATE WITH MORE DEBT THAN SMARTS.
THAT'S SIMPLY WRONG.
PRETTY PEOPLE IOULD NEVER WORRY ABOUT MONEY.
YOU DON'T KNOW ME VERY WELL.
GOSH. YOU'RE SWEET, ARENTCHA...
Hmph--
OKAY. TELL ME YOUR NAME.
JACK.
THERE. "HIYA, JACK." NOW I KNOW YA.
SO HOW LONG YOU GONNA BE IN GOTHAM?

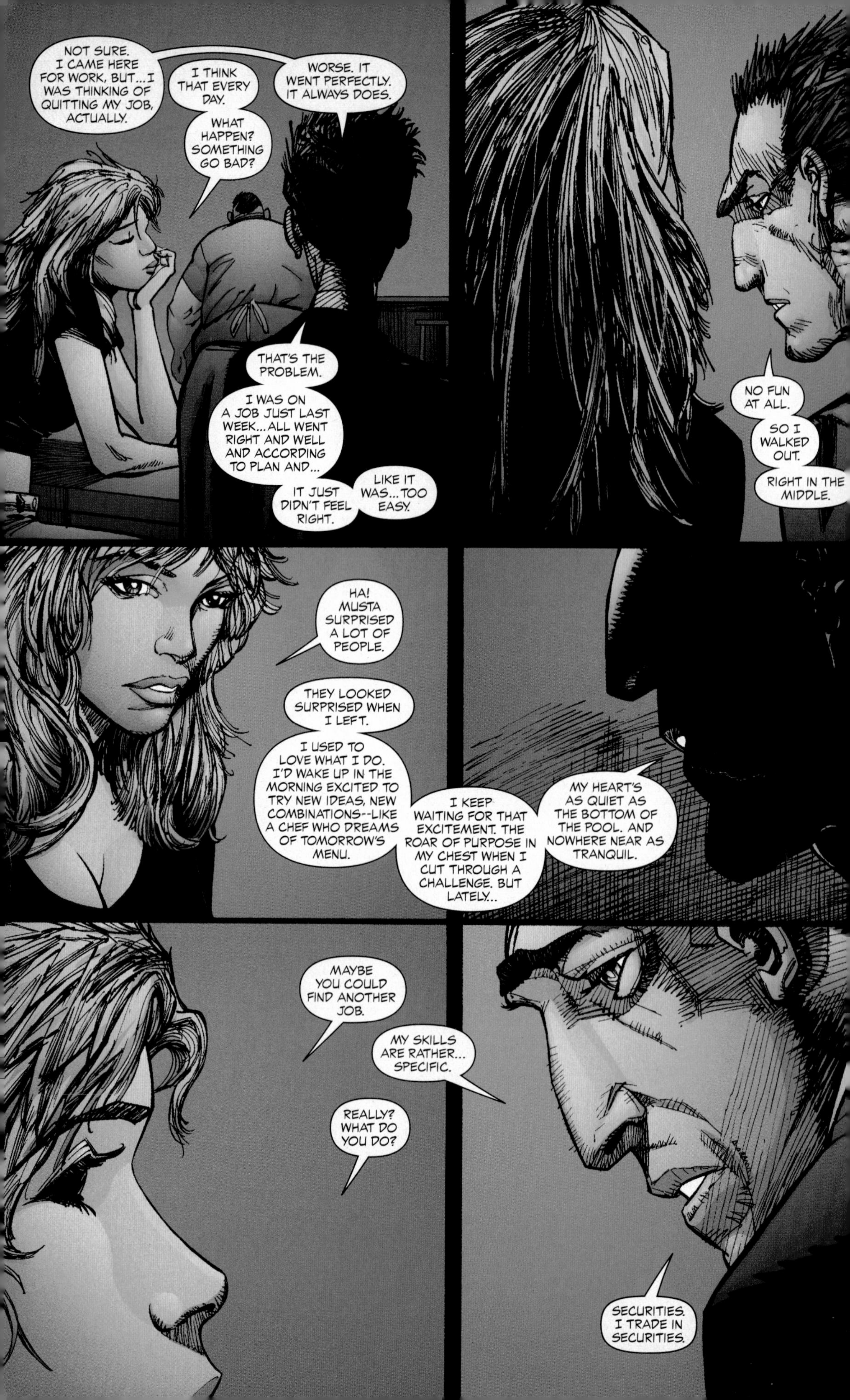
NOT SURE. I CAME HERE FOR WORK, BUT... I WAS THINKING OF QUITTING MY JOB, ACTUALLY.
I THINK THAT EVERY DAY.
WHAT HAPPEN? SOMETHING GO BAD?
WORSE. IT WENT PERFECTLY. IT ALWAYS DOES.
THAT'S THE PROBLEM.
I WAS ON A JOB JUST LAST WEEK... ALL WENT RIGHT AND WELL AND ACCORDING TO PLAN AND...
IT JUST DIDN'T FEEL RIGHT.
LIKE IT WAS... TOO EASY.
NO FUN AT ALL.
SO I WALKED OUT.
RIGHT IN THE MIDDLE.
HA! MUSTA SURPRISED A LOT OF PEOPLE.
THEY LOOKED SURPRISED WHEN I LEFT.
I USED TO LOVE WHAT I DO. I'D WAKE UP IN THE MORNING EXCITED TO TRY NEW IDEAS, NEW COMBINATIONS--LIKE A CHEF WHO DREAMS OF TOMORROW'S MENU.
I KEEP WAITING FOR THAT EXCITEMENT. THE ROAR OF PURPOSE IN MY CHEST WHEN I CUT THROUGH A CHALLENGE. BUT LATELY...
MY HEART'S AS QUIET AS THE BOTTOM OF THE POOL. AND NOWHERE NEAR AS TRANQUIL.
MAYBE YOU COULD FIND ANOTHER JOB.
MY SKILLS ARE RATHER... SPECIFIC.
REALLY? WHAT DO YOU DO?
SECURITIES. I TRADE IN SECURITIES.

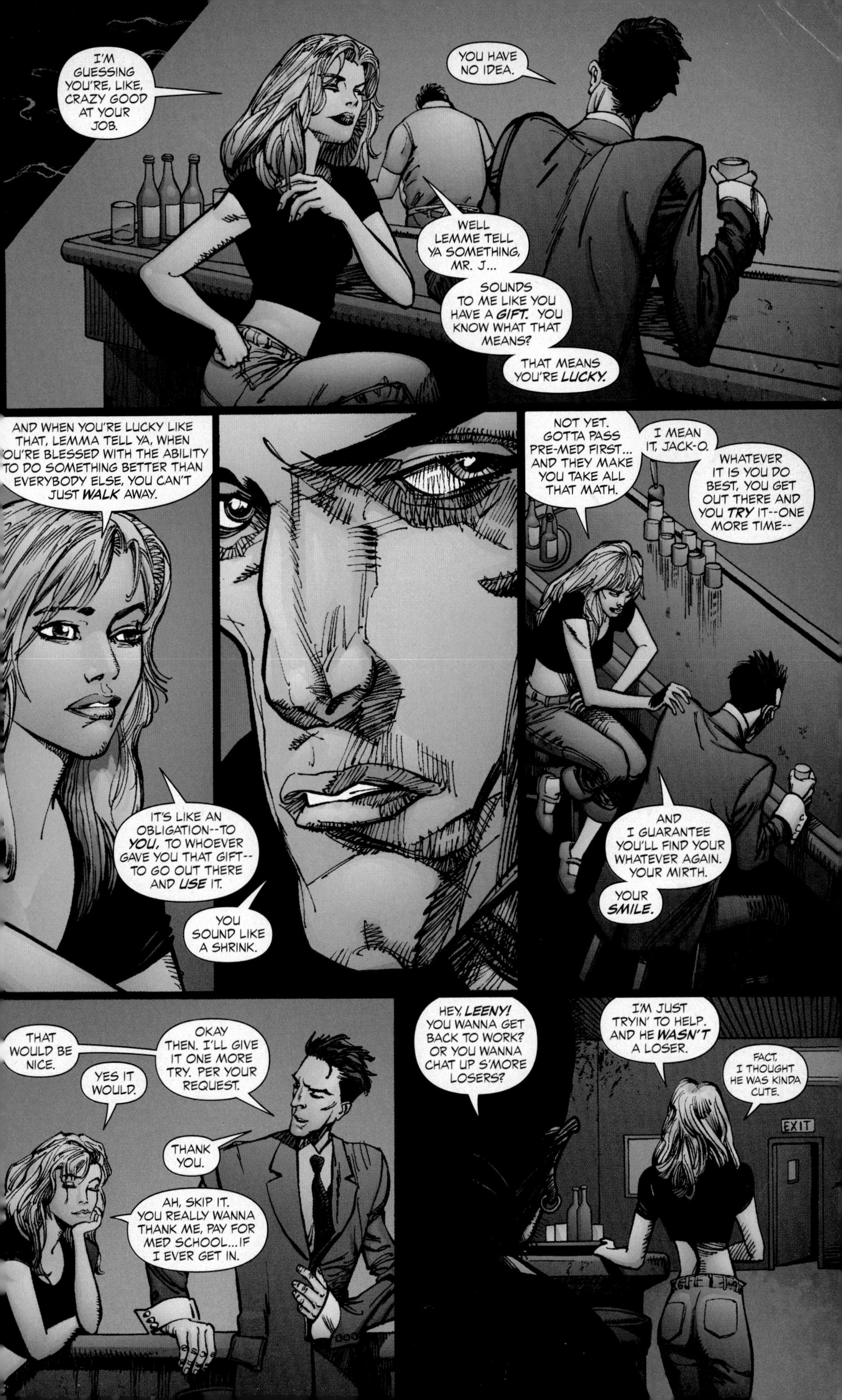

I'M GUESSING YOU'RE, LIKE, CRAZY GOOD AT YOUR JOB.
YOU HAVE NO IDEA.
WELL LEMME TELL YA SOMETHING, MR. J...
SOUNDS TO ME LIKE YOU HAVE A GIFT. YOU KNOW WHAT THAT MEANS?
THAT MEANS YOU'RE LUCKY.
AND WHEN YOU'RE LUCKY LIKE THAT, LEMMA TELL YA, WHEN OU'RE BLESSED WITH THE ABILITY TO DO SOMETHING BETTER THAN EVERYBODY ELSE, YOU CAN'T JUST WALK AWAY.
IT'S LIKE AN OBLIGATION--TO YOU, TO WHOEVER GAVE YOU THAT GIFT--TO GO OUT THERE AND USE IT.
YOU SOUND LIKE A SHRINK.
NOT YET. GOTTA PASS PRE-MED FIRST... AND THEY MAKE YOU TAKE ALL THAT MATH.
I MEAN IT, JACK-O.
WHATEVER IT IS YOU DO BEST, YOU GET OUT THERE AND YOU TRY IT--ONE MORE TIME--
AND I GUARANTEE YOU'LL FIND YOUR WHATEVER AGAIN. YOUR MIRTH.
YOUR SMILE.
THAT WOULD BE NICE.
YES IT WOULD.
OKAY THEN. I'LL GIVE IT ONE MORE TRY. PER YOUR REQUEST.
THANK YOU.
AH, SKIP IT. YOU REALLY WANNA THANK ME, PAY FOR MED SCHOOL...IF I EVER GET IN.
HEY, LEENY! YOU WANNA GET BACK TO WORK? OR YOU WANNA CHAT UP S'MORE LOSERS?
I'M JUST TRYIN' TO HELP. AND HE WASN'T A LOSER.
FACT, I THOUGHT HE WAS KINDA CUTE.
EXIT

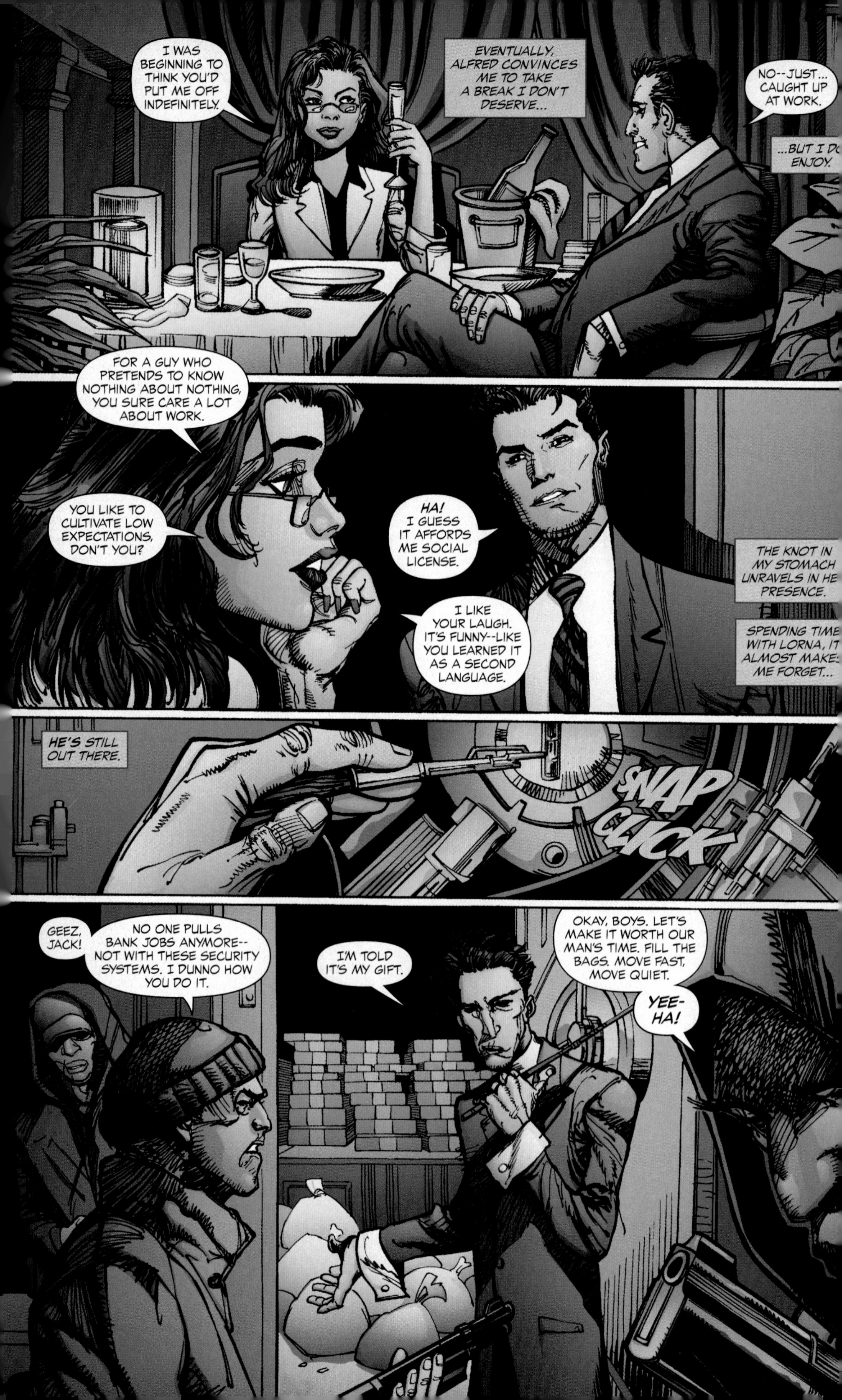
I WAS BEGINNING TO THINK YOU'D PUT ME OFF INDEFINITELY.
EVENTUALLY, ALFRED CONVINCES ME TO TAKE A BREAK I DON'T DESERVE...
NO--JUST... CAUGHT UP AT WORK.
...BUT I DO ENJOY.
FOR A GUY WHO PRETENDS TO KNOW NOTHING ABOUT NOTHING, YOU SURE CARE A LOT ABOUT WORK.
YOU LIKE TO CULTIVATE LOW EXPECTATIONS, DON'T YOU?
HA! I GUESS IT AFFORDS ME SOCIAL LICENSE.
I LIKE YOUR LAUGH. IT'S FUNNY--LIKE YOU LEARNED IT AS A SECOND LANGUAGE.
THE KNOT IN MY STOMACH UNRAVELS IN HER PRESENCE.
SPENDING TIME WITH LORNA, IT ALMOST MAKES ME FORGET...
HE'S STILL OUT THERE.
SNAP
CLICK
GEEZ, JACK!
NO ONE PULLS BANK JOBS ANYMORE--NOT WITH THESE SECURITY SYSTEMS. I DUNNO HOW YOU DO IT.
I'M TOLD IT'S MY GIFT.
OKAY, BOYS. LET'S MAKE IT WORTH OUR MAN'S TIME. FILL THE BAGS. MOVE FAST, MOVE QUIET.
YEE-HA!

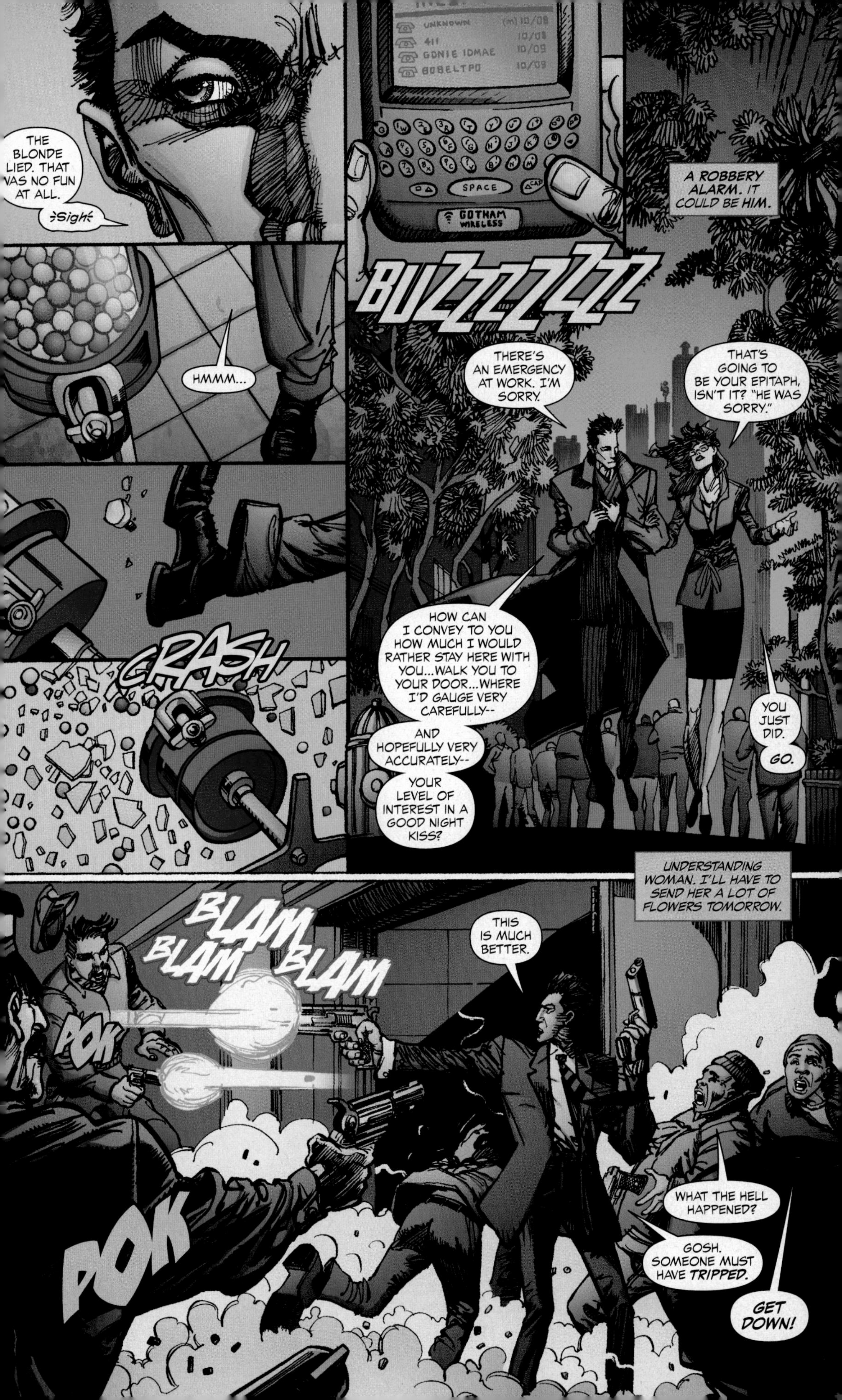

THE BLONDE LIED. THAT WAS NO FUN AT ALL.
Sigh
UNKNOWN (m) 10/09
411 10/09
GDNIE IDMAE 10/09
BOBELTPO 10/09
SPACE
GOTHAM WIRELESS
A ROBBERY ALARM. IT COULD BE HIM.
HMMM...
BUZZZZZZZ
THERE'S AN EMERGENCY AT WORK. I'M SORRY.
THAT'S GOING TO BE YOUR EPITAPH, ISN'T IT? "HE WAS SORRY."
CRASH
HOW CAN I CONVEY TO YOU HOW MUCH I WOULD RATHER STAY HERE WITH YOU...WALK YOU TO YOUR DOOR...WHERE I'D GAUGE VERY CAREFULLY--
AND HOPEFULLY VERY ACCURATELY--
YOUR LEVEL OF INTEREST IN A GOOD NIGHT KISS?
YOU JUST DID.
GO.
UNDERSTANDING WOMAN. I'LL HAVE TO SEND HER A LOT OF FLOWERS TOMORROW.
BLAM BLAM BLAM BLAM
THIS IS MUCH BETTER.
POK
POK
WHAT THE HELL HAPPENED?
GOSH. SOMEONE MUST HAVE TRIPPED.
GET DOWN!

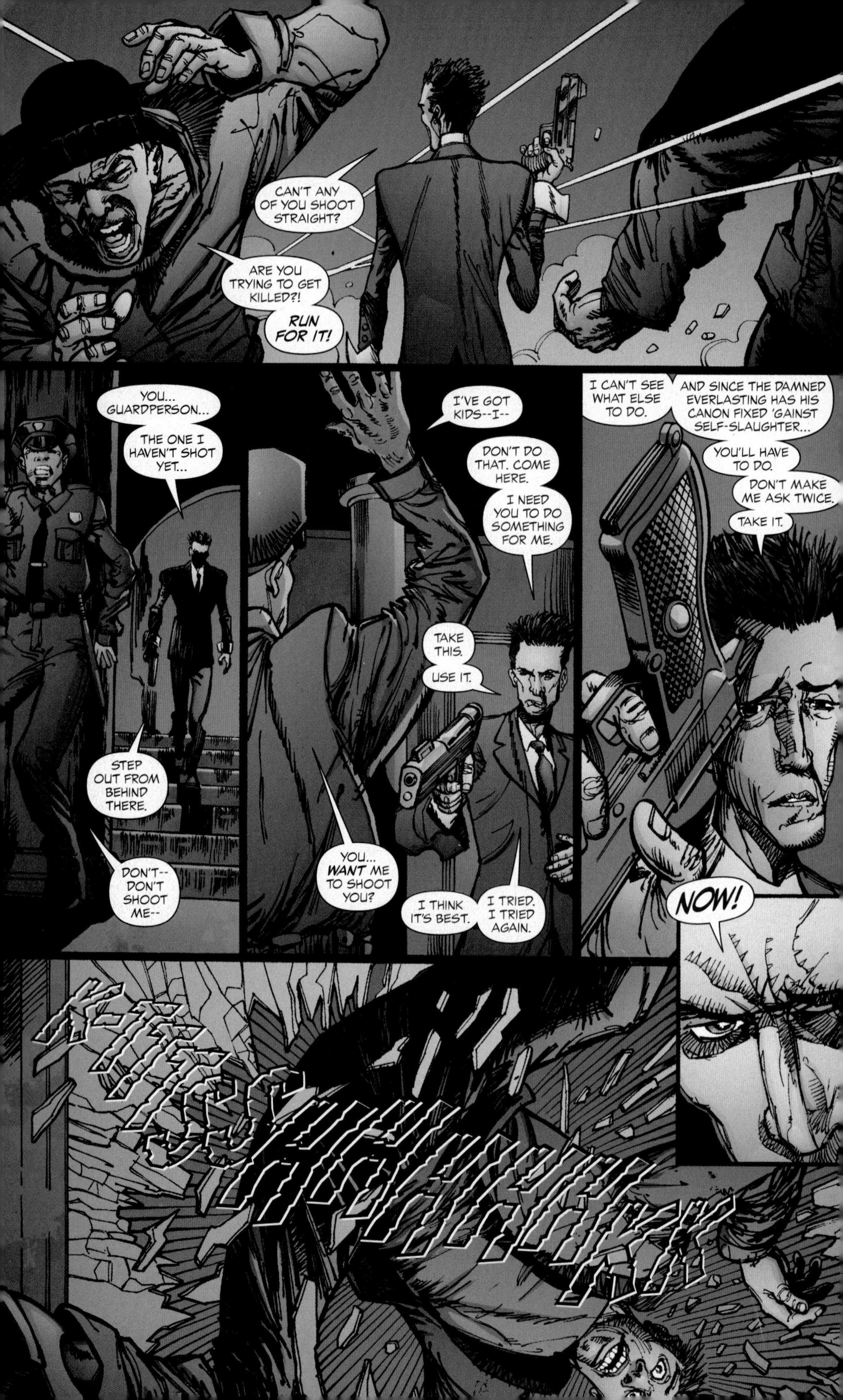

CAN'T ANY OF YOU SHOOT STRAIGHT?
ARE YOU TRYING TO GET KILLED?!
RUN FOR IT!
YOU... GUARDPERSON...
THE ONE I HAVEN'T SHOT YET...
STEP OUT FROM BEHIND THERE.
DON'T-- DON'T SHOOT ME--
I'VE GOT KIDS--I--
DON'T DO THAT. COME HERE.
I NEED YOU TO DO SOMETHING FOR ME.
TAKE THIS.
USE IT.
YOU... WANT ME TO SHOOT YOU?
I THINK IT'S BEST.
I TRIED. I TRIED AGAIN.
I CAN'T SEE WHAT ELSE TO DO.
AND SINCE THE DAMNED EVERLASTING HAS HIS CANON FIXED 'GAINST SELF-SLAUGHTER...
YOU'LL HAVE TO DO.
DON'T MAKE ME ASK TWICE.
TAKE IT.
NOW!

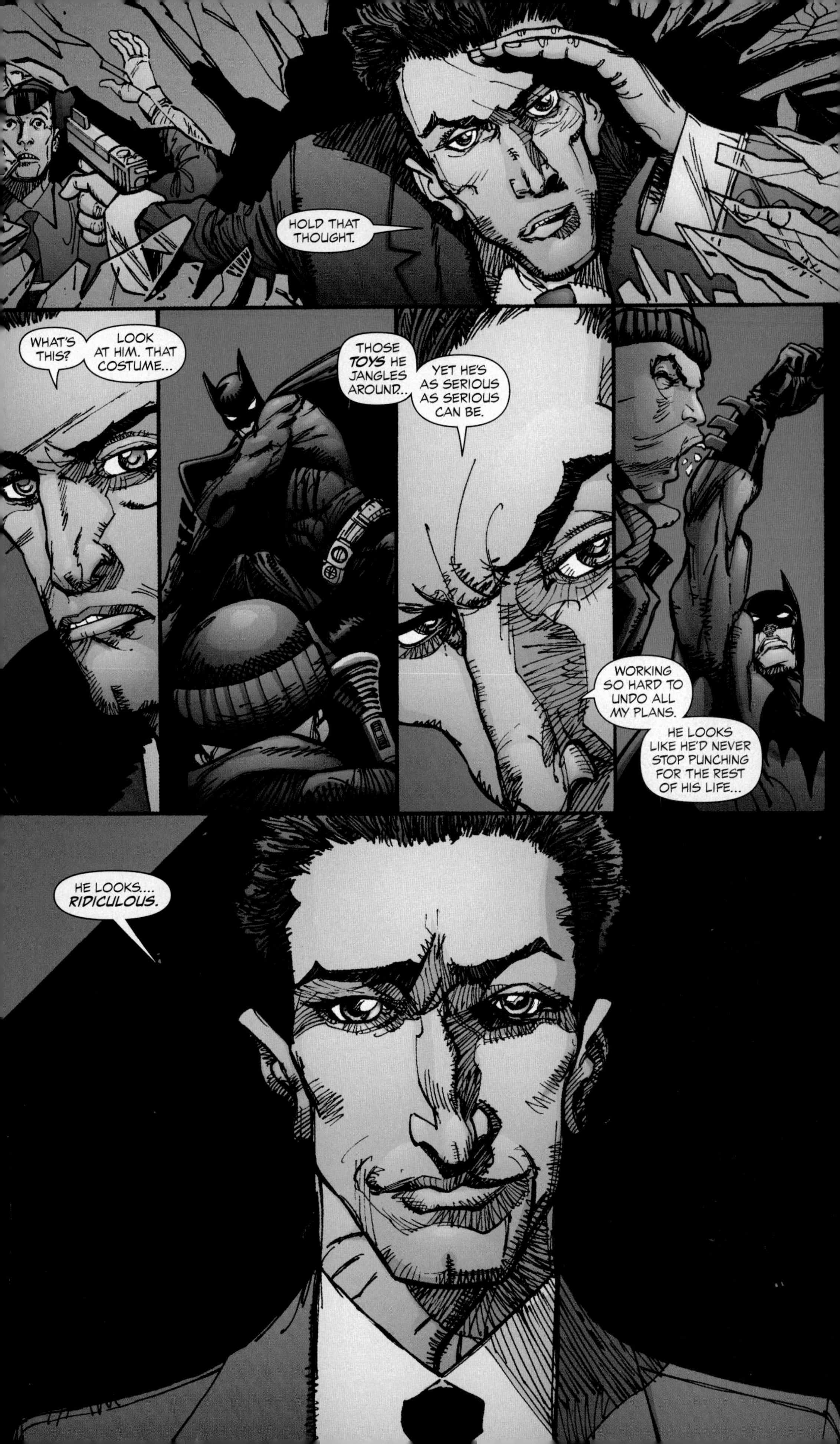
HOLD THAT THOUGHT.
WHAT'S THIS?
LOOK AT HIM. THAT COSTUME...
THOSE TOYS HE JANGLES AROUND...
YET HE'S AS SERIOUS AS SERIOUS CAN BE.
WORKING SO HARD TO UNDO ALL MY PLANS.
HE LOOKS LIKE HE'D NEVER STOP PUNCHING FOR THE REST OF HIS LIFE...
HE LOOKS.... RIDICULOUS.

chapter two **PEACE IN ARMS**

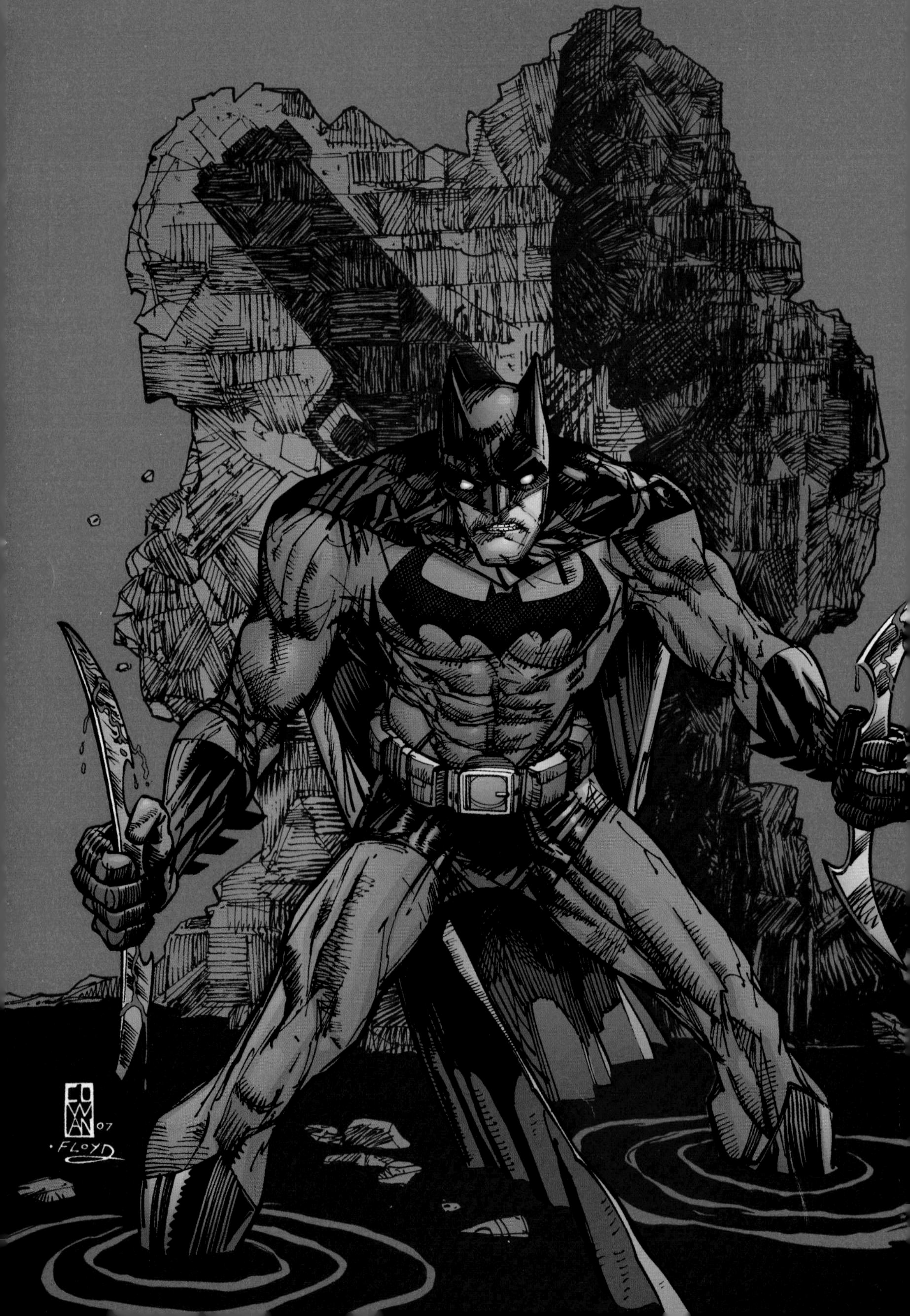
COWAN 07
FLOYD

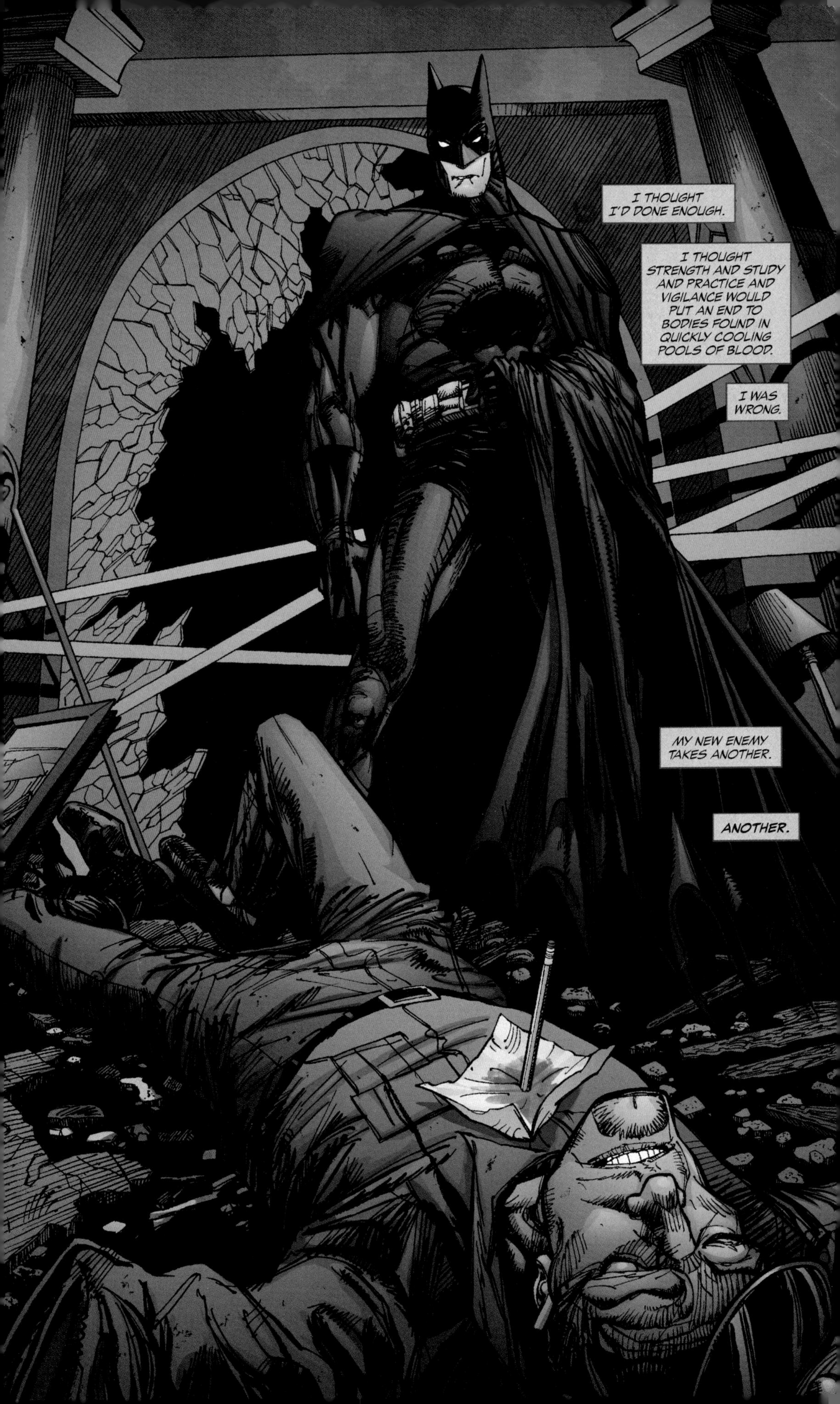
I THOUGHT I'D DONE ENOUGH.
I THOUGHT STRENGTH AND STUDY AND PRACTICE AND VIGILANCE WOULD PUT AN END TO BODIES FOUND IN QUICKLY COOLING POOLS OF BLOOD.
I WAS WRONG.
MY NEW ENEMY TAKES ANOTHER.
ANOTHER.

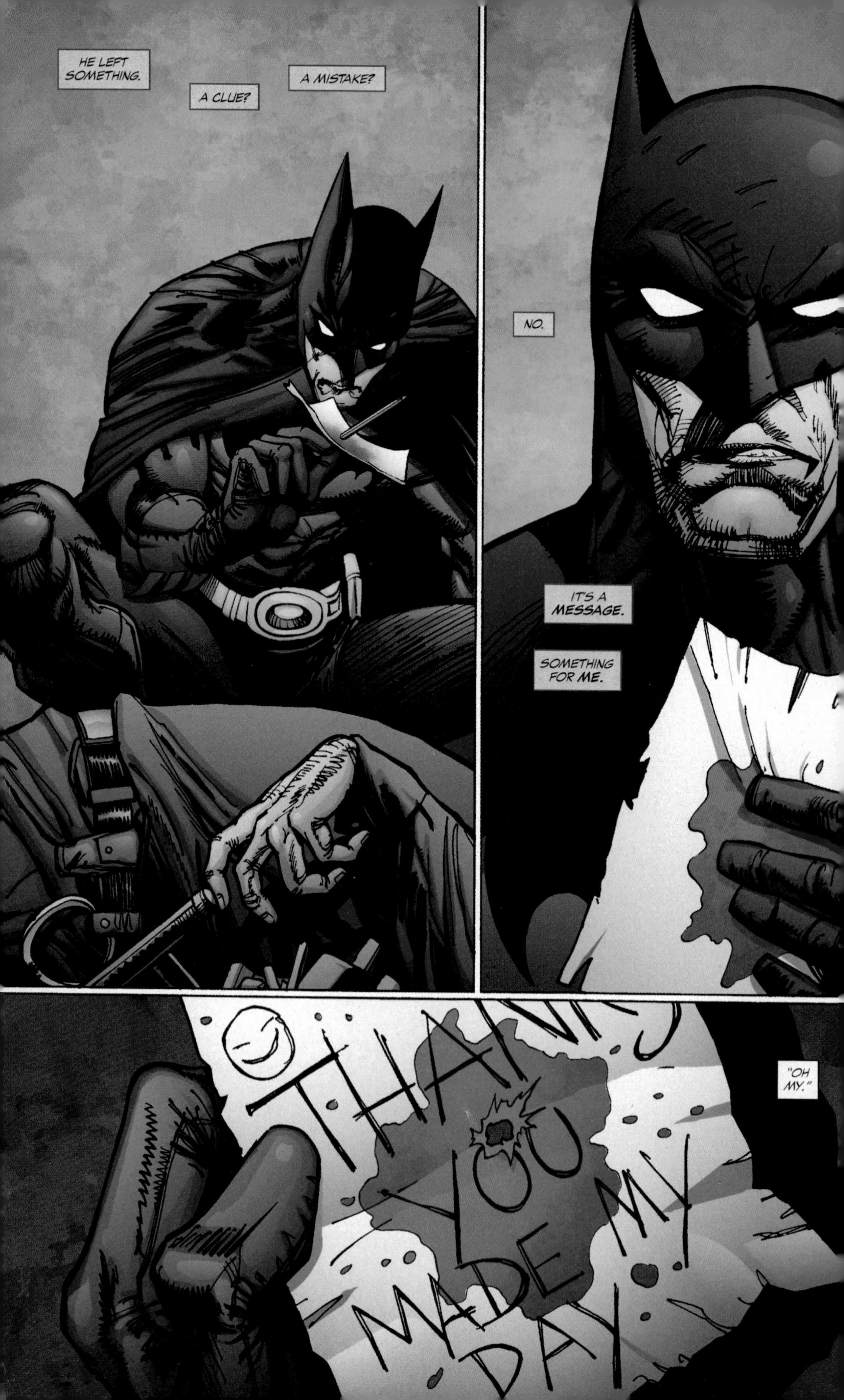
HE LEFT SOMETHING.
A CLUE?
A MISTAKE?
NO.
IT'S A MESSAGE.
SOMETHING FOR ME.
THANKS
YOU MADE MY DAY
"OH MY."

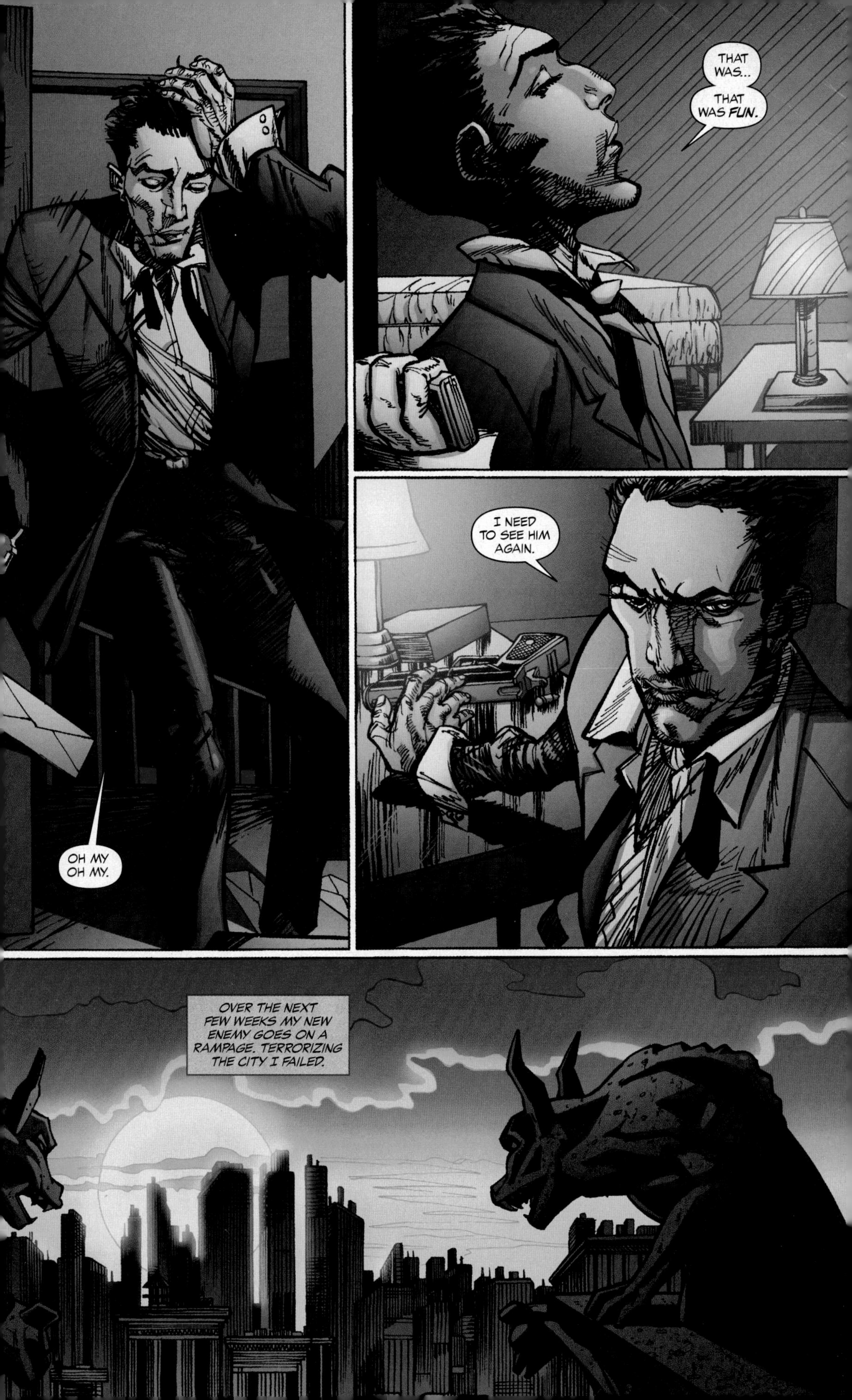
OH MY
OH MY.
THAT WAS...
THAT WAS FUN.
I NEED TO SEE HIM AGAIN.
OVER THE NEXT FEW WEEKS MY NEW ENEMY GOES ON A RAMPAGE. TERRORIZING THE CITY I FAILED.

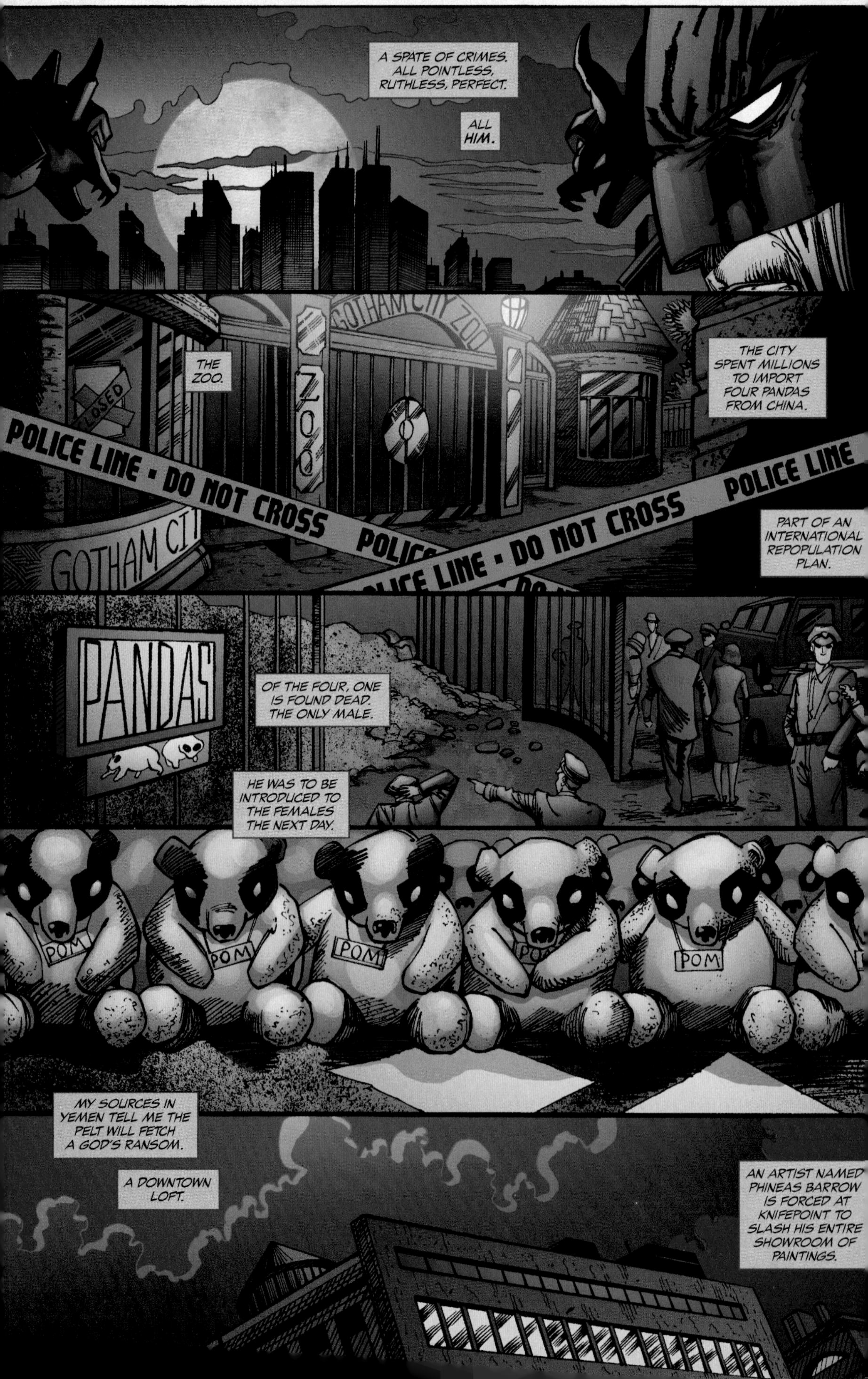
A SPATE OF CRIMES. ALL POINTLESS, RUTHLESS, PERFECT.
ALL HIM.
THE ZOO.
GOTHAM CITY ZOO
ZOO
CLOSED
THE CITY SPENT MILLIONS TO IMPORT FOUR PANDAS FROM CHINA.
POLICE LINE - DO NOT CROSS
POLICE LINE - DO NOT CROSS
POLICE LINE
GOTHAM CITY
PART OF AN INTERNATIONAL REPOPULATION PLAN.
PANDAS
OF THE FOUR, ONE IS FOUND DEAD. THE ONLY MALE.
HE WAS TO BE INTRODUCED TO THE FEMALES THE NEXT DAY.
POM
POM
POM
POM
MY SOURCES IN YEMEN TELL ME THE PELT WILL FETCH A GOD'S RANSOM.
A DOWNTOWN LOFT.
AN ARTIST NAMED PHINEAS BARROW IS FORCED AT KNIFEPOINT TO SLASH HIS ENTIRE SHOWROOM OF PAINTINGS.

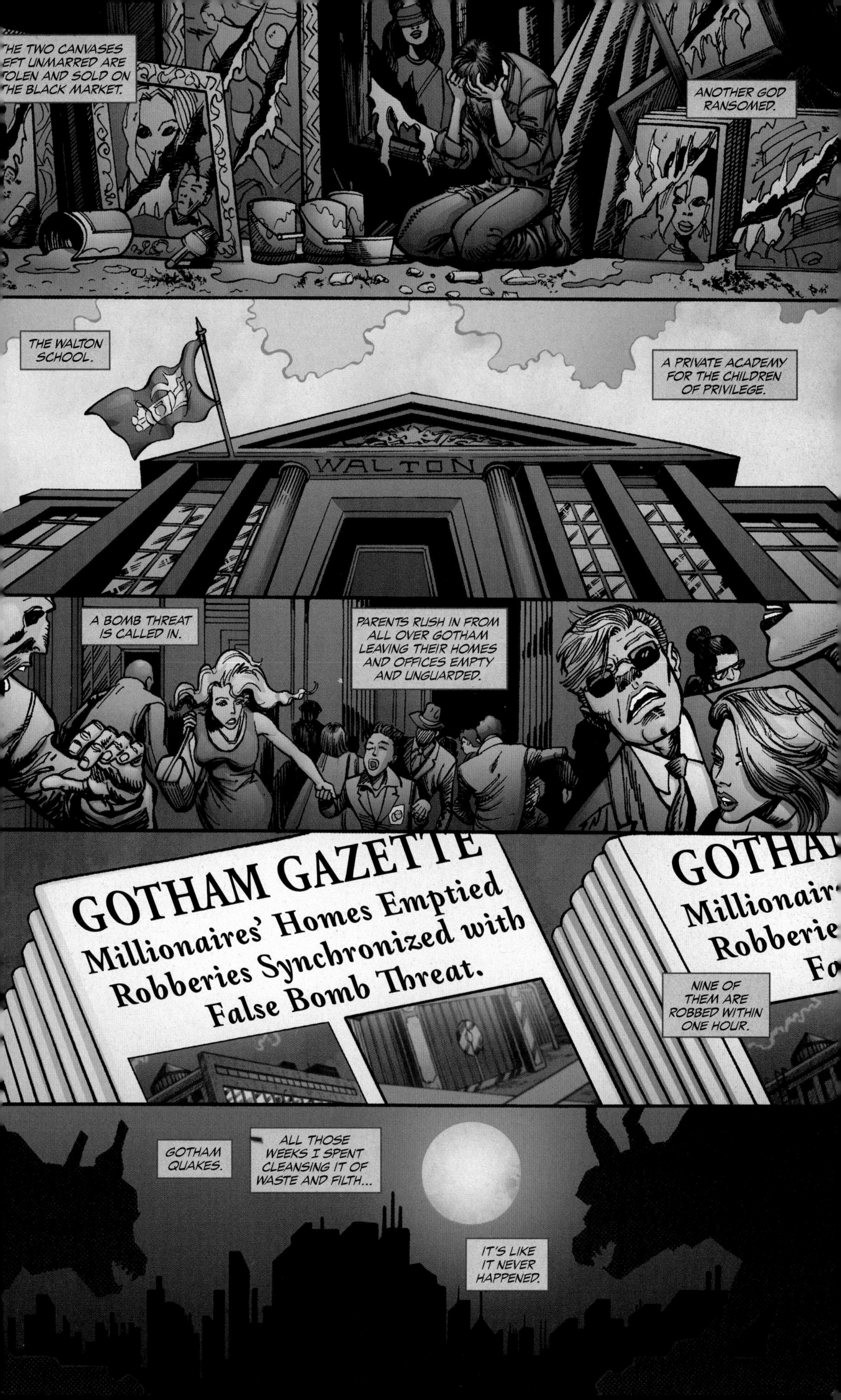
THE TWO CANVASES
EFT UNMARRED ARE
TOLEN AND SOLD ON
THE BLACK MARKET.
ANOTHER GOD RANSOMED.
THE WALTON SCHOOL.
A PRIVATE ACADEMY FOR THE CHILDREN OF PRIVILEGE.
WALTON
A BOMB THREAT IS CALLED IN.
PARENTS RUSH IN FROM ALL OVER GOTHAM LEAVING THEIR HOMES AND OFFICES EMPTY AND UNGUARDED.
GOTHAM GAZETTE
Millionaires' Homes Emptied
Robberies Synchronized with
False Bomb Threat.
NINE OF THEM ARE ROBBED WITHIN ONE HOUR.
GOTHAM QUAKES.
ALL THOSE WEEKS I SPENT CLEANSING IT OF WASTE AND FILTH...
IT'S LIKE IT NEVER HAPPENED.

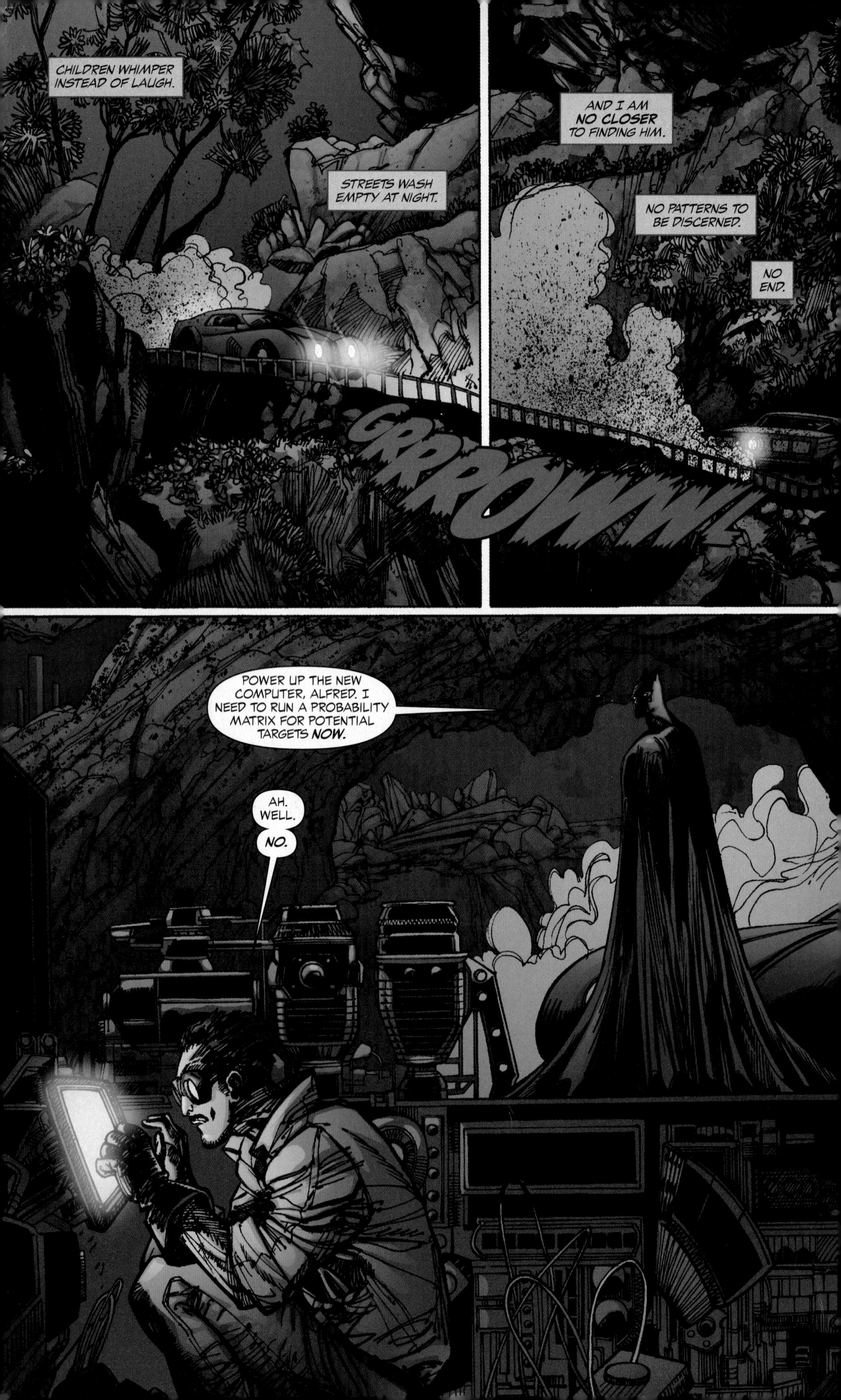
CHILDREN WHIMPER INSTEAD OF LAUGH.
STREETS WASH EMPTY AT NIGHT.
AND I AM NO CLOSER TO FINDING HIM.
NO PATTERNS TO BE DISCERNED.
NO END.
GRRROWWW!
POWER UP THE NEW COMPUTER, ALFRED. I NEED TO RUN A PROBABILITY MATRIX FOR POTENTIAL TARGETS NOW.
AH. WELL.
NO.

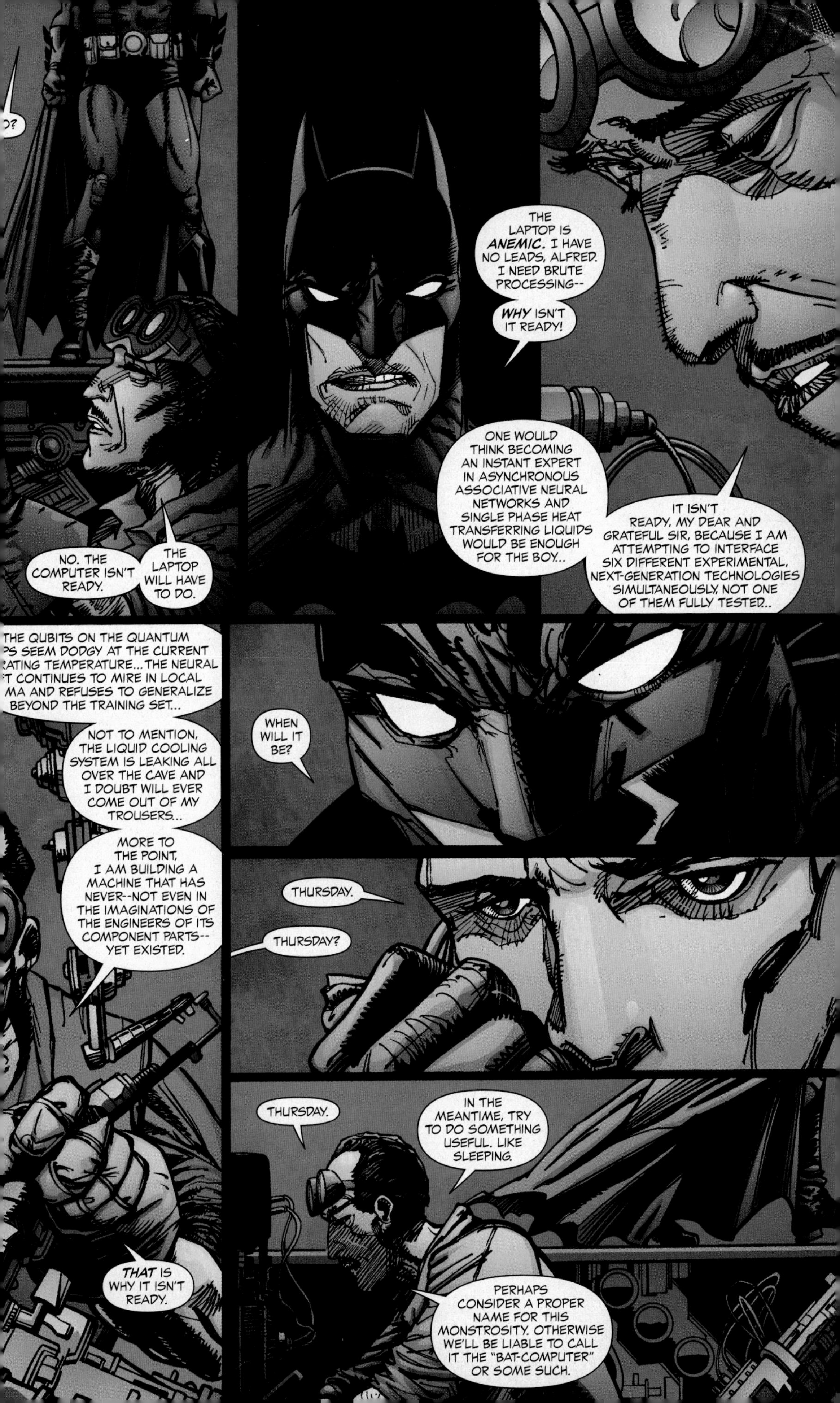

NO. THE COMPUTER ISN'T READY.
THE LAPTOP WILL HAVE TO DO.
THE LAPTOP IS ANEMIC. I HAVE NO LEADS, ALFRED. I NEED BRUTE PROCESSING--
WHY ISN'T IT READY!
ONE WOULD THINK BECOMING AN INSTANT EXPERT IN ASYNCHRONOUS ASSOCIATIVE NEURAL NETWORKS AND SINGLE PHASE HEAT TRANSFERRING LIQUIDS WOULD BE ENOUGH FOR THE BOY...
IT ISN'T READY, MY DEAR AND GRATEFUL SIR, BECAUSE I AM ATTEMPTING TO INTERFACE SIX DIFFERENT EXPERIMENTAL, NEXT-GENERATION TECHNOLOGIES SIMULTANEOUSLY, NOT ONE OF THEM FULLY TESTED...
THE QUBITS ON THE QUANTUM PS SEEM DODGY AT THE CURRENT RATING TEMPERATURE... THE NEURAL T CONTINUES TO MIRE IN LOCAL MA AND REFUSES TO GENERALIZE BEYOND THE TRAINING SET...
NOT TO MENTION, THE LIQUID COOLING SYSTEM IS LEAKING ALL OVER THE CAVE AND I DOUBT WILL EVER COME OUT OF MY TROUSERS...
MORE TO THE POINT, I AM BUILDING A MACHINE THAT HAS NEVER--NOT EVEN IN THE IMAGINATIONS OF THE ENGINEERS OF ITS COMPONENT PARTS--YET EXISTED.
THAT IS WHY IT ISN'T READY.
WHEN WILL IT BE?
THURSDAY.
THURSDAY?
THURSDAY.
IN THE MEANTIME, TRY TO DO SOMETHING USEFUL. LIKE SLEEPING.
PERHAPS CONSIDER A PROPER NAME FOR THIS MONSTROSITY. OTHERWISE WE'LL BE LIABLE TO CALL IT THE "BAT-COMPUTER" OR SOME SUCH.

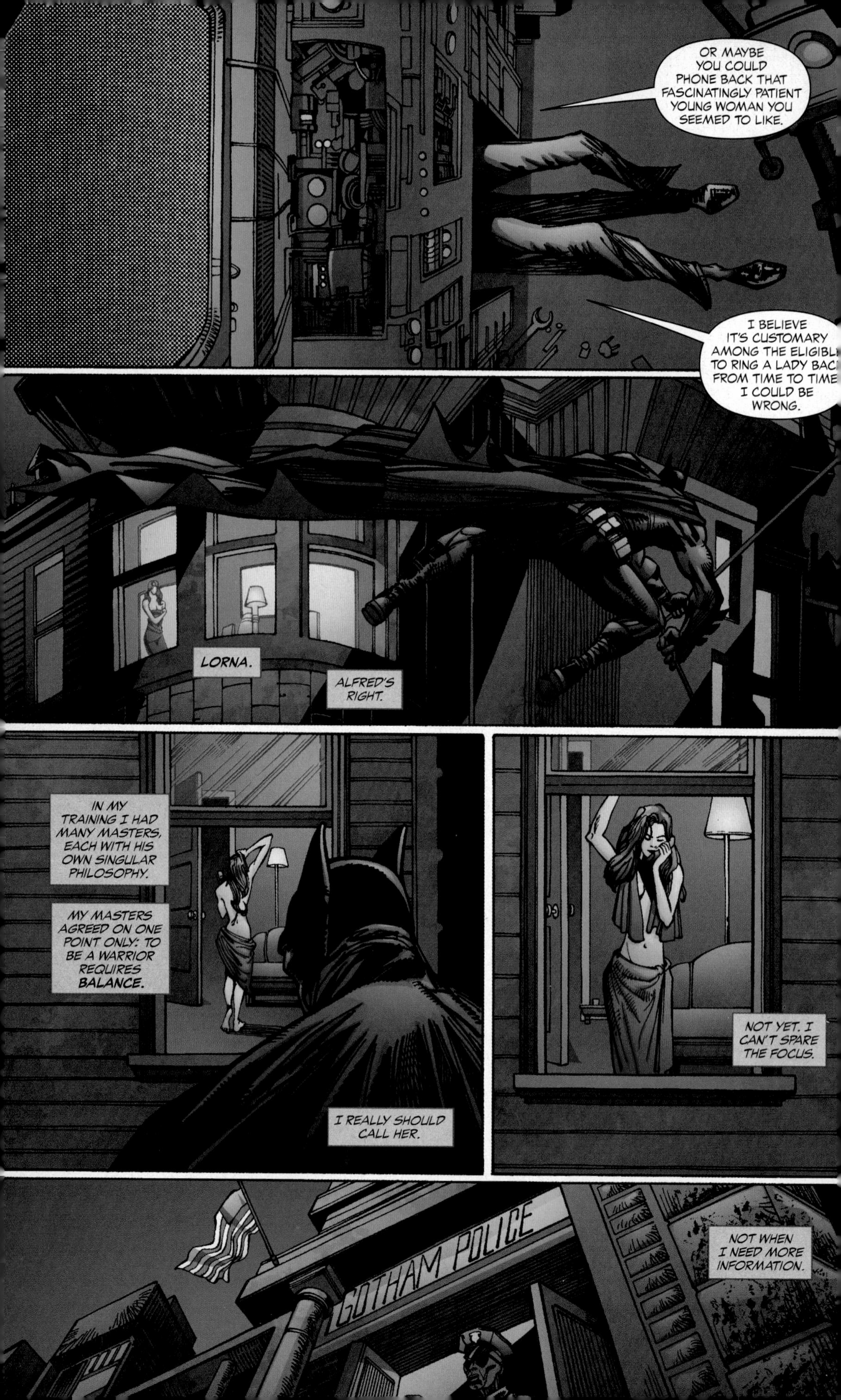

OR MAYBE YOU COULD PHONE BACK THAT FASCINATINGLY PATIENT YOUNG WOMAN YOU SEEMED TO LIKE.
I BELIEVE IT'S CUSTOMARY AMONG THE ELIGIBL TO RING A LADY BAC FROM TIME TO TIME I COULD BE WRONG.
LORNA.
ALFRED'S RIGHT.
IN MY TRAINING I HAD MANY MASTERS, EACH WITH HIS OWN SINGULAR PHILOSOPHY.
MY MASTERS AGREED ON ONE POINT ONLY: TO BE A WARRIOR REQUIRES BALANCE.
I REALLY SHOULD CALL HER.
NOT YET. I CAN'T SPARE THE FOCUS.
NOT WHEN I NEED MORE INFORMATION.
GOTHAM POLICE

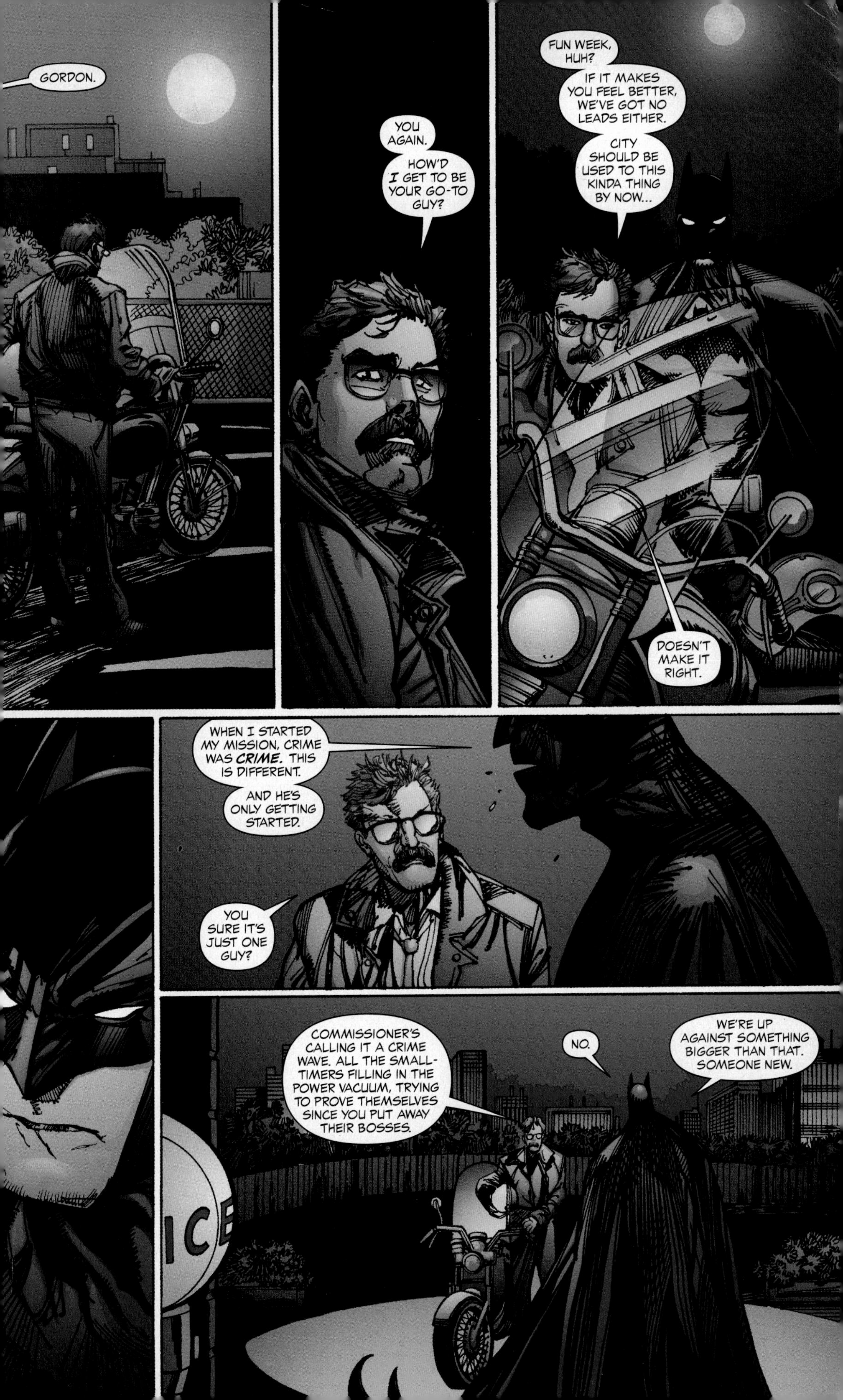
GORDON.
YOU AGAIN.
HOW'D *I* GET TO BE YOUR GO-TO GUY?
FUN WEEK, HUH?
IF IT MAKES YOU FEEL BETTER, WE'VE GOT NO LEADS EITHER.
CITY SHOULD BE USED TO THIS KINDA THING BY NOW...
DOESN'T MAKE IT RIGHT.
WHEN I STARTED MY MISSION, CRIME WAS *CRIME.* THIS IS DIFFERENT.
AND HE'S ONLY GETTING STARTED.
YOU SURE IT'S JUST ONE GUY?
COMMISSIONER'S CALLING IT A CRIME WAVE. ALL THE SMALL-TIMERS FILLING IN THE POWER VACUUM, TRYING TO PROVE THEMSELVES SINCE YOU PUT AWAY THEIR BOSSES.
NO.
WE'RE UP AGAINST SOMETHING BIGGER THAN THAT. SOMEONE NEW.
ICE

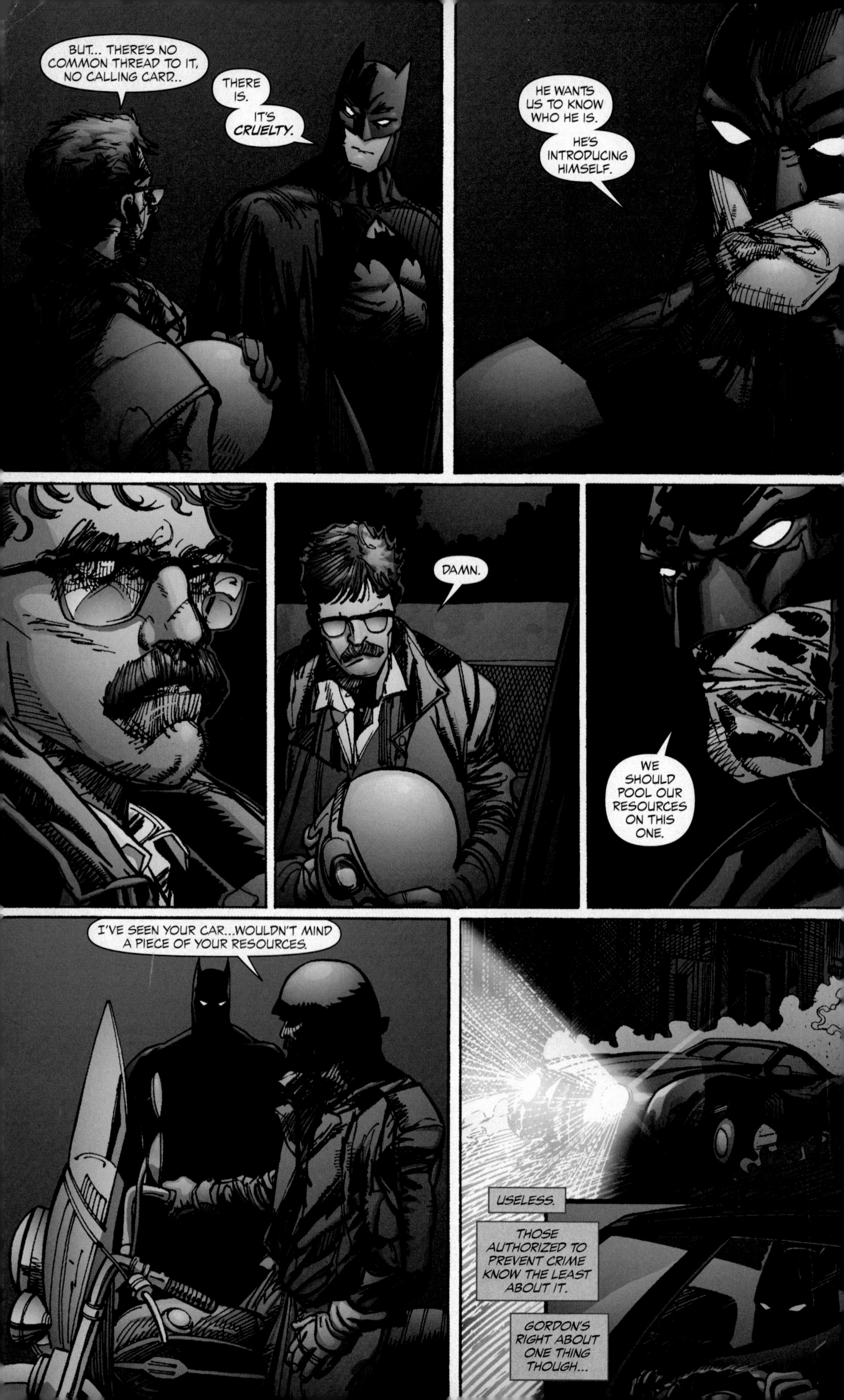
BUT... THERE'S NO COMMON THREAD TO IT, NO CALLING CARD...
THERE IS.
IT'S *CRUELTY.*
HE WANTS US TO KNOW WHO HE IS.
HE'S INTRODUCING HIMSELF.
DAMN.
WE SHOULD POOL OUR RESOURCES ON THIS ONE.
I'VE SEEN YOUR CAR...WOULDN'T MIND A PIECE OF YOUR RESOURCES.
USELESS.
THOSE AUTHORIZED TO PREVENT CRIME KNOW THE LEAST ABOUT IT.
GORDON'S RIGHT ABOUT ONE THING THOUGH...

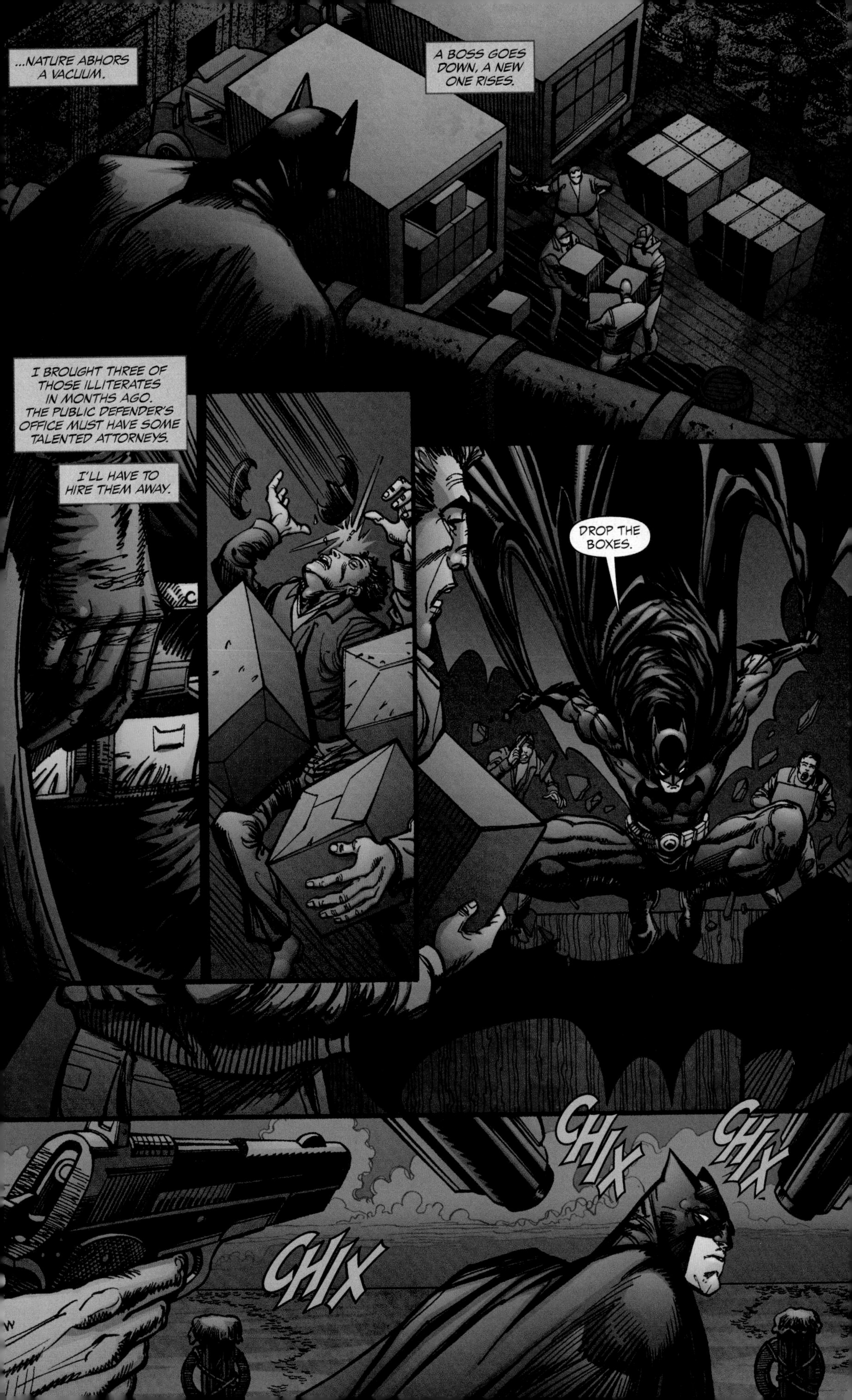
...NATURE ABHORS A VACUUM.
A BOSS GOES DOWN, A NEW ONE RISES.
I BROUGHT THREE OF THOSE ILLITERATES IN MONTHS AGO. THE PUBLIC DEFENDER'S OFFICE MUST HAVE SOME TALENTED ATTORNEYS.
I'LL HAVE TO HIRE THEM AWAY.
DROP THE BOXES.
CHIX
CHIX
CHIX

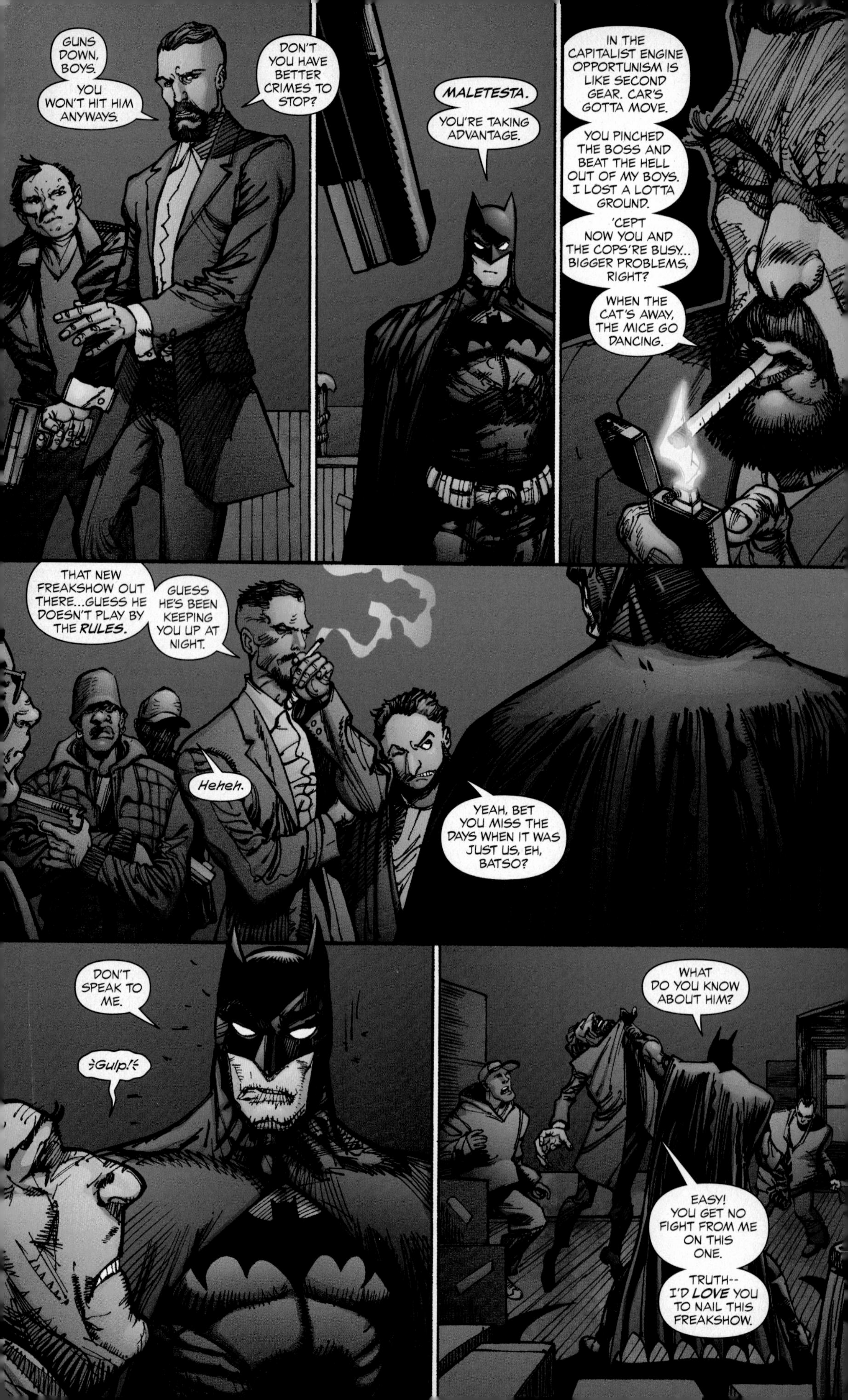
GUNS DOWN, BOYS.
YOU WON'T HIT HIM ANYWAYS.
DON'T YOU HAVE BETTER CRIMES TO STOP?
MALETESTA.
YOU'RE TAKING ADVANTAGE.
IN THE CAPITALIST ENGINE OPPORTUNISM IS LIKE SECOND GEAR. CAR'S GOTTA MOVE.
YOU PINCHED THE BOSS AND BEAT THE HELL OUT OF MY BOYS. I LOST A LOTTA GROUND.
'CEPT NOW YOU AND THE COPS'RE BUSY... BIGGER PROBLEMS, RIGHT?
WHEN THE CAT'S AWAY, THE MICE GO DANCING.
THAT NEW FREAKSHOW OUT THERE...GUESS HE DOESN'T PLAY BY THE RULES.
GUESS HE'S BEEN KEEPING YOU UP AT NIGHT.
Heheh.
YEAH, BET YOU MISS THE DAYS WHEN IT WAS JUST US, EH, BATSO?
DON'T SPEAK TO ME.
Gulp!
WHAT DO YOU KNOW ABOUT HIM?
EASY! YOU GET NO FIGHT FROM ME ON THIS ONE.
TRUTH-- I'D LOVE YOU TO NAIL THIS FREAKSHOW.

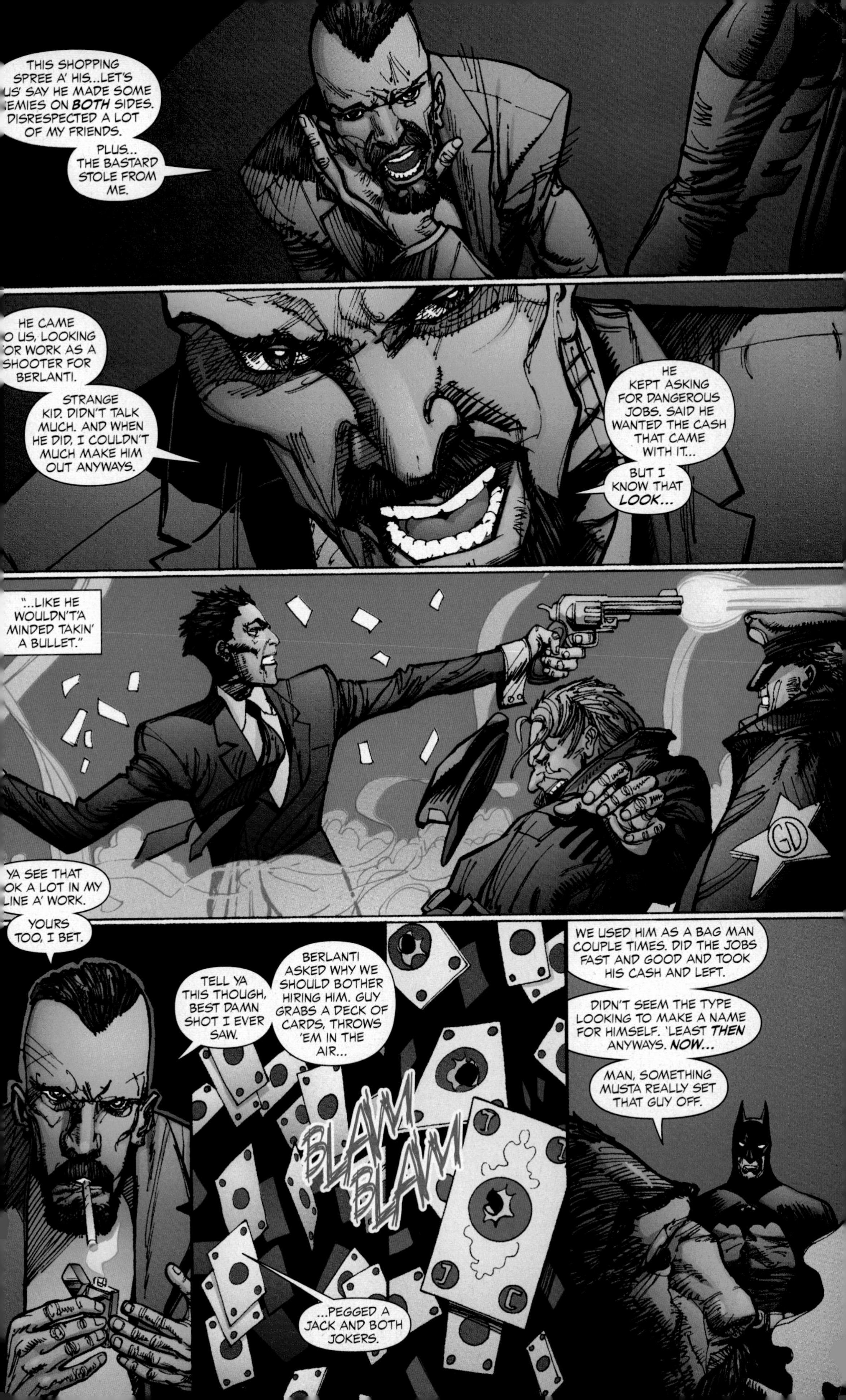

THIS SHOPPING SPREE A' HIS...LET'S US' SAY HE MADE SOME EMIES ON **BOTH** SIDES. DISRESPECTED A LOT OF MY FRIENDS.
PLUS... THE BASTARD STOLE FROM ME.
HE CAME O US, LOOKING OR WORK AS A SHOOTER FOR BERLANTI.
STRANGE KID. DIDN'T TALK MUCH. AND WHEN HE DID, I COULDN'T MUCH MAKE HIM OUT ANYWAYS.
HE KEPT ASKING FOR DANGEROUS JOBS. SAID HE WANTED THE CASH THAT CAME WITH IT...
BUT I KNOW THAT ***LOOK...***
"...LIKE HE WOULDN'T'A MINDED TAKIN' A BULLET."
YA SEE THAT OK A LOT IN MY LINE A' WORK.
YOURS TOO, I BET.
TELL YA THIS THOUGH, BEST DAMN SHOT I EVER SAW.
BERLANTI ASKED WHY WE SHOULD BOTHER HIRING HIM. GUY GRABS A DECK OF CARDS, THROWS 'EM IN THE AIR...
BLAM BLAM
...PEGGED A JACK AND BOTH JOKERS.
WE USED HIM AS A BAG MAN COUPLE TIMES. DID THE JOBS FAST AND GOOD AND TOOK HIS CASH AND LEFT.
DIDN'T SEEM THE TYPE LOOKING TO MAKE A NAME FOR HIMSELF. 'LEAST ***THEN*** ANYWAYS. ***NOW...***
MAN, SOMETHING MUSTA REALLY SET THAT GUY OFF.

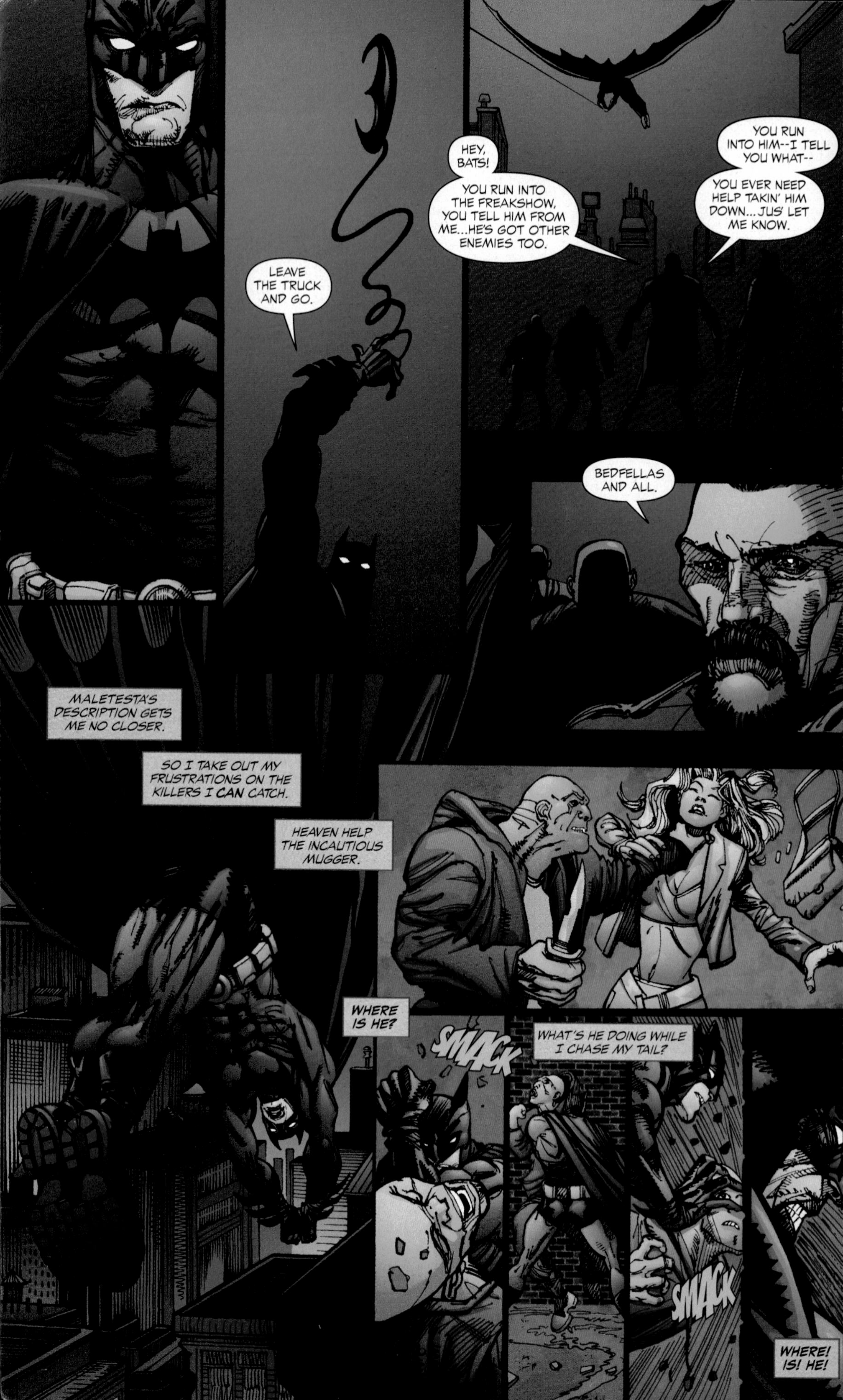

LEAVE THE TRUCK AND GO.
HEY, BATS!
YOU RUN INTO THE FREAKSHOW, YOU TELL HIM FROM ME...HE'S GOT OTHER ENEMIES TOO.
YOU RUN INTO HIM--I TELL YOU WHAT--
YOU EVER NEED HELP TAKIN' HIM DOWN...JUS' LET ME KNOW.
BEDFELLAS AND ALL.
MALETESTA'S DESCRIPTION GETS ME NO CLOSER.
SO I TAKE OUT MY FRUSTRATIONS ON THE KILLERS I CAN CATCH.
HEAVEN HELP THE INCAUTIOUS MUGGER.
WHERE IS HE?
SMACK
WHAT'S HE DOING WHILE I CHASE MY TAIL?
SMACK
WHERE! IS! HE!

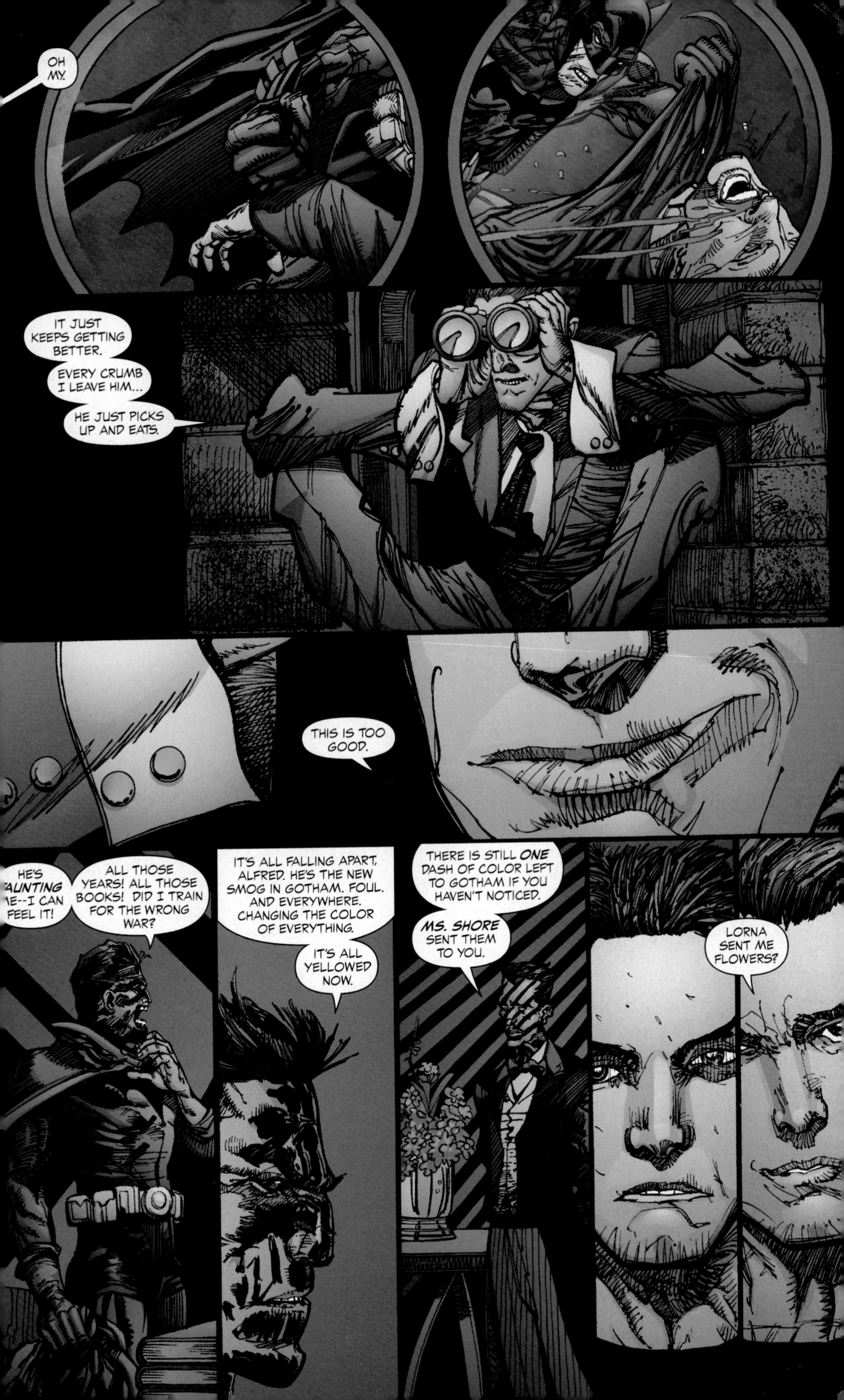
OH MY.
IT JUST KEEPS GETTING BETTER.
EVERY CRUMB I LEAVE HIM...
HE JUST PICKS UP AND EATS.
THIS IS TOO GOOD.
HE'S TAUNTING ME--I CAN FEEL IT!
ALL THOSE YEARS! ALL THOSE BOOKS! DID I TRAIN FOR THE WRONG WAR?
IT'S ALL FALLING APART, ALFRED. HE'S THE NEW SMOG IN GOTHAM. FOUL. AND EVERYWHERE. CHANGING THE COLOR OF EVERYTHING.
IT'S ALL YELLOWED NOW.
THERE IS STILL ONE DASH OF COLOR LEFT TO GOTHAM IF YOU HAVEN'T NOTICED.
MS. SHORE SENT THEM TO YOU.
LORNA SENT ME FLOWERS?

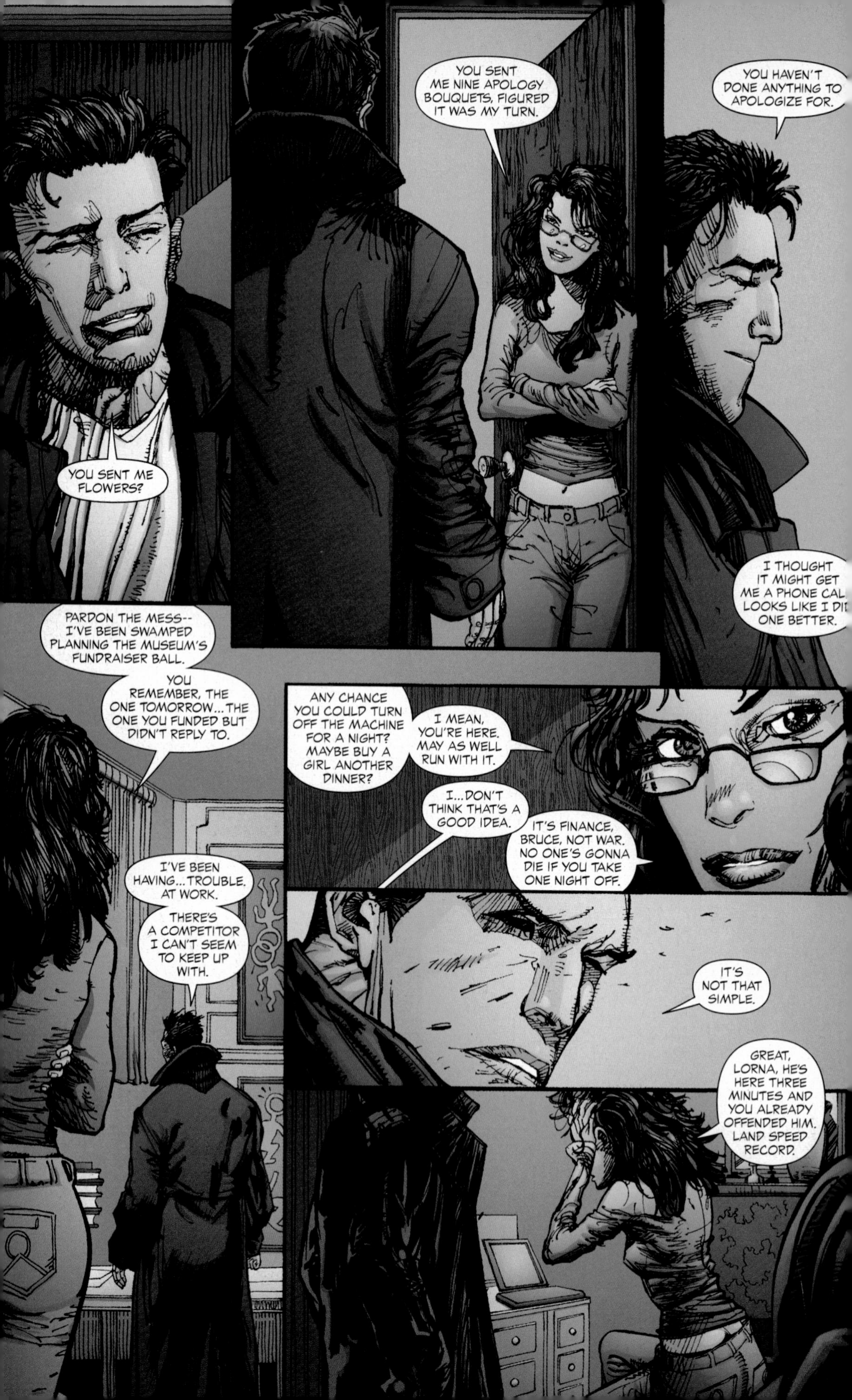
YOU SENT ME FLOWERS?
YOU SENT ME NINE APOLOGY BOUQUETS, FIGURED IT WAS MY TURN.
YOU HAVEN'T DONE ANYTHING TO APOLOGIZE FOR.
I THOUGHT IT MIGHT GET ME A PHONE CAL LOOKS LIKE I DI ONE BETTER.
PARDON THE MESS-- I'VE BEEN SWAMPED PLANNING THE MUSEUM'S FUNDRAISER BALL.
YOU REMEMBER, THE ONE TOMORROW... THE ONE YOU FUNDED BUT DIDN'T REPLY TO.
I'VE BEEN HAVING... TROUBLE. AT WORK.
THERE'S A COMPETITOR I CAN'T SEEM TO KEEP UP WITH.
I MEAN, YOU'RE HERE. MAY AS WELL RUN WITH IT.
ANY CHANCE YOU COULD TURN OFF THE MACHINE FOR A NIGHT? MAYBE BUY A GIRL ANOTHER DINNER?
I... DON'T THINK THAT'S A GOOD IDEA.
IT'S FINANCE, BRUCE, NOT WAR. NO ONE'S GONNA DIE IF YOU TAKE ONE NIGHT OFF.
IT'S NOT THAT SIMPLE.
GREAT, LORNA, HE'S HERE THREE MINUTES AND YOU ALREADY OFFENDED HIM. LAND SPEED RECORD.

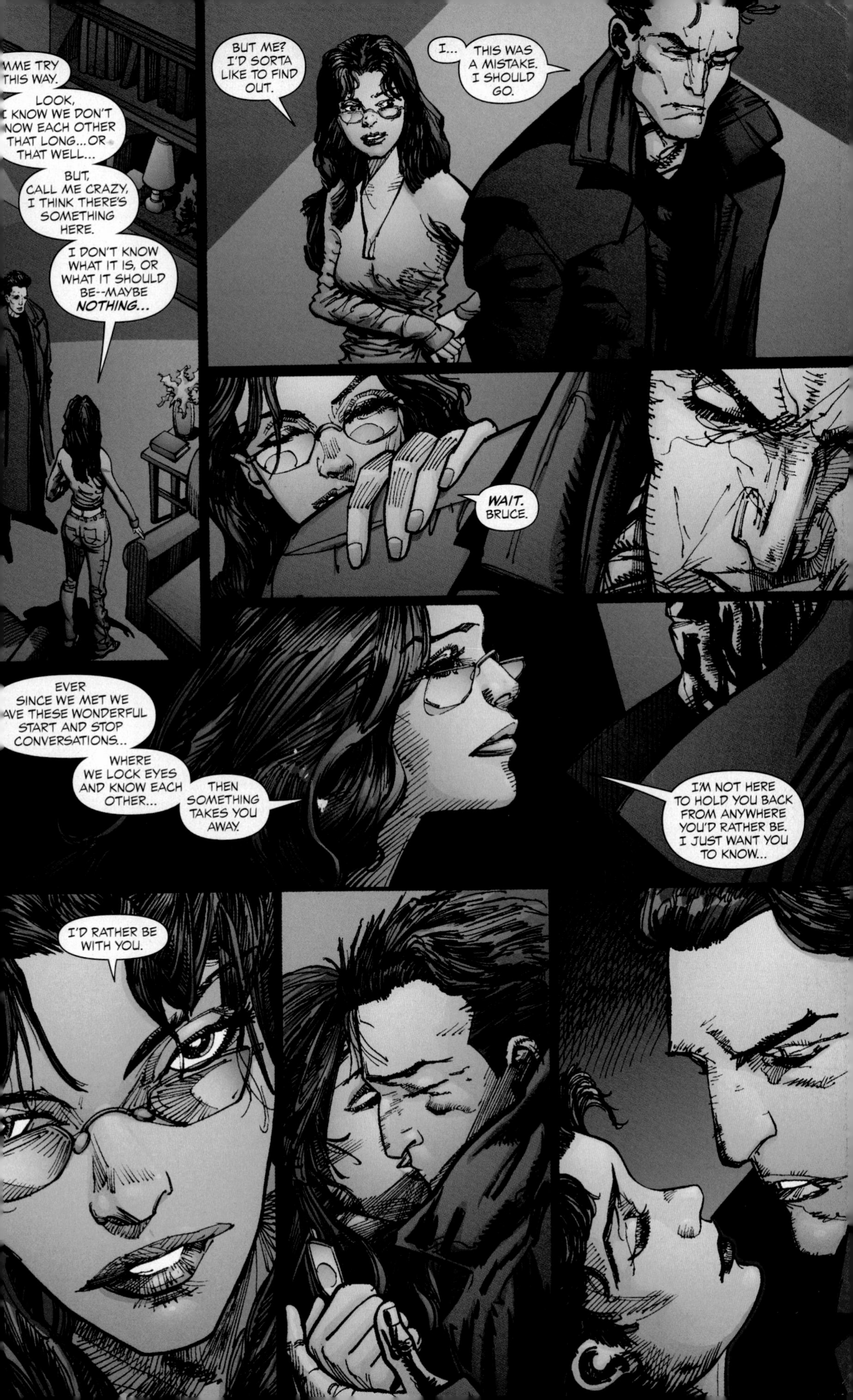
MME TRY THIS WAY.
LOOK, I KNOW WE DON'T NOW EACH OTHER THAT LONG...OR THAT WELL...
BUT, CALL ME CRAZY, I THINK THERE'S SOMETHING HERE.
I DON'T KNOW WHAT IT IS, OR WHAT IT SHOULD BE--MAYBE *NOTHING...*
BUT ME? I'D SORTA LIKE TO FIND OUT.
I...
THIS WAS A MISTAKE. I SHOULD GO.
WAIT. BRUCE.
EVER SINCE WE MET WE AVE THESE WONDERFUL START AND STOP CONVERSATIONS...
WHERE WE LOCK EYES AND KNOW EACH OTHER...
THEN SOMETHING TAKES YOU AWAY.
I'M NOT HERE TO HOLD YOU BACK FROM ANYWHERE YOU'D RATHER BE. I JUST WANT YOU TO KNOW...
I'D RATHER BE WITH YOU.

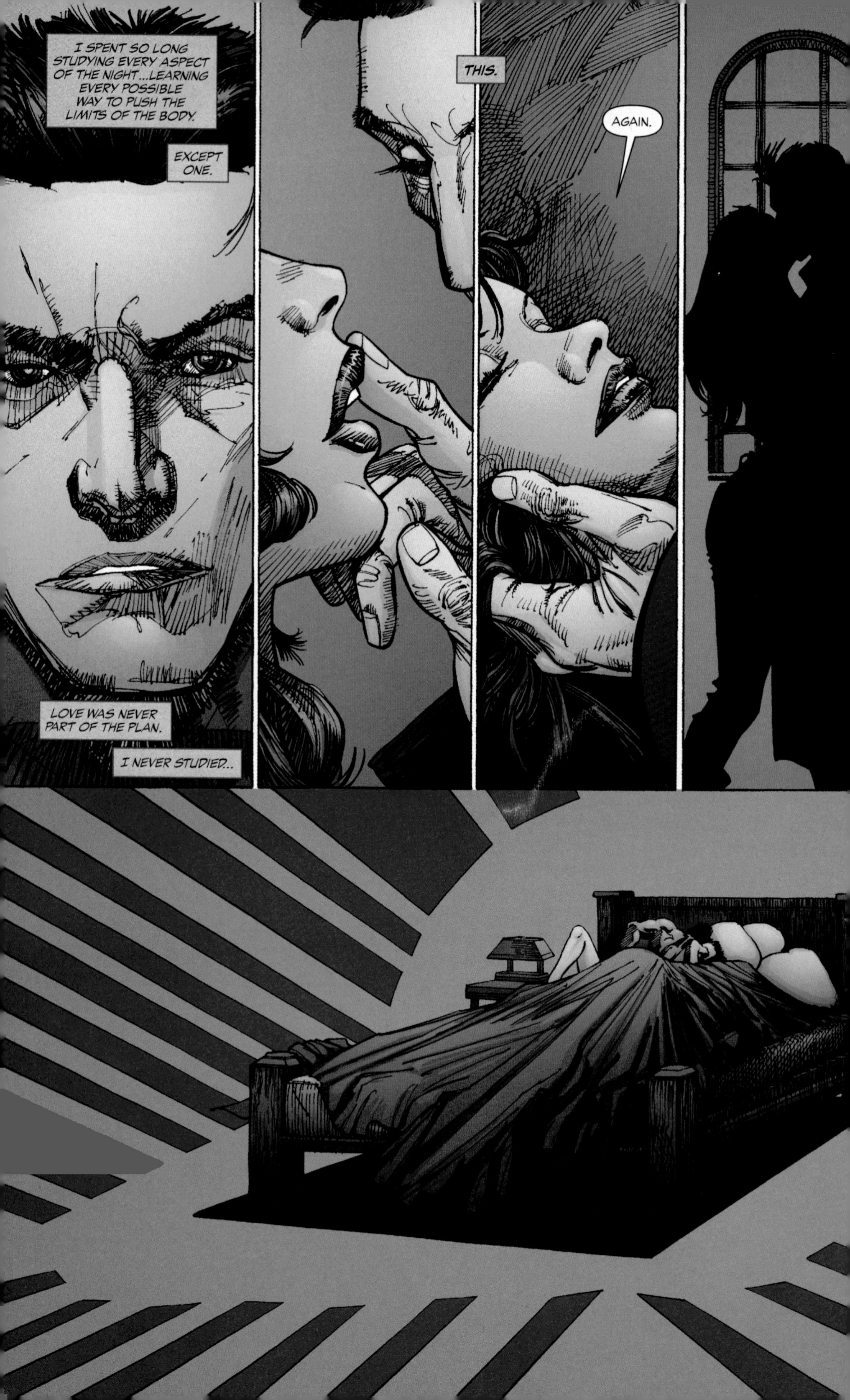
I SPENT SO LONG STUDYING EVERY ASPECT OF THE NIGHT...LEARNING EVERY POSSIBLE WAY TO PUSH THE LIMITS OF THE BODY.
EXCEPT ONE.
LOVE WAS NEVER PART OF THE PLAN.
I NEVER STUDIED...
THIS.
AGAIN.

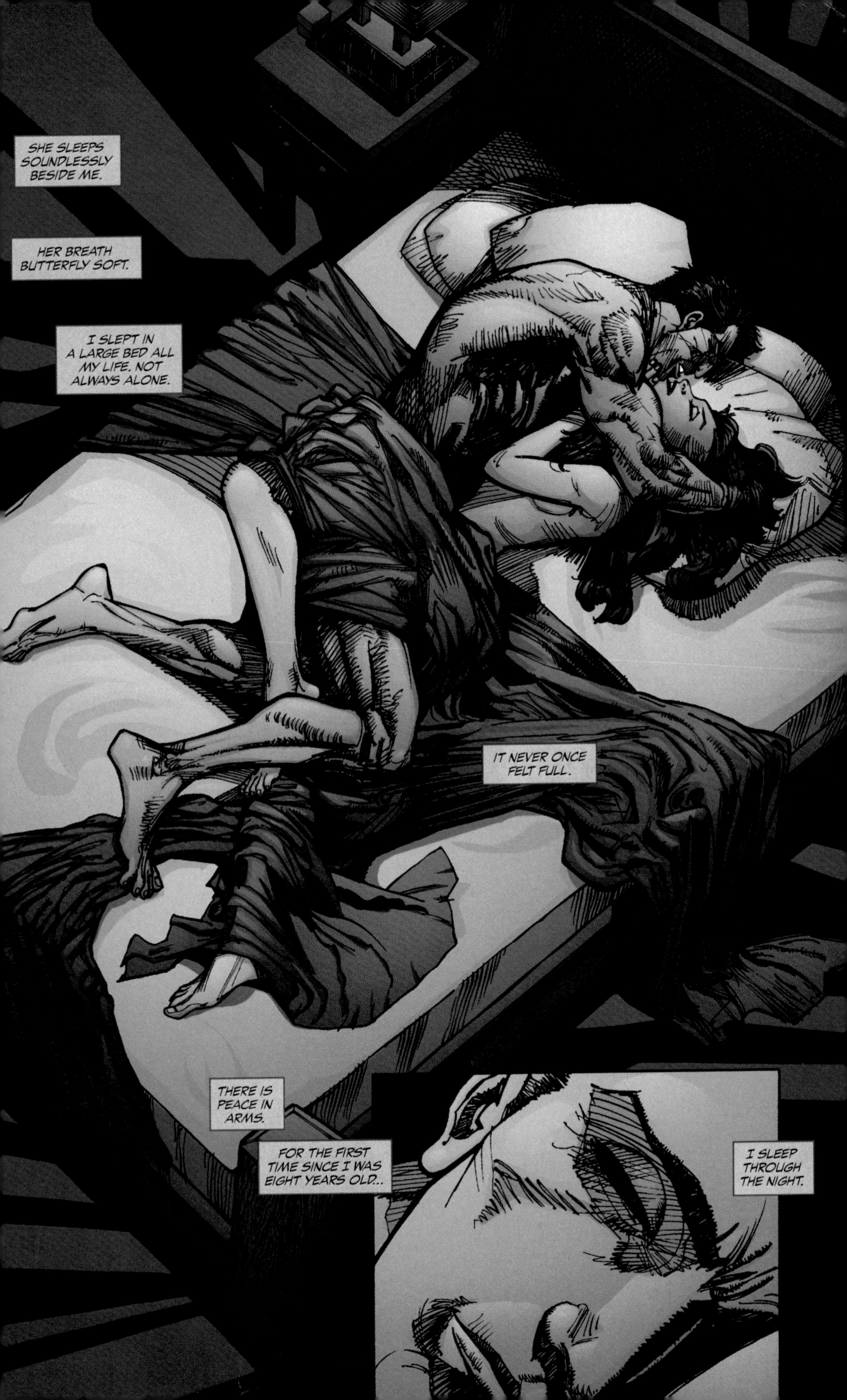
SHE SLEEPS SOUNDLESSLY BESIDE ME.
HER BREATH BUTTERFLY SOFT.
I SLEPT IN A LARGE BED ALL MY LIFE. NOT ALWAYS ALONE.
IT NEVER ONCE FELT FULL.
THERE IS PEACE IN ARMS.
FOR THE FIRST TIME SINCE I WAS EIGHT YEARS OLD...
I SLEEP THROUGH THE NIGHT.

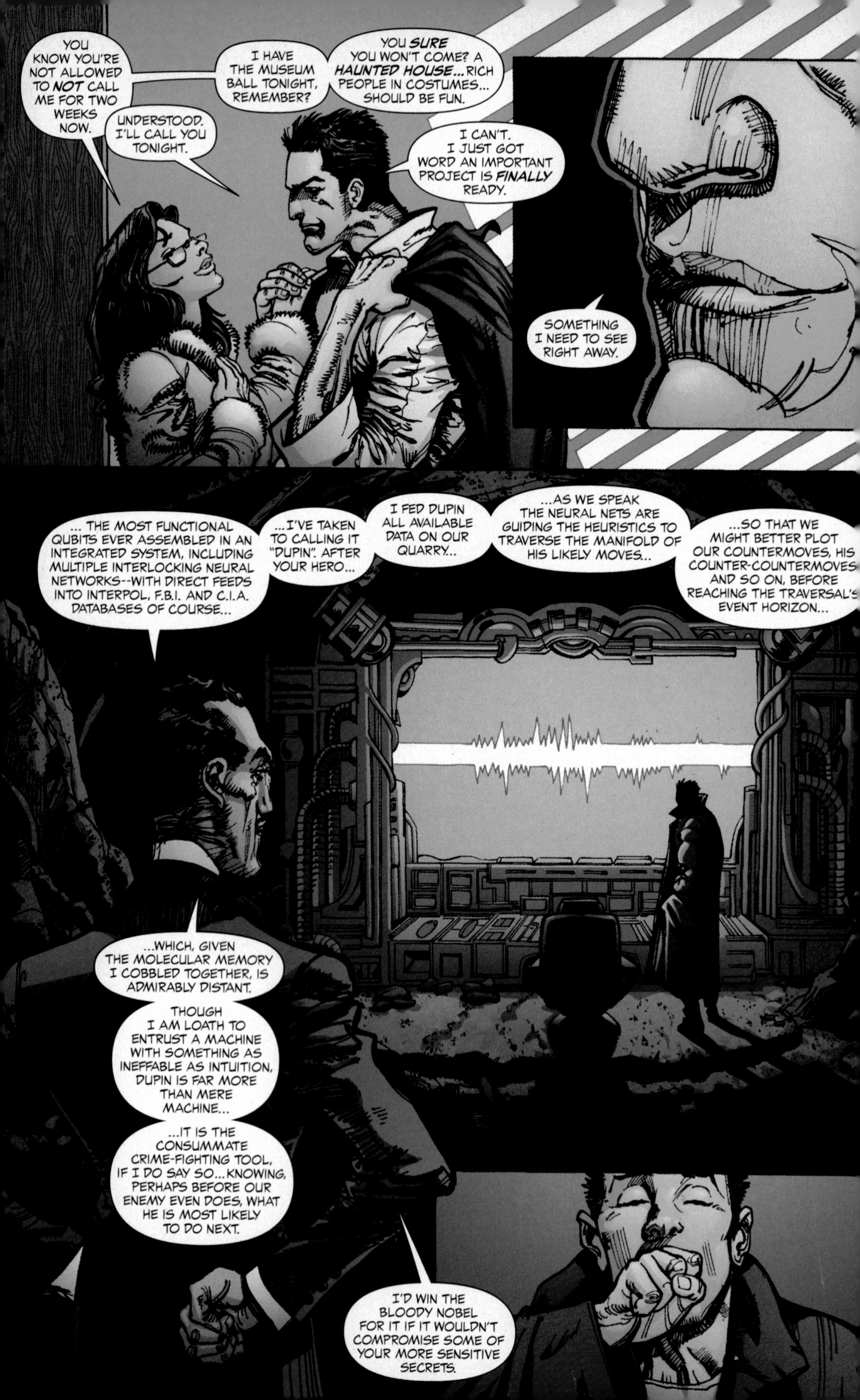

YOU KNOW YOU'RE NOT ALLOWED TO NOT CALL ME FOR TWO WEEKS NOW.
I HAVE THE MUSEUM BALL TONIGHT, REMEMBER?
YOU SURE YOU WON'T COME? A HAUNTED HOUSE... RICH PEOPLE IN COSTUMES... SHOULD BE FUN.
UNDERSTOOD. I'LL CALL YOU TONIGHT.
I CAN'T. I JUST GOT WORD AN IMPORTANT PROJECT IS FINALLY READY.
SOMETHING I NEED TO SEE RIGHT AWAY.
... THE MOST FUNCTIONAL QUBITS EVER ASSEMBLED IN AN INTEGRATED SYSTEM, INCLUDING MULTIPLE INTERLOCKING NEURAL NETWORKS--WITH DIRECT FEEDS INTO INTERPOL, F.B.I. AND C.I.A. DATABASES OF COURSE...
...I'VE TAKEN TO CALLING IT "DUPIN". AFTER YOUR HERO...
I FED DUPIN ALL AVAILABLE DATA ON OUR QUARRY...
...AS WE SPEAK THE NEURAL NETS ARE GUIDING THE HEURISTICS TO TRAVERSE THE MANIFOLD OF HIS LIKELY MOVES...
...SO THAT WE MIGHT BETTER PLOT OUR COUNTERMOVES, HIS COUNTER-COUNTERMOVES AND SO ON, BEFORE REACHING THE TRAVERSAL'S EVENT HORIZON...
...WHICH, GIVEN THE MOLECULAR MEMORY I COBBLED TOGETHER, IS ADMIRABLY DISTANT.
THOUGH I AM LOATH TO ENTRUST A MACHINE WITH SOMETHING AS INEFFABLE AS INTUITION, DUPIN IS FAR MORE THAN MERE MACHINE...
...IT IS THE CONSUMMATE CRIME-FIGHTING TOOL, IF I DO SAY SO... KNOWING, PERHAPS BEFORE OUR ENEMY EVEN DOES, WHAT HE IS MOST LIKELY TO DO NEXT.
I'D WIN THE BLOODY NOBEL FOR IT IF IT WOULDN'T COMPROMISE SOME OF YOUR MORE SENSITIVE SECRETS.

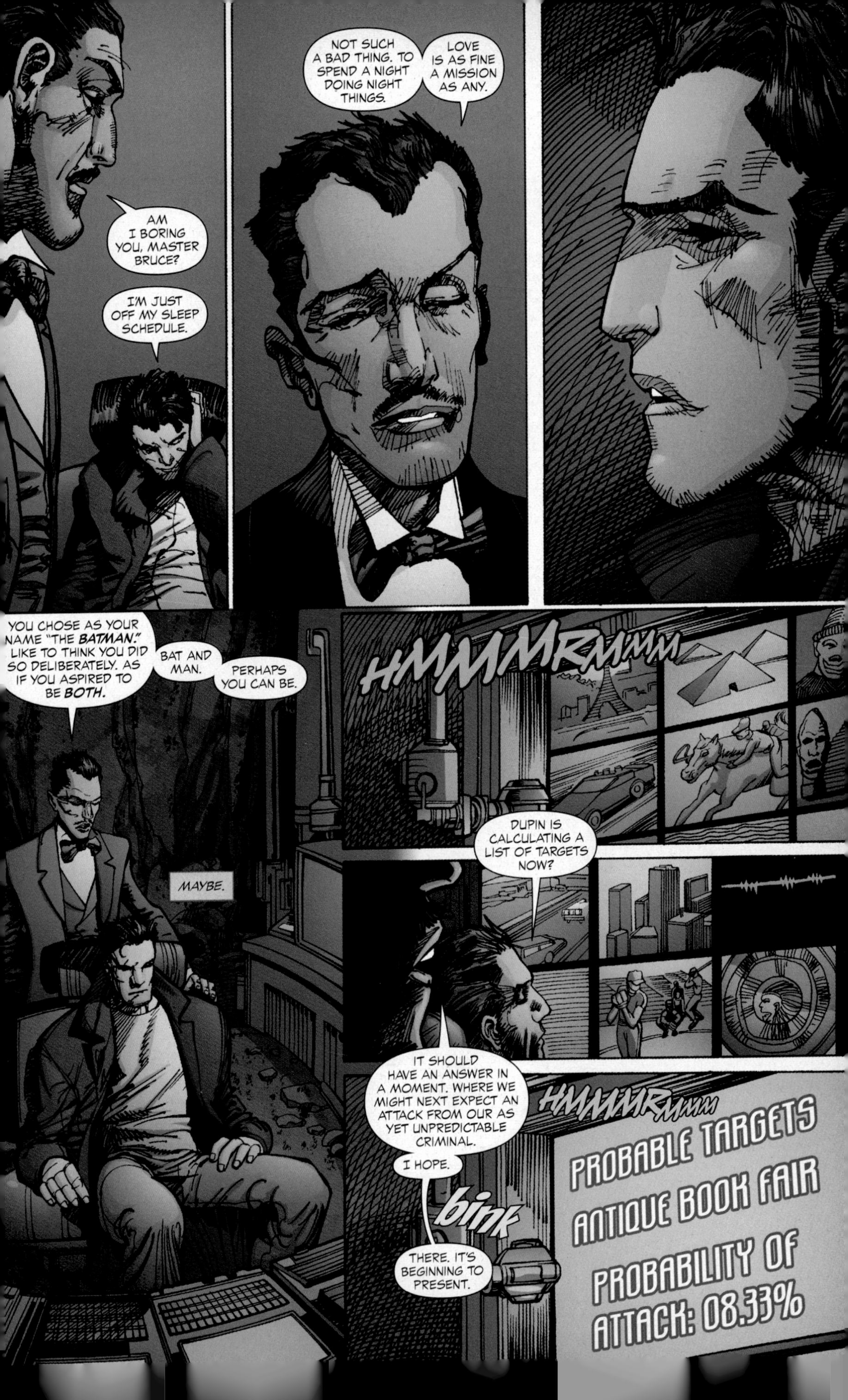
AM I BORING YOU, MASTER BRUCE?
I'M JUST OFF MY SLEEP SCHEDULE.
NOT SUCH A BAD THING. TO SPEND A NIGHT DOING NIGHT THINGS.
LOVE IS AS FINE A MISSION AS ANY.
YOU CHOSE AS YOUR NAME "THE BATMAN." LIKE TO THINK YOU DID SO DELIBERATELY. AS IF YOU ASPIRED TO BE BOTH.
BAT AND MAN.
PERHAPS YOU CAN BE.
MAYBE.
HMMMRMMM
DUPIN IS CALCULATING A LIST OF TARGETS NOW?
IT SHOULD HAVE AN ANSWER IN A MOMENT. WHERE WE MIGHT NEXT EXPECT AN ATTACK FROM OUR AS YET UNPREDICTABLE CRIMINAL.
I HOPE.
HMMMRMMM
bink
THERE. IT'S BEGINNING TO PRESENT.
PROBABLE TARGETS
ANTIQUE BOOK FAIR
PROBABILITY OF ATTACK: 08.33%

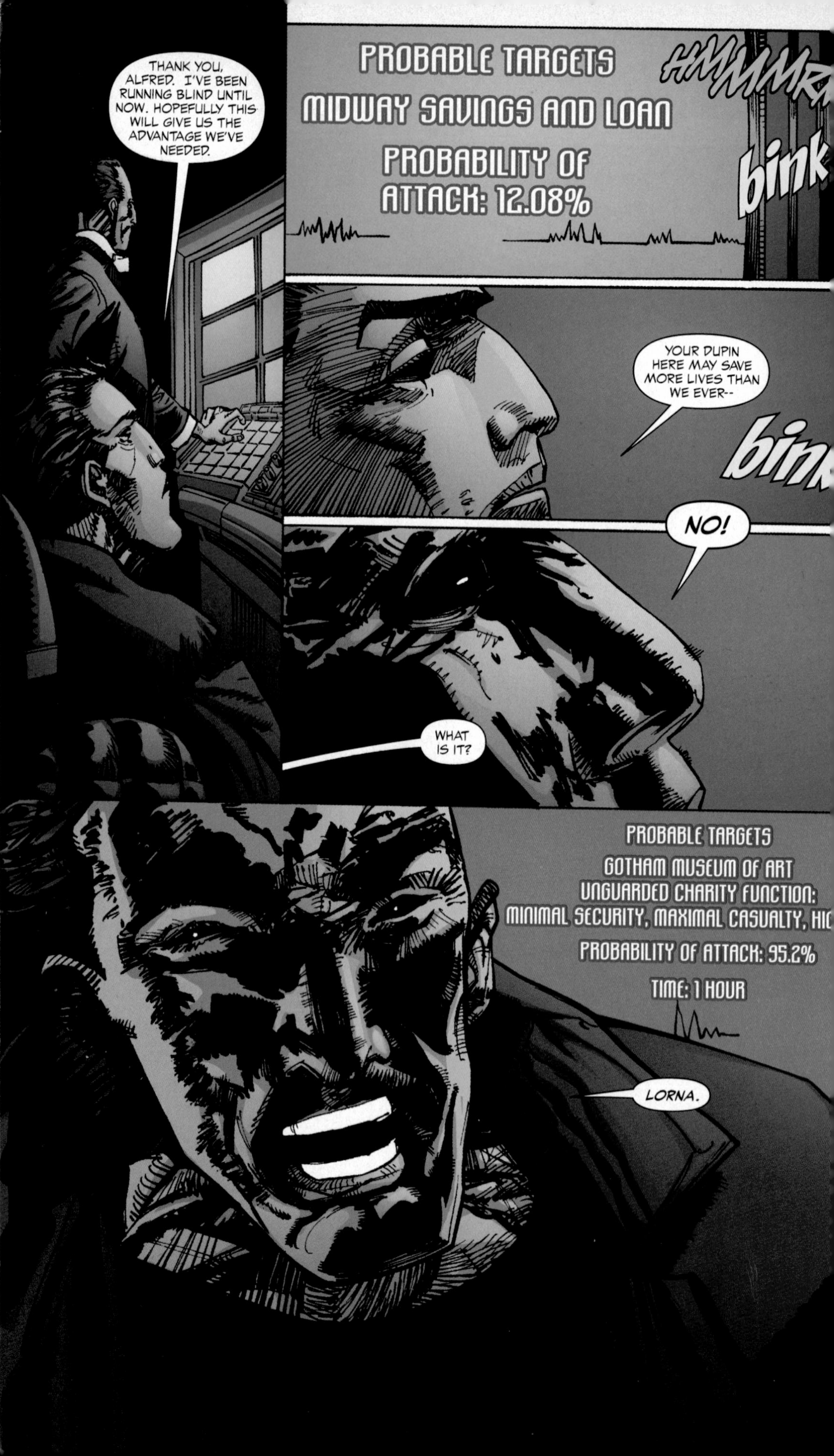
THANK YOU, ALFRED. I'VE BEEN RUNNING BLIND UNTIL NOW. HOPEFULLY THIS WILL GIVE US THE ADVANTAGE WE'VE NEEDED.
PROBABLE TARGETS
MIDWAY SAVINGS AND LOAN
PROBABILITY OF ATTACK: 12.08%
HMMMR
bink
YOUR DUPIN HERE MAY SAVE MORE LIVES THAN WE EVER--
bink
NO!
WHAT IS IT?
PROBABLE TARGETS
GOTHAM MUSEUM OF ART
UNGUARDED CHARITY FUNCTION:
MINIMAL SECURITY, MAXIMAL CASUALTY, HIG
PROBABILITY OF ATTACK: 95.2%
TIME: 1 HOUR
LORNA.

chapter three **CRIME'S NEW FACE**

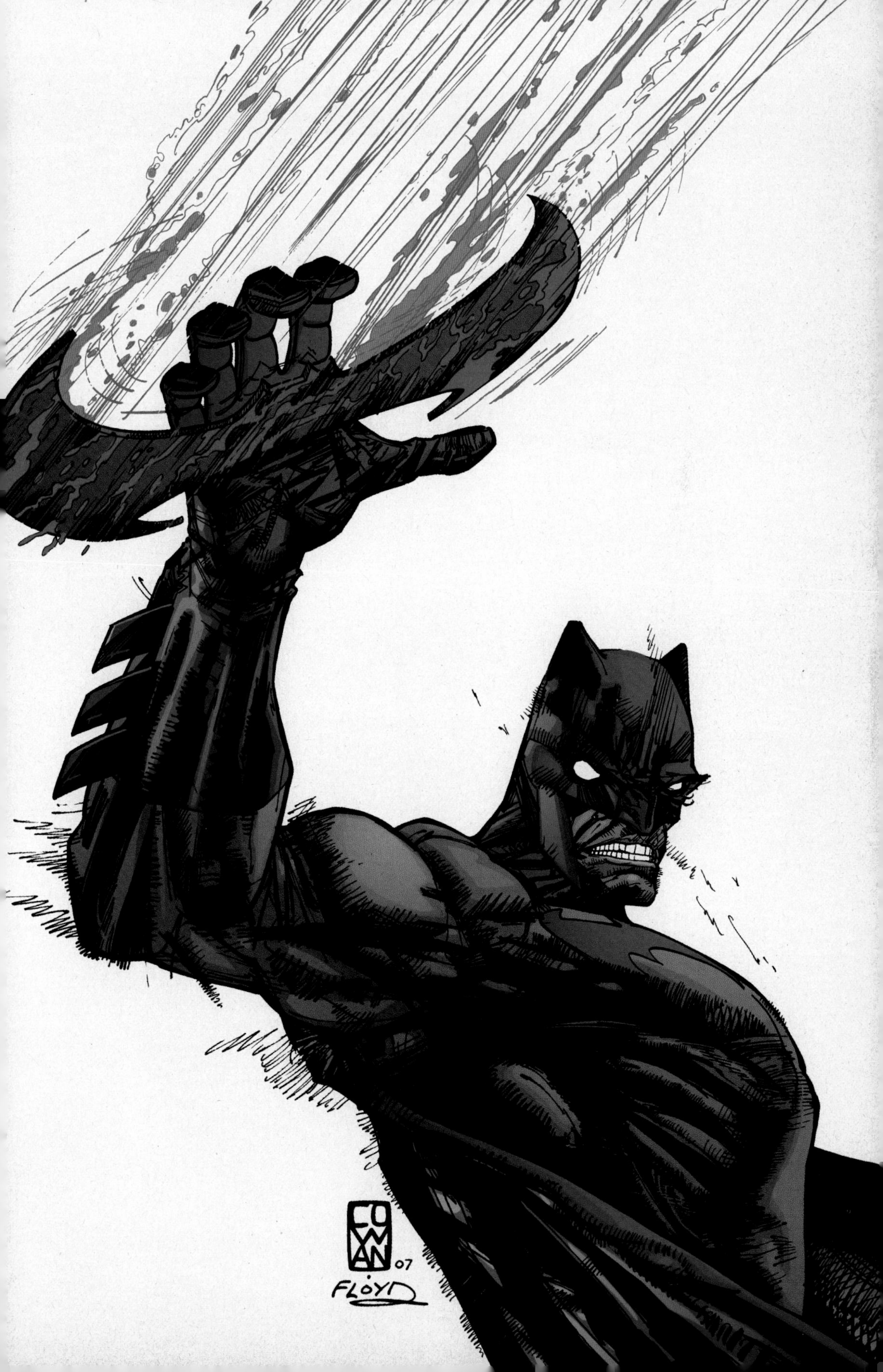
COWAN 07
FLOYD

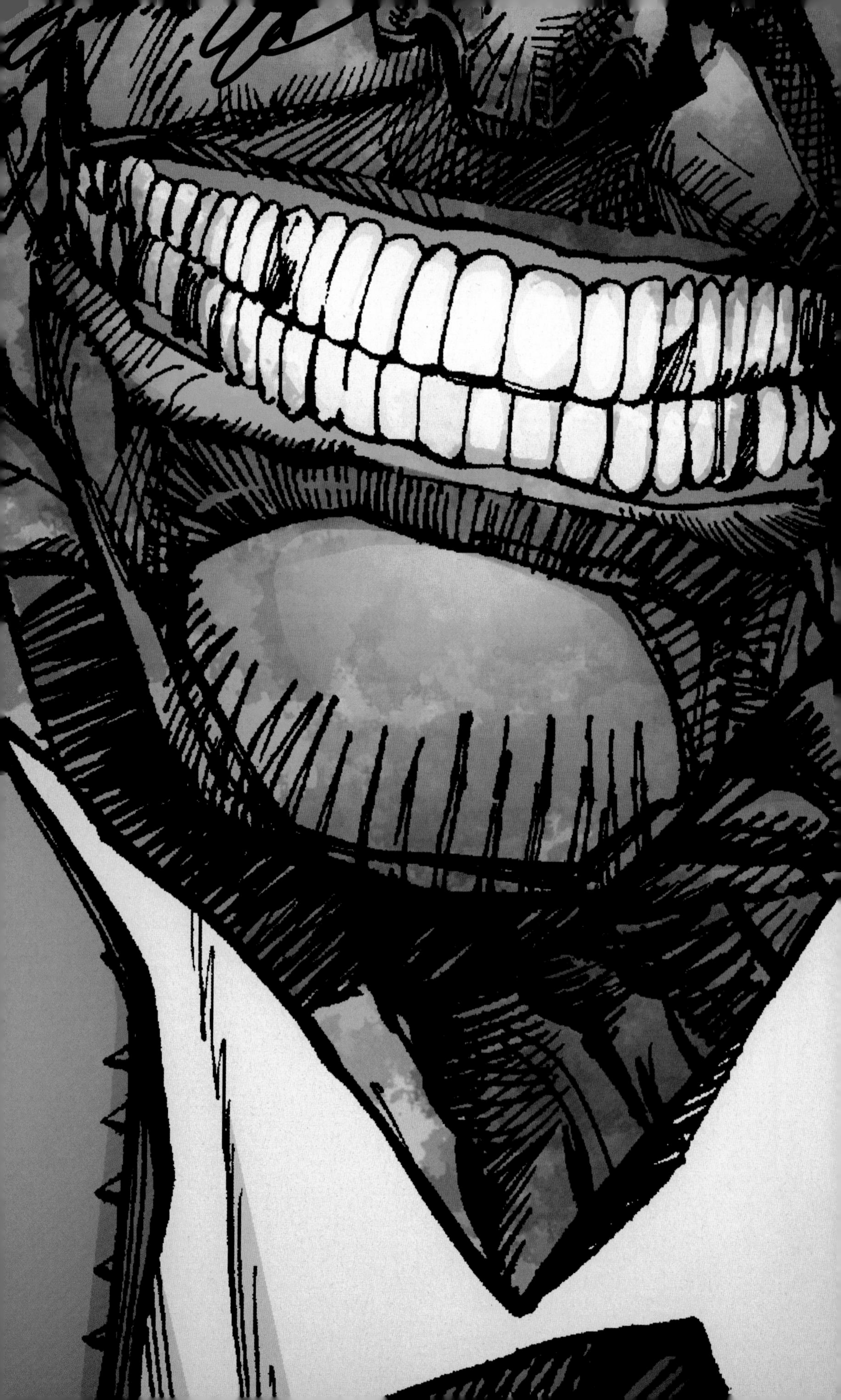

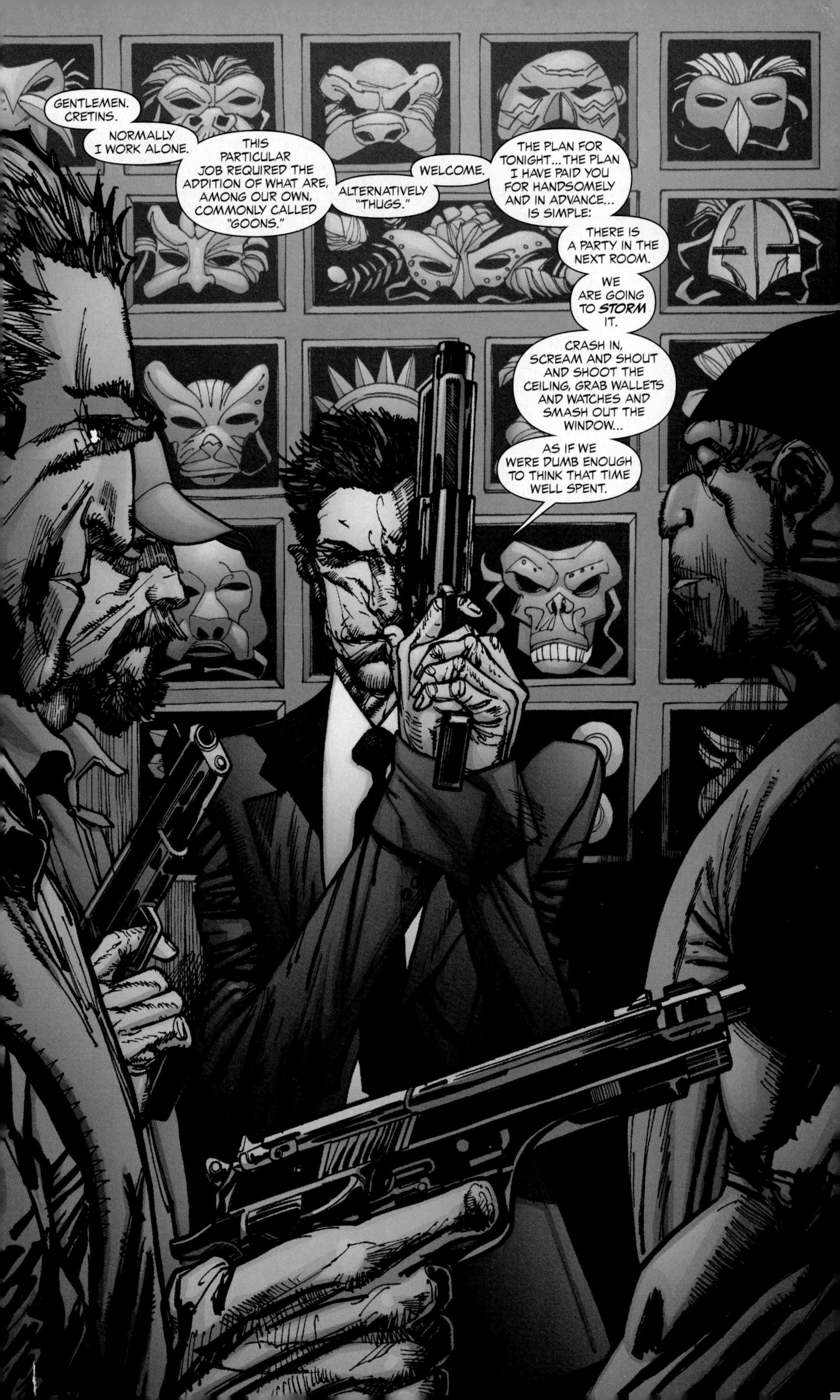
GENTLEMEN. CRETINS.
NORMALLY I WORK ALONE.
THIS PARTICULAR JOB REQUIRED THE ADDITION OF WHAT ARE, AMONG OUR OWN, COMMONLY CALLED "GOONS."
ALTERNATIVELY "THUGS."
WELCOME.
THE PLAN FOR TONIGHT... THE PLAN I HAVE PAID YOU FOR HANDSOMELY AND IN ADVANCE... IS SIMPLE:
THERE IS A PARTY IN THE NEXT ROOM.
WE ARE GOING TO *STORM* IT.
CRASH IN, SCREAM AND SHOUT AND SHOOT THE CEILING, GRAB WALLETS AND WATCHES AND SMASH OUT THE WINDOW...
AS IF WE WERE DUMB ENOUGH TO THINK THAT TIME WELL SPENT.

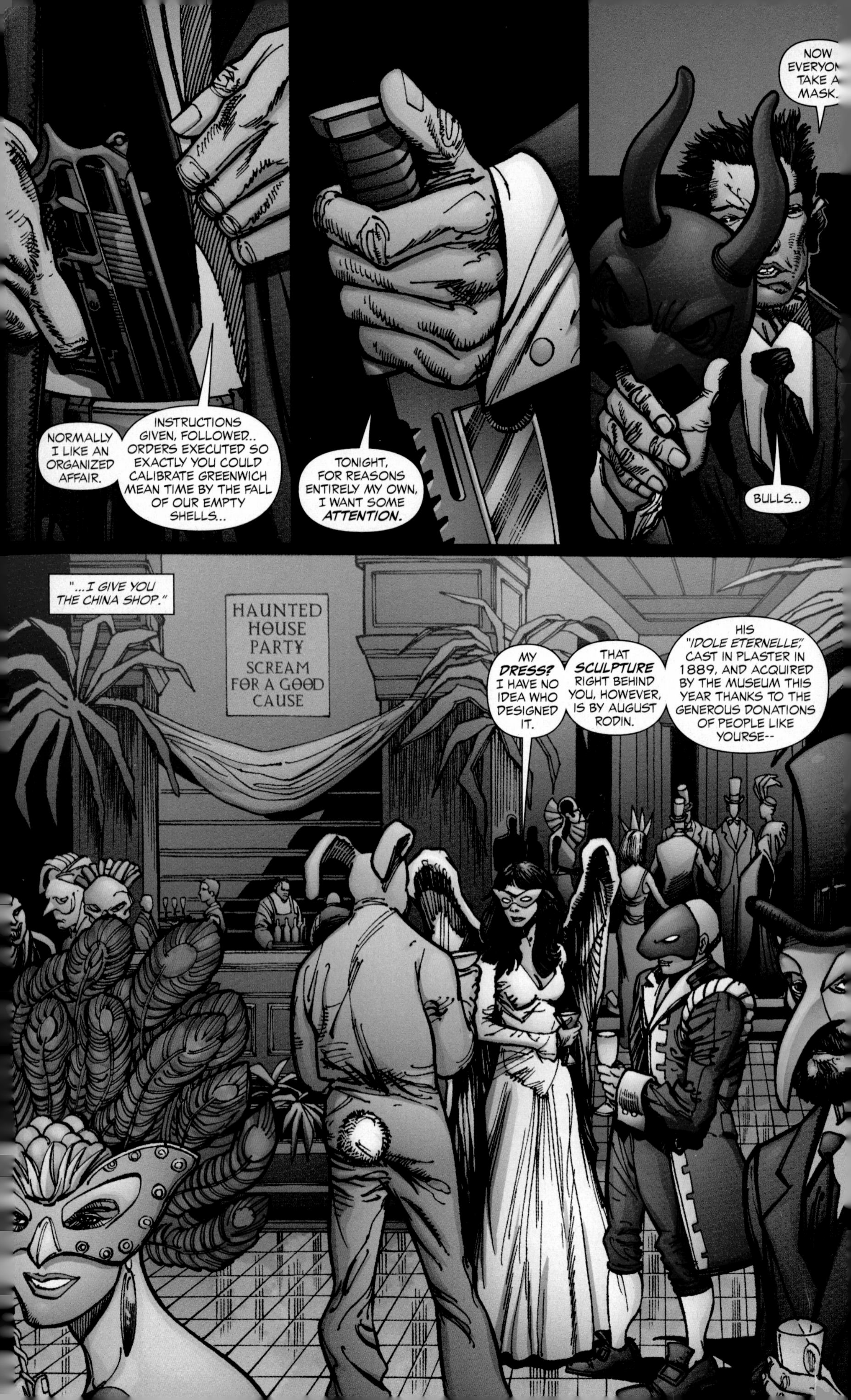
NORMALLY I LIKE AN ORGANIZED AFFAIR.
INSTRUCTIONS GIVEN, FOLLOWED... ORDERS EXECUTED SO EXACTLY YOU COULD CALIBRATE GREENWICH MEAN TIME BY THE FALL OF OUR EMPTY SHELLS...
TONIGHT, FOR REASONS ENTIRELY MY OWN, I WANT SOME ATTENTION.
NOW EVERYON TAKE A MASK.
BULLS...
"...I GIVE YOU THE CHINA SHOP."
HAUNTED HOUSE PARTY SCREAM FOR A GOOD CAUSE
MY DRESS? I HAVE NO IDEA WHO DESIGNED IT.
THAT SCULPTURE RIGHT BEHIND YOU, HOWEVER, IS BY AUGUST RODIN.
HIS "IDOLE ETERNELLE," CAST IN PLASTER IN 1889, AND ACQUIRED BY THE MUSEUM THIS YEAR THANKS TO THE GENEROUS DONATIONS OF PEOPLE LIKE YOURSE--

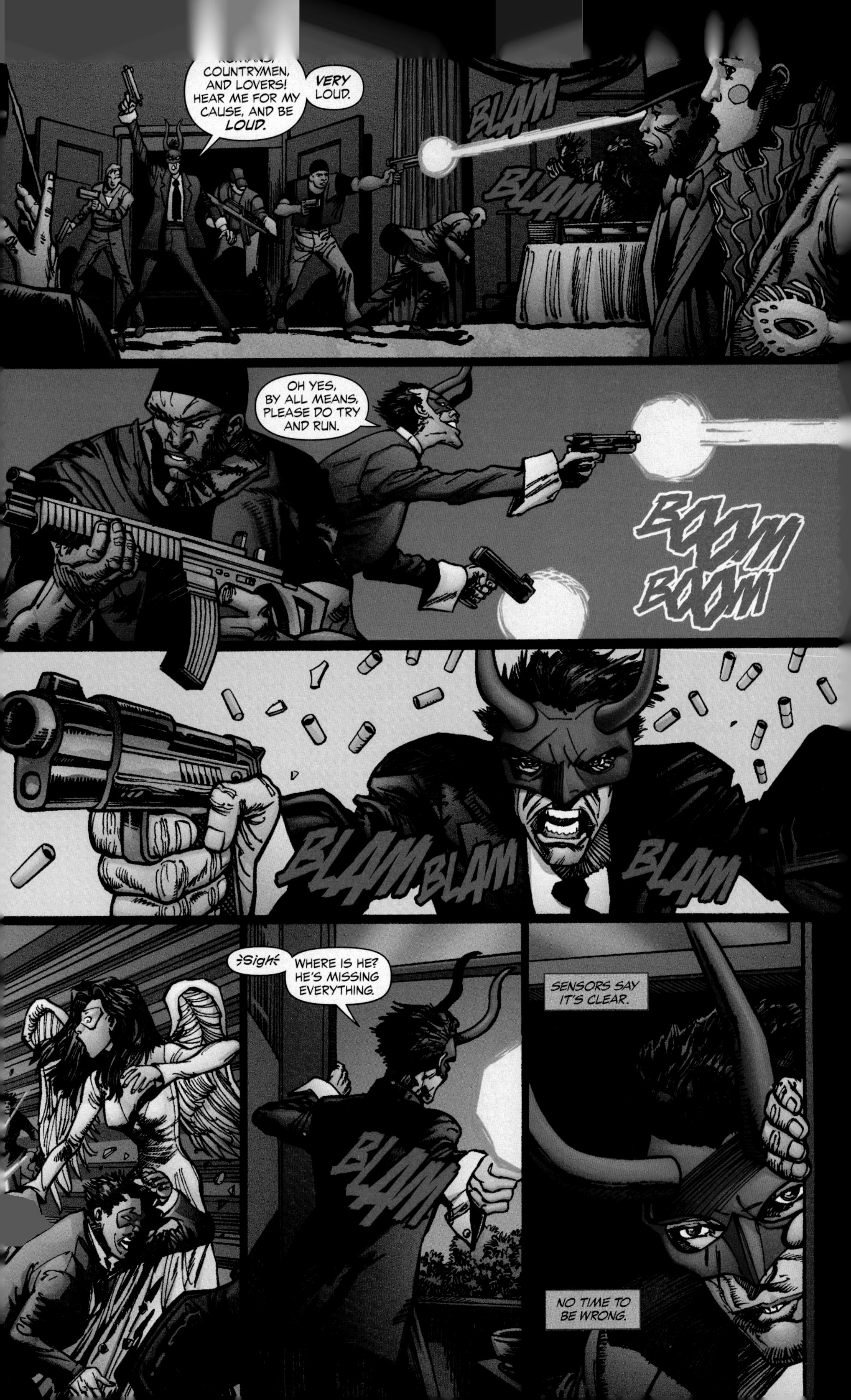
ROMANS, COUNTRYMEN, AND LOVERS! HEAR ME FOR MY CAUSE, AND BE LOUD.
VERY LOUD.
BLAM
BLAM
OH YES, BY ALL MEANS, PLEASE DO TRY AND RUN.
BOOM
BOOM
BLAM BLAM BLAM
Sigh
WHERE IS HE? HE'S MISSING EVERYTHING.
BLAM
SENSORS SAY IT'S CLEAR.
NO TIME TO BE WRONG.

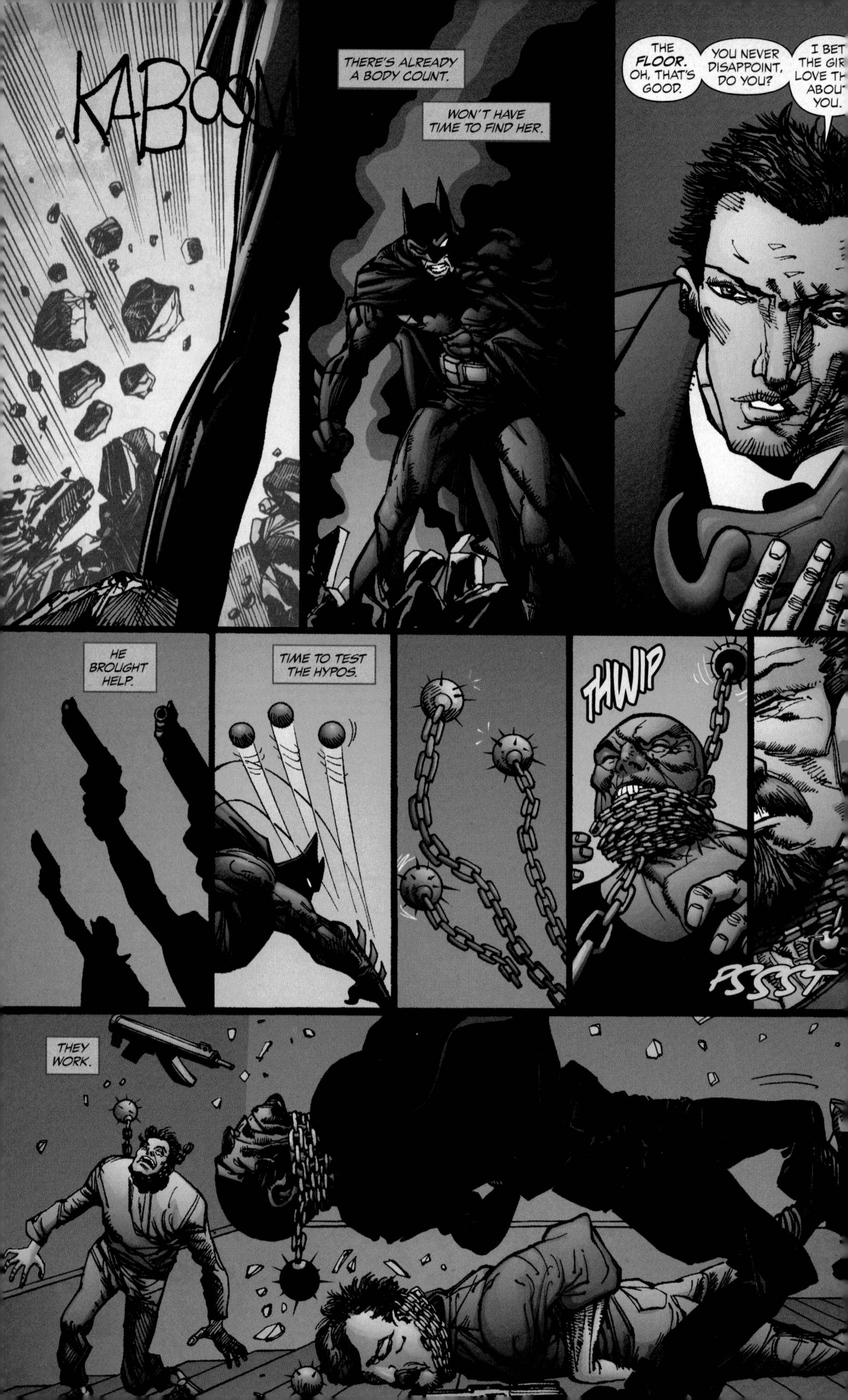
KABOOM
THERE'S ALREADY A BODY COUNT.
WON'T HAVE TIME TO FIND HER.
THE FLOOR. OH, THAT'S GOOD.
YOU NEVER DISAPPOINT, DO YOU?
I BET THE GIR LOVE TH ABOUT YOU.
HE BROUGHT HELP.
TIME TO TEST THE HYPOS.
THWIP
PSSST
THEY WORK.

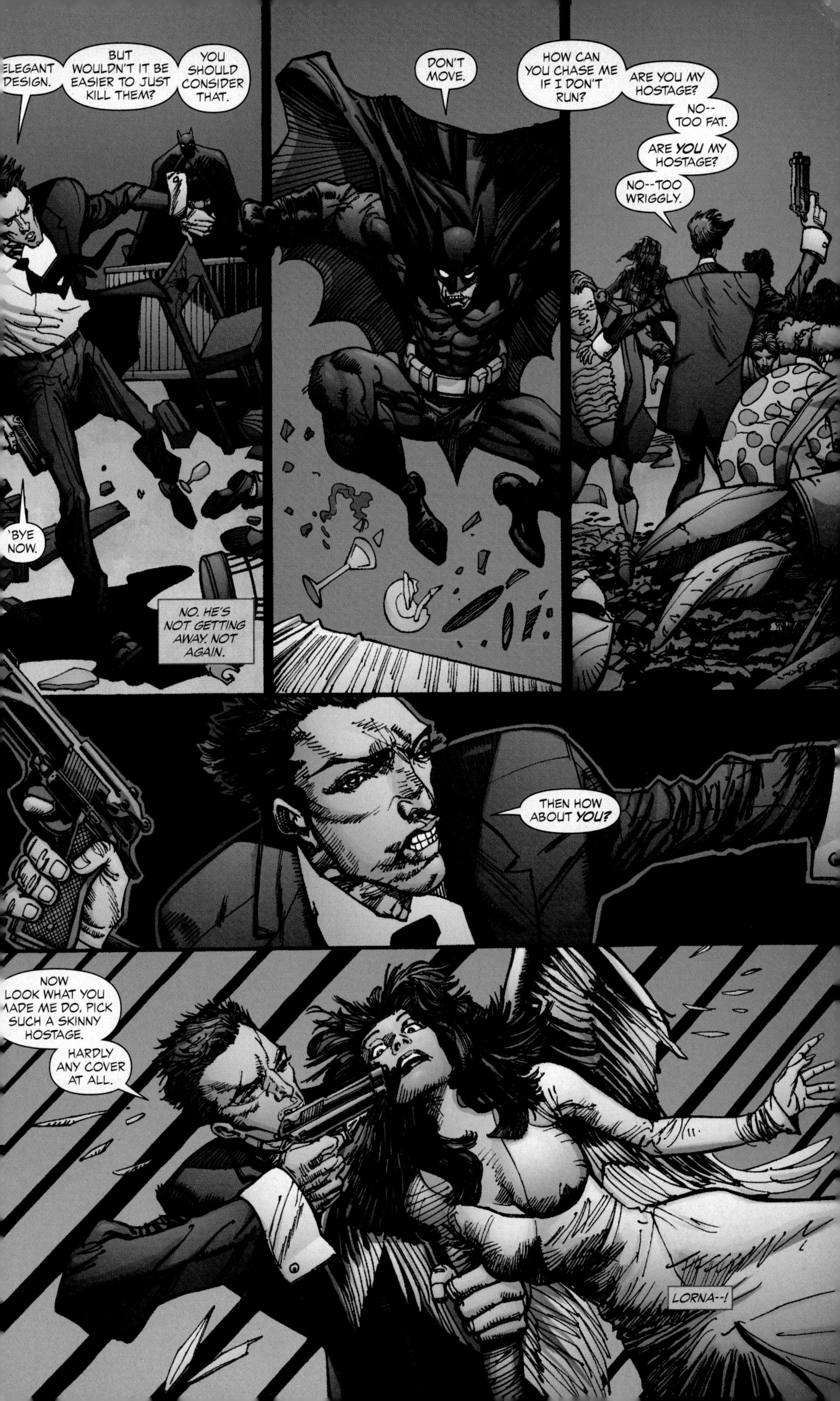

ELEGANT DESIGN.
BUT WOULDN'T IT BE EASIER TO JUST KILL THEM?
YOU SHOULD CONSIDER THAT.
'BYE NOW.
NO. HE'S NOT GETTING AWAY. NOT AGAIN.
DON'T MOVE.
HOW CAN YOU CHASE ME IF I DON'T RUN?
ARE YOU MY HOSTAGE?
NO-- TOO FAT.
ARE YOU MY HOSTAGE?
NO--TOO WRIGGLY.
THEN HOW ABOUT YOU?
NOW LOOK WHAT YOU MADE ME DO, PICK SUCH A SKINNY HOSTAGE.
HARDLY ANY COVER AT ALL.
LORNA--!

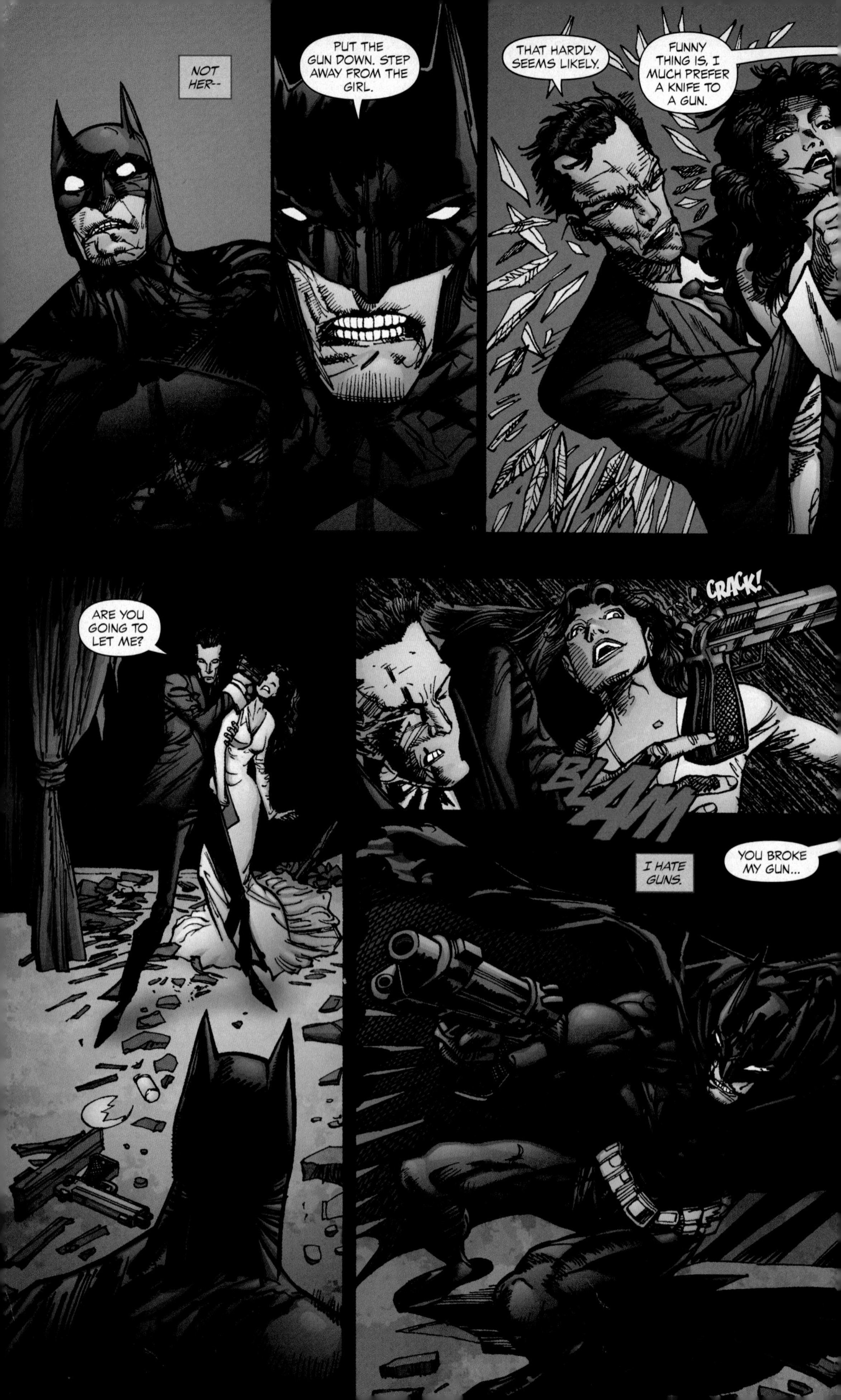

NOT HER--
PUT THE GUN DOWN. STEP AWAY FROM THE GIRL.
THAT HARDLY SEEMS LIKELY.
FUNNY THING IS, I MUCH PREFER A KNIFE TO A GUN.
ARE YOU GOING TO LET ME?
CRACK!
BLAM
I HATE GUNS.
YOU BROKE MY GUN...

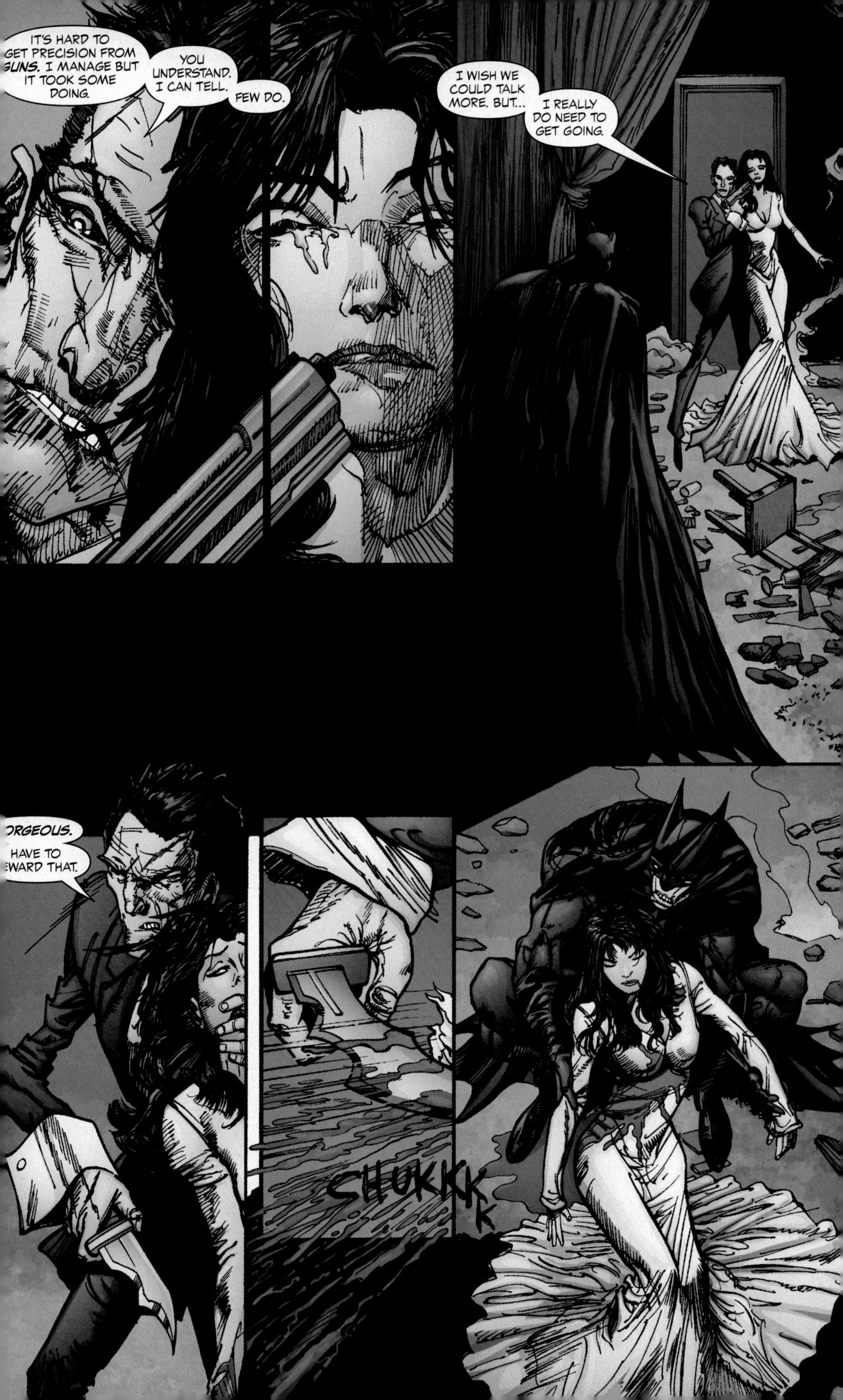

IT'S HARD TO GET PRECISION FROM GUNS. I MANAGE BUT IT TOOK SOME DOING.
YOU UNDERSTAND. I CAN TELL.
FEW DO.
I WISH WE COULD TALK MORE. BUT...
I REALLY DO NEED TO GET GOING.
ORGEOUS.
HAVE TO EWARD THAT.
CHUKKKK

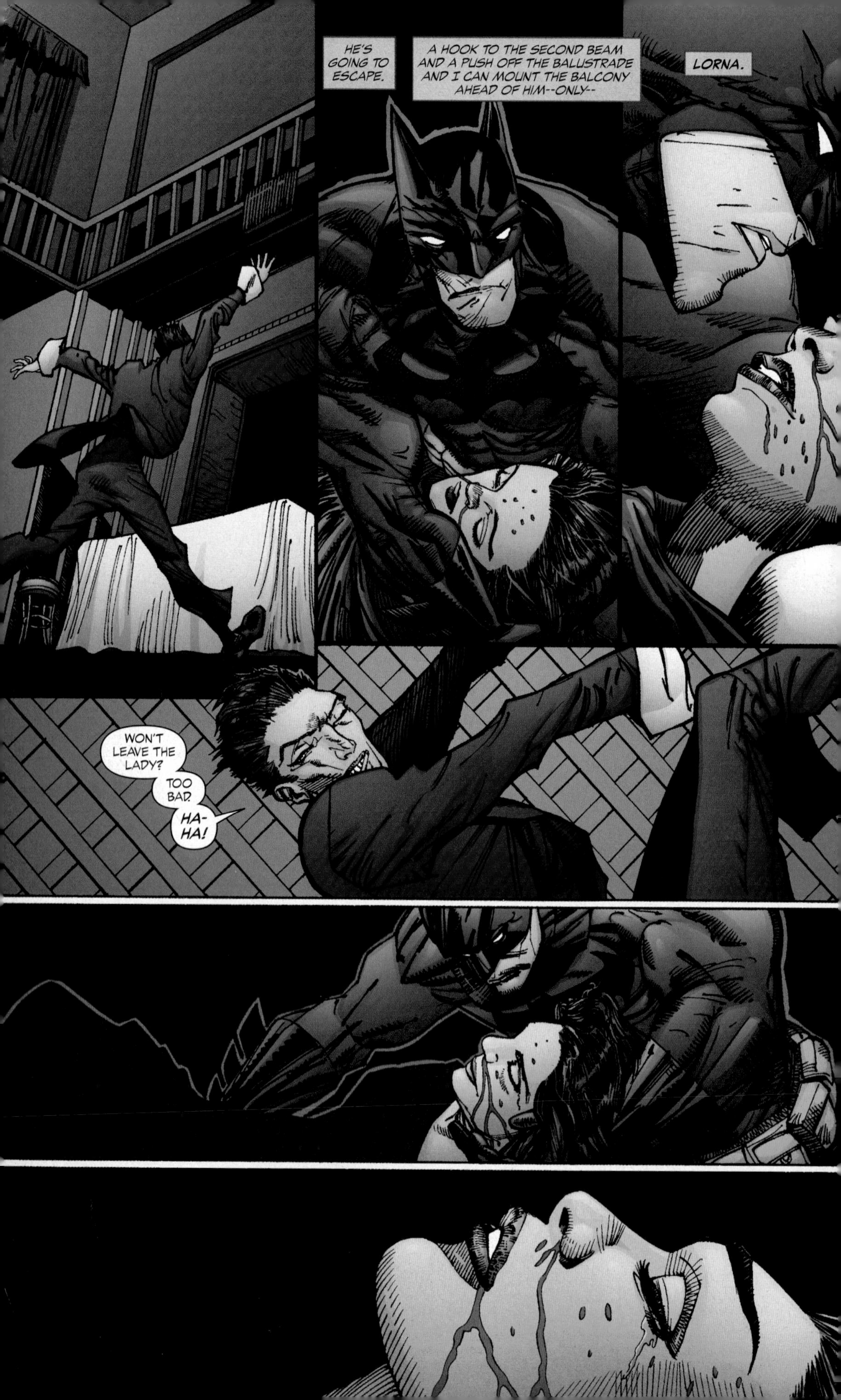
HE'S GOING TO ESCAPE.
A HOOK TO THE SECOND BEAM AND A PUSH OFF THE BALUSTRADE AND I CAN MOUNT THE BALCONY AHEAD OF HIM--ONLY--
LORNA.
WON'T LEAVE THE LADY?
TOO BAD.
HA-HA!

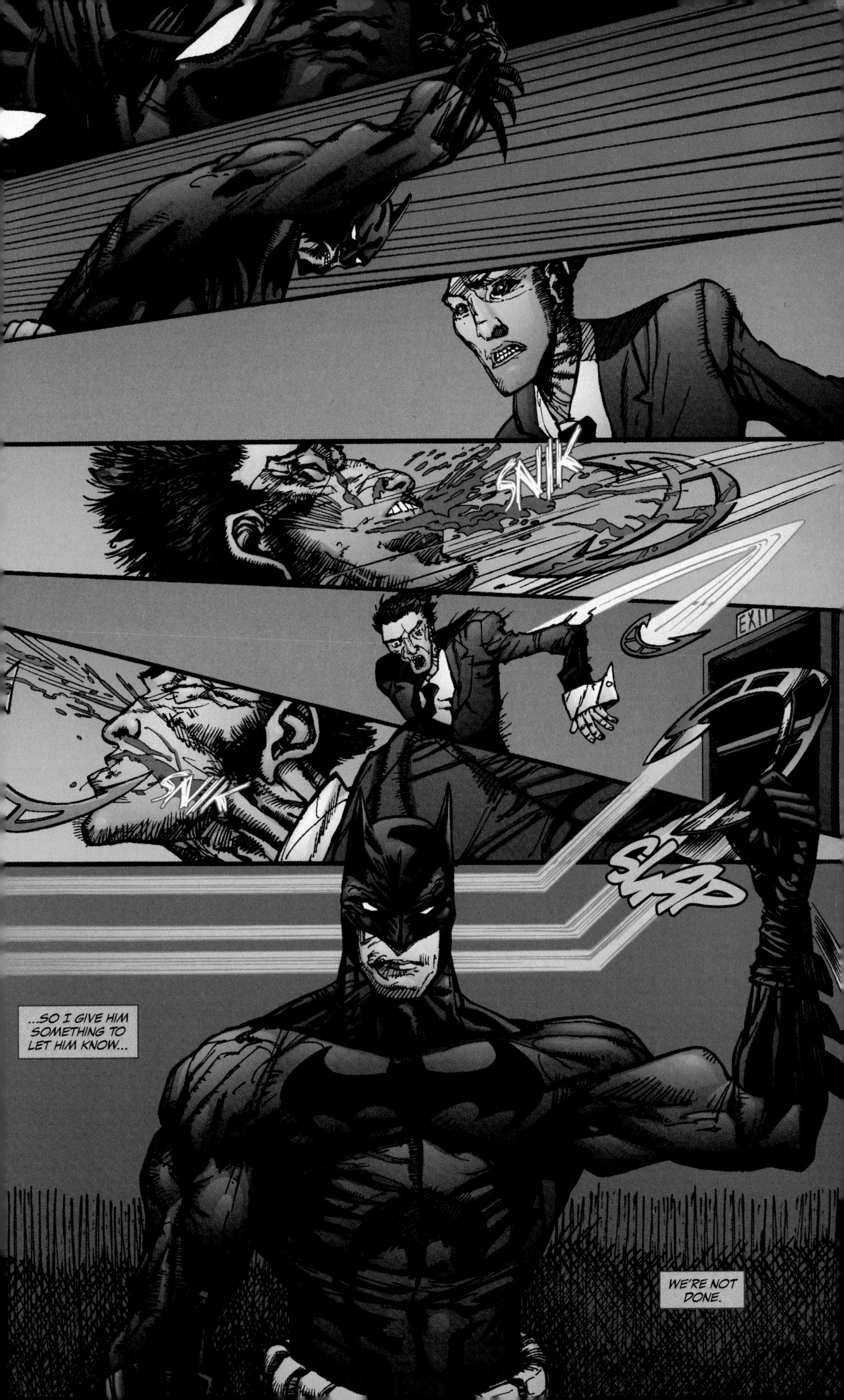
SNIK
SNIK
SLAP
...SO I GIVE HIM SOMETHING TO LET HIM KNOW...
WE'RE NOT DONE.

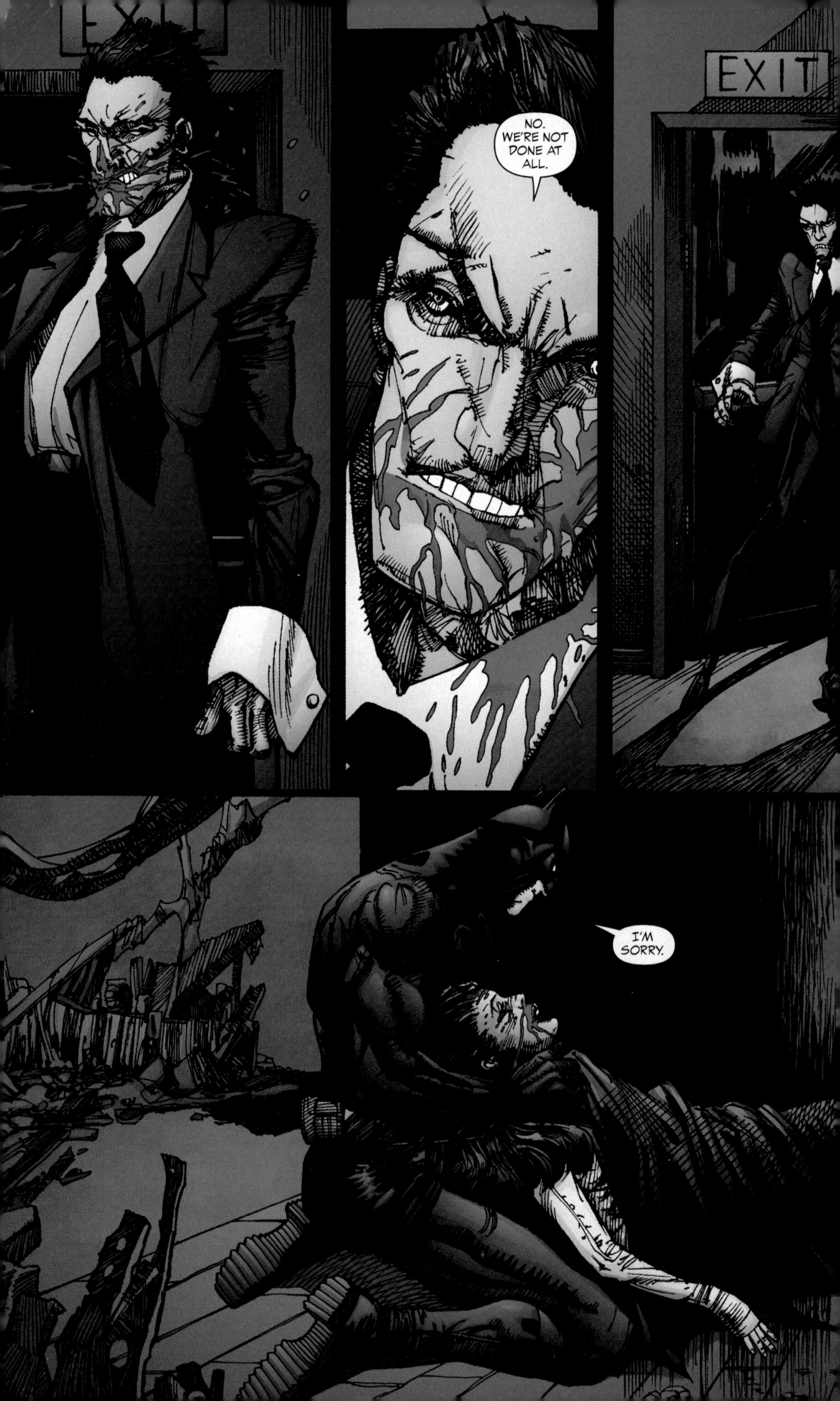
EXIT
NO. WE'RE NOT DONE AT ALL.
EXIT
I'M SORRY.

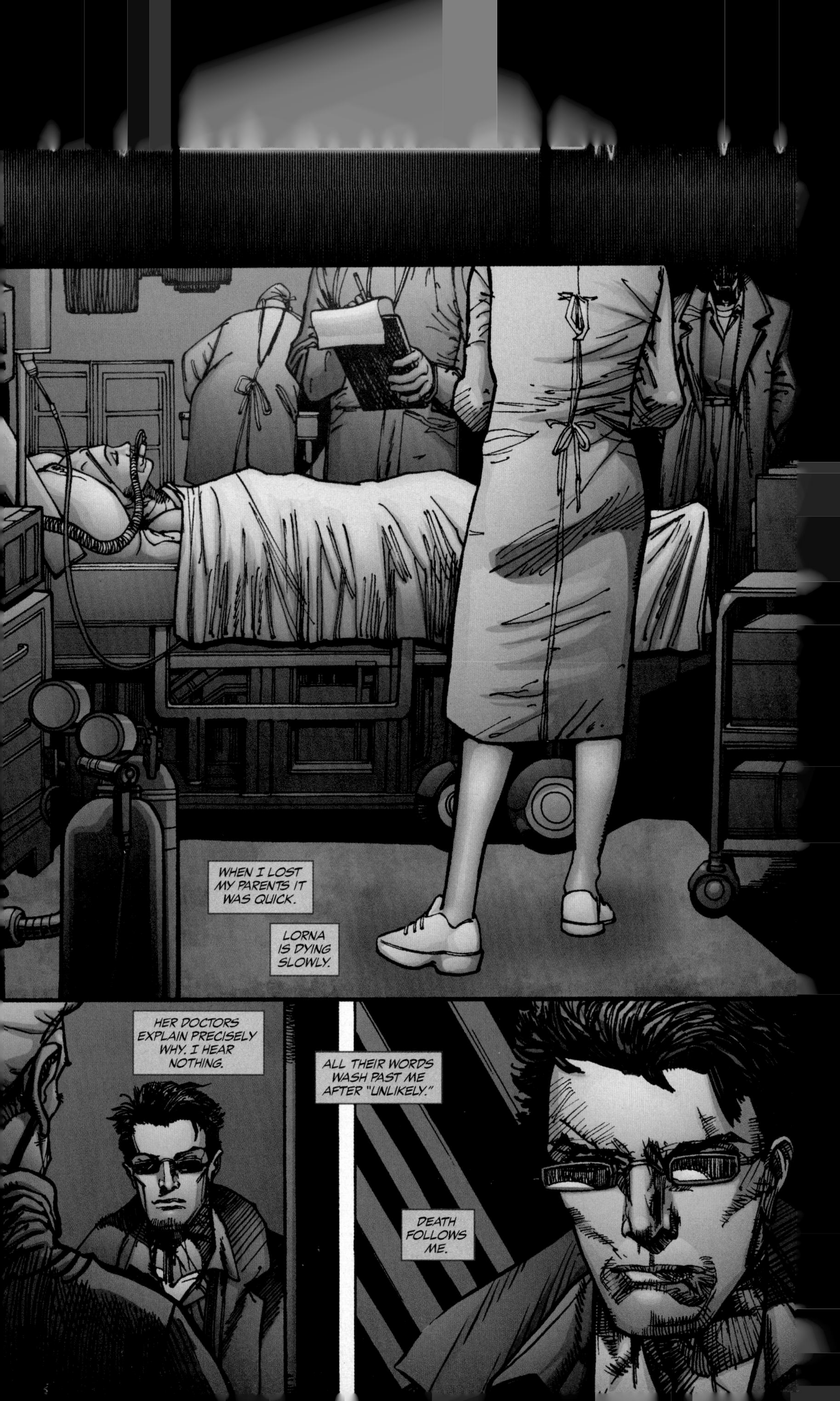
WHEN I LOST MY PARENTS IT WAS QUICK.
LORNA IS DYING SLOWLY.
HER DOCTORS EXPLAIN PRECISELY WHY. I HEAR NOTHING.
ALL THEIR WORDS WASH PAST ME AFTER "UNLIKELY."
DEATH FOLLOWS ME.

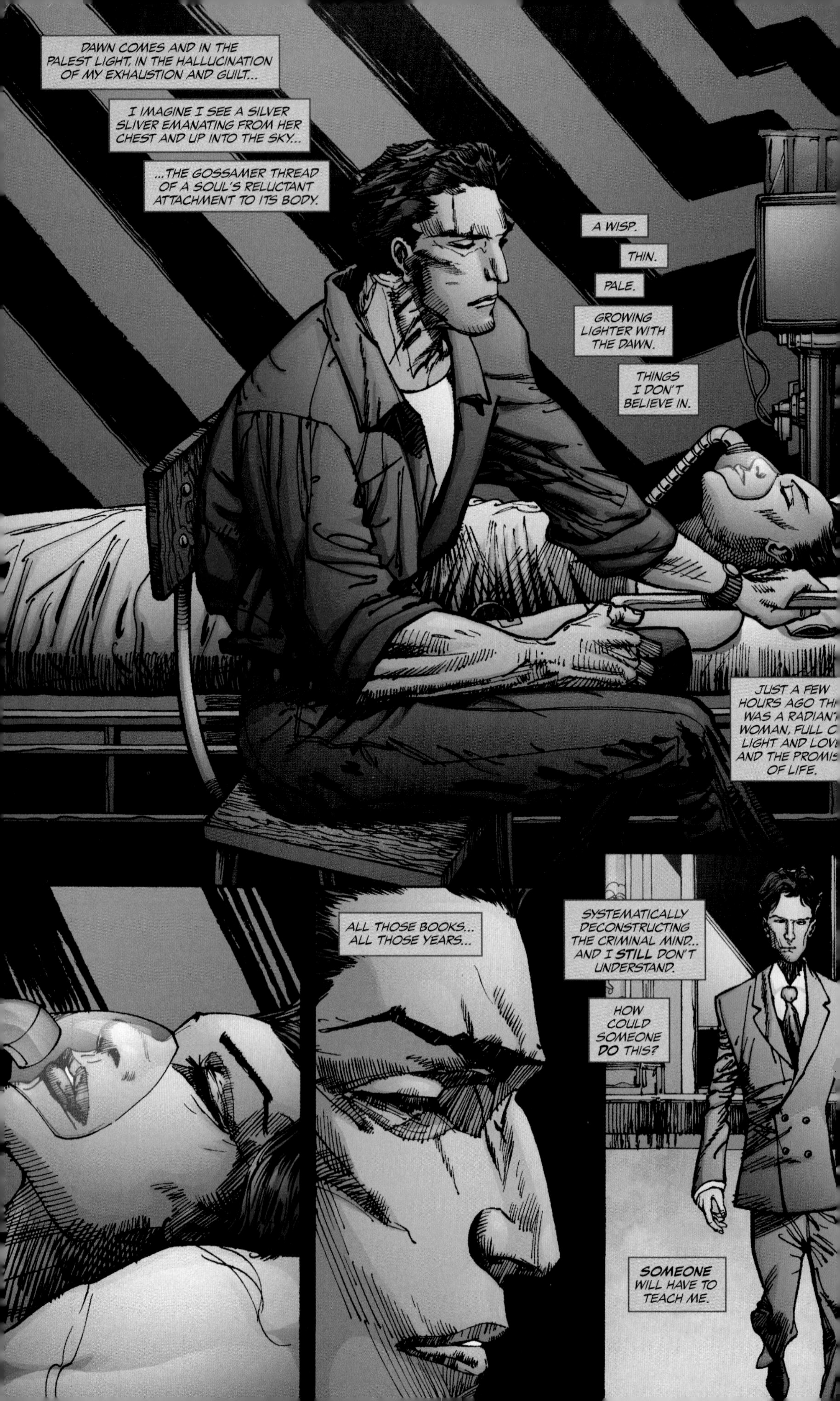

DAWN COMES AND IN THE PALEST LIGHT, IN THE HALLUCINATION OF MY EXHAUSTION AND GUILT...
I IMAGINE I SEE A SILVER SLIVER EMANATING FROM HER CHEST AND UP INTO THE SKY...
...THE GOSSAMER THREAD OF A SOUL'S RELUCTANT ATTACHMENT TO ITS BODY.
A WISP.
THIN.
PALE.
GROWING LIGHTER WITH THE DAWN.
THINGS I DON'T BELIEVE IN.
JUST A FEW HOURS AGO TH WAS A RADIAN WOMAN, FULL O LIGHT AND LOV AND THE PROMIS OF LIFE.
ALL THOSE BOOKS... ALL THOSE YEARS...
SYSTEMATICALLY DECONSTRUCTING THE CRIMINAL MIND... AND I **STILL** DON'T UNDERSTAND.
HOW COULD SOMEONE **DO** THIS?
SOMEONE WILL HAVE TO TEACH ME.

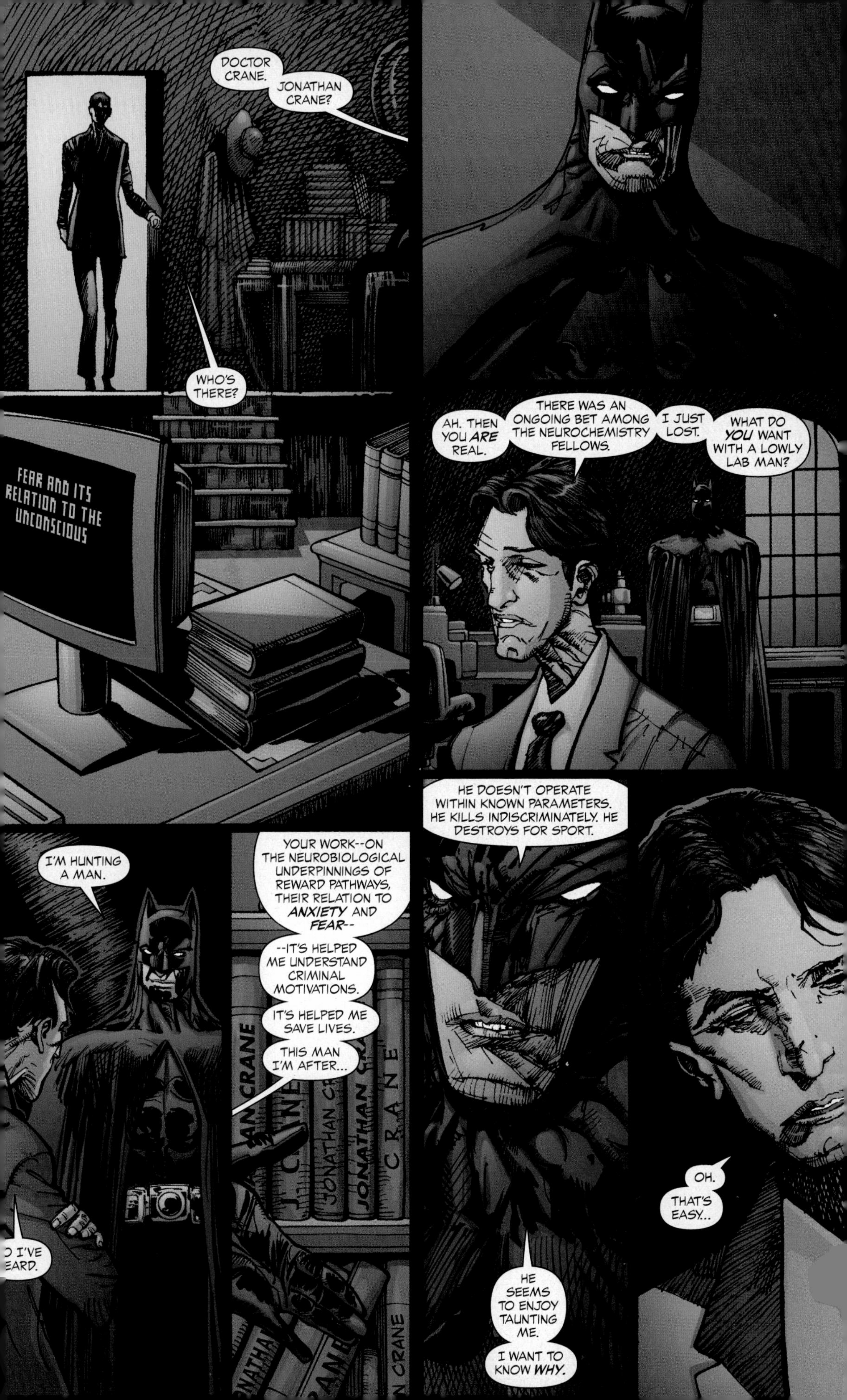
DOCTOR CRANE.
JONATHAN CRANE?
WHO'S THERE?
FEAR AND ITS RELATION TO THE UNCONSCIOUS
AH. THEN YOU *ARE* REAL.
THERE WAS AN ONGOING BET AMONG THE NEUROCHEMISTRY FELLOWS.
I JUST LOST.
WHAT DO *YOU* WANT WITH A LOWLY LAB MAN?
I'M HUNTING A MAN.
YOUR WORK--ON THE NEUROBIOLOGICAL UNDERPINNINGS OF REWARD PATHWAYS, THEIR RELATION TO *ANXIETY* AND *FEAR*--
--IT'S HELPED ME UNDERSTAND CRIMINAL MOTIVATIONS.
IT'S HELPED ME SAVE LIVES.
THIS MAN I'M AFTER...
HE DOESN'T OPERATE WITHIN KNOWN PARAMETERS. HE KILLS INDISCRIMINATELY. HE DESTROYS FOR SPORT.
HE SEEMS TO ENJOY TAUNTING ME.
I WANT TO KNOW *WHY*.
OH.
THAT'S EASY...

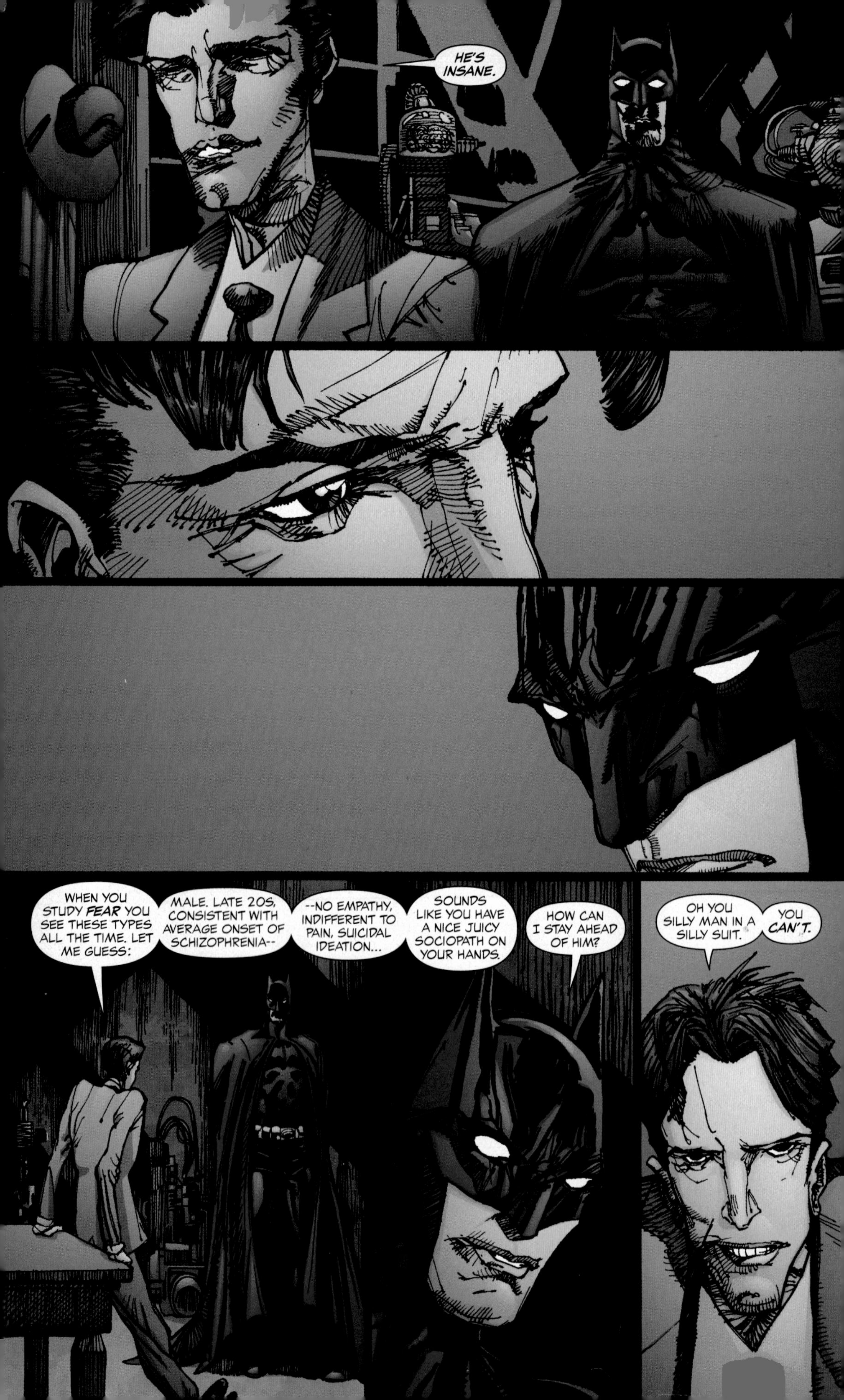
HE'S INSANE.
WHEN YOU STUDY **FEAR** YOU SEE THESE TYPES ALL THE TIME. LET ME GUESS:
MALE. LATE 20S, CONSISTENT WITH AVERAGE ONSET OF SCHIZOPHRENIA--
--NO EMPATHY, INDIFFERENT TO PAIN, SUICIDAL IDEATION...
SOUNDS LIKE YOU HAVE A NICE JUICY SOCIOPATH ON YOUR HANDS.
HOW CAN I STAY AHEAD OF HIM?
OH YOU SILLY MAN IN A SILLY SUIT.
YOU **CAN'T.**

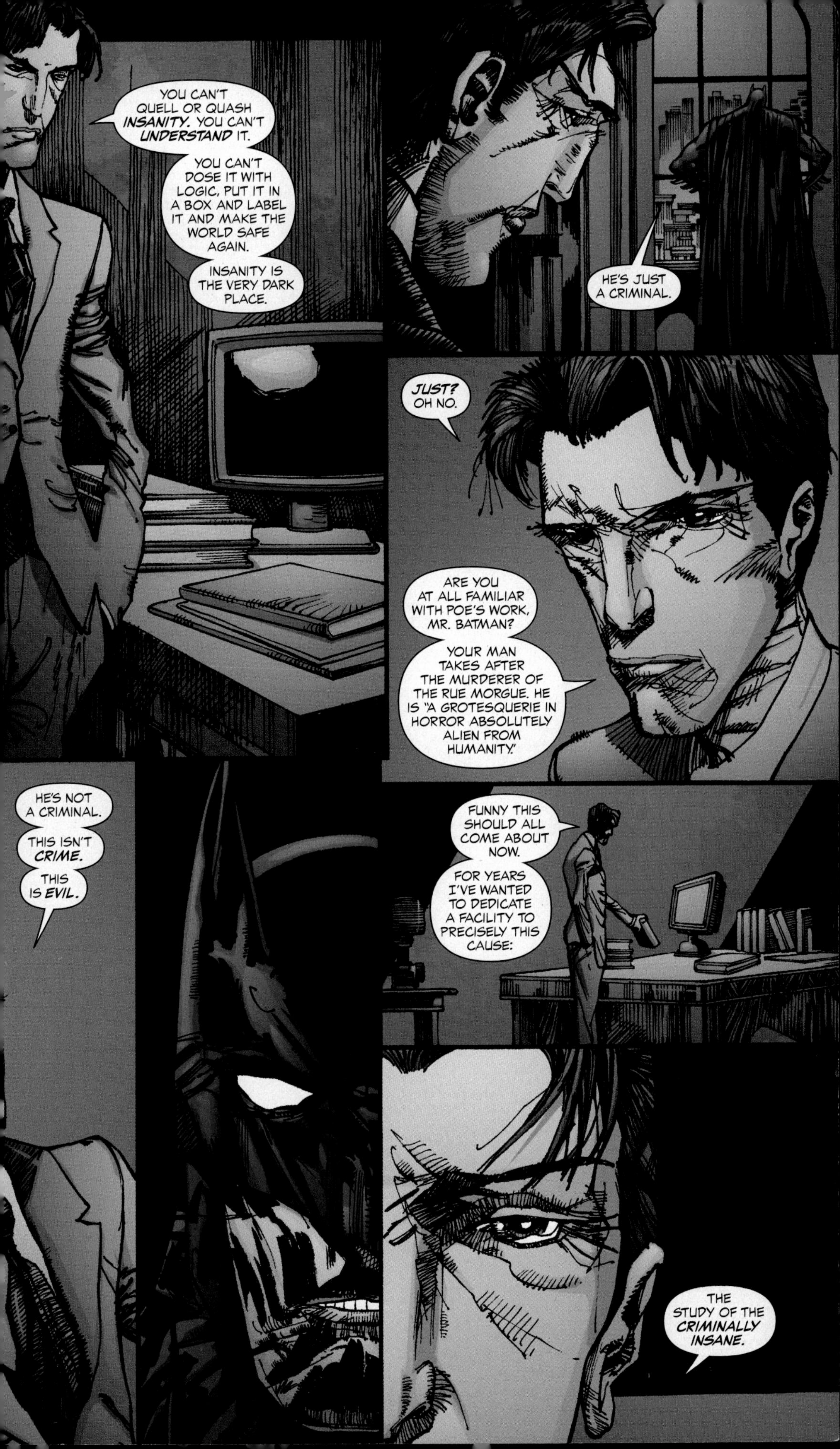
YOU CAN'T QUELL OR QUASH INSANITY. YOU CAN'T UNDERSTAND IT.
YOU CAN'T DOSE IT WITH LOGIC, PUT IT IN A BOX AND LABEL IT AND MAKE THE WORLD SAFE AGAIN.
INSANITY IS THE VERY DARK PLACE.
HE'S JUST A CRIMINAL.
JUST? OH NO.
ARE YOU AT ALL FAMILIAR WITH POE'S WORK, MR. BATMAN?
YOUR MAN TAKES AFTER THE MURDERER OF THE RUE MORGUE. HE IS "A GROTESQUERIE IN HORROR ABSOLUTELY ALIEN FROM HUMANITY."
HE'S NOT A CRIMINAL.
THIS ISN'T CRIME.
THIS IS EVIL.
FUNNY THIS SHOULD ALL COME ABOUT NOW.
FOR YEARS I'VE WANTED TO DEDICATE A FACILITY TO PRECISELY THIS CAUSE:
THE STUDY OF THE CRIMINALLY INSANE.

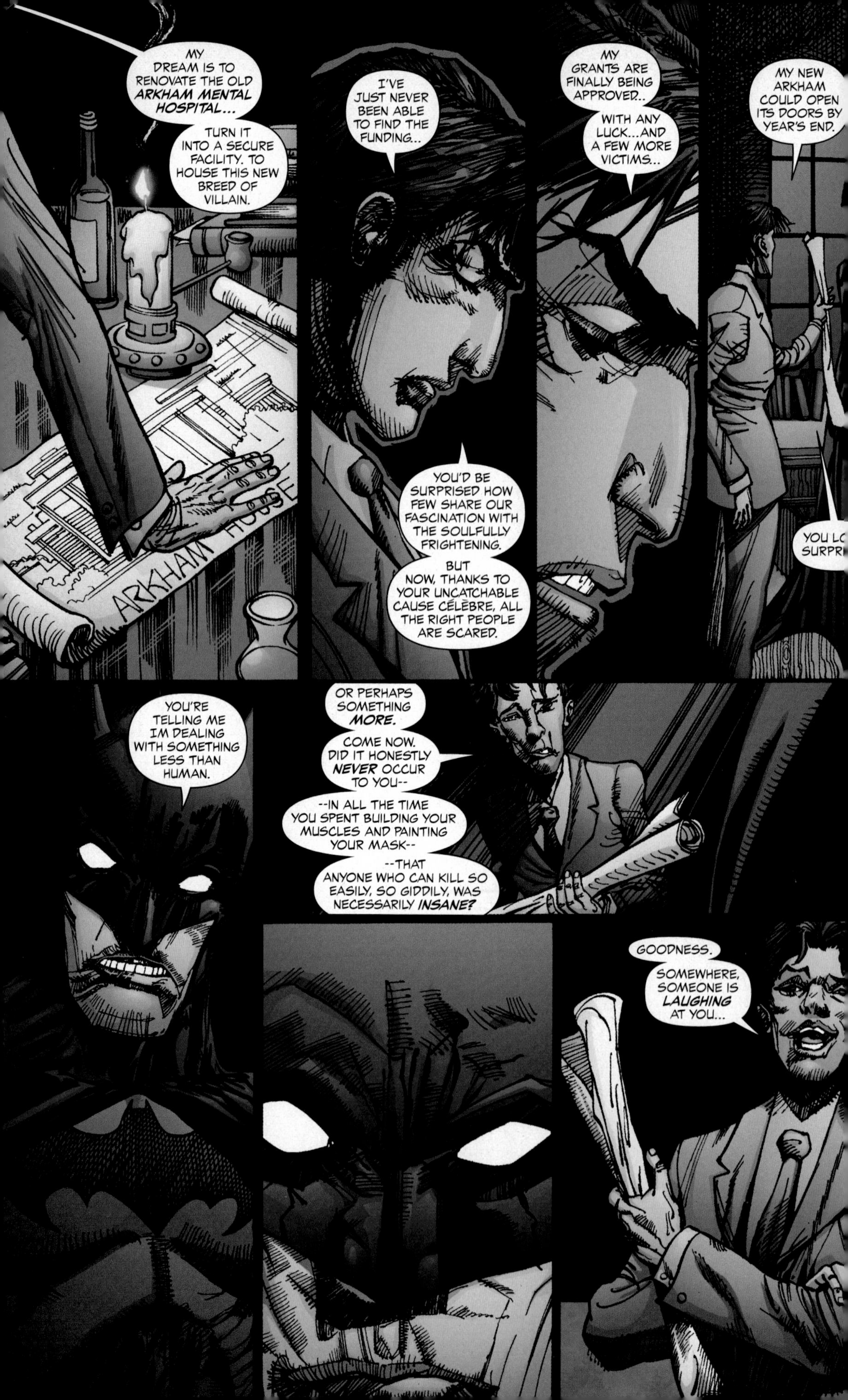
MY DREAM IS TO RENOVATE THE OLD ARKHAM MENTAL HOSPITAL...
TURN IT INTO A SECURE FACILITY. TO HOUSE THIS NEW BREED OF VILLAIN.
ARKHAM HOUSE
I'VE JUST NEVER BEEN ABLE TO FIND THE FUNDING...
YOU'D BE SURPRISED HOW FEW SHARE OUR FASCINATION WITH THE SOULFULLY FRIGHTENING.
BUT NOW, THANKS TO YOUR UNCATCHABLE CAUSE CÉLEBRE, ALL THE RIGHT PEOPLE ARE SCARED.
MY GRANTS ARE FINALLY BEING APPROVED..
WITH ANY LUCK...AND A FEW MORE VICTIMS...
MY NEW ARKHAM COULD OPEN ITS DOORS BY YEAR'S END.
YOU'RE TELLING ME IM DEALING WITH SOMETHING LESS THAN HUMAN.
OR PERHAPS SOMETHING MORE.
COME NOW. DID IT HONESTLY NEVER OCCUR TO YOU--
--IN ALL THE TIME YOU SPENT BUILDING YOUR MUSCLES AND PAINTING YOUR MASK--
--THAT ANYONE WHO CAN KILL SO EASILY, SO GIDDILY, WAS NECESSARILY INSANE?
GOODNESS.
SOMEWHERE, SOMEONE IS LAUGHING AT YOU...

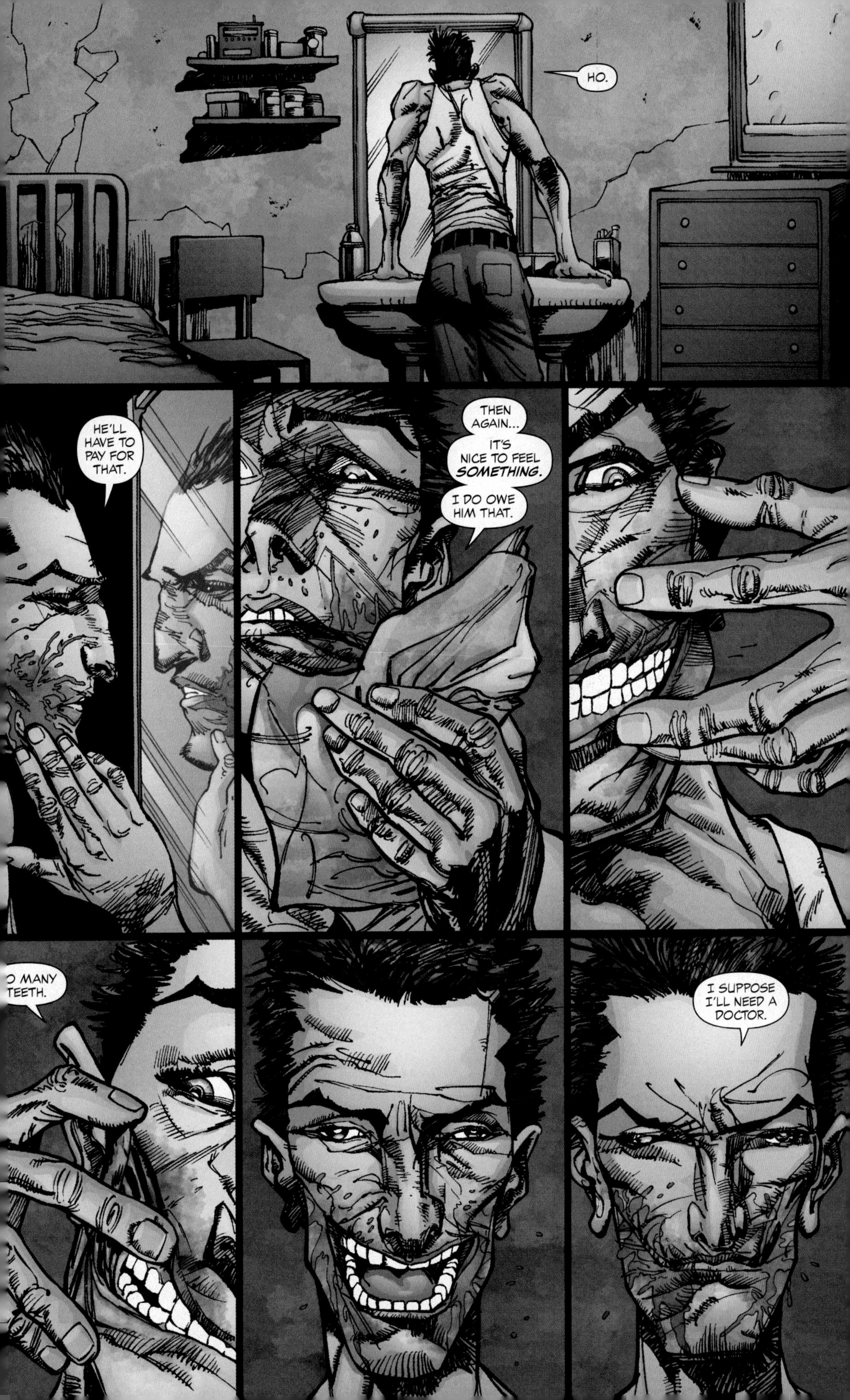
HO.
HE'LL HAVE TO PAY FOR THAT.
THEN AGAIN...
IT'S NICE TO FEEL *SOMETHING*.
I DO OWE HIM THAT.
O MANY TEETH.
I SUPPOSE I'LL NEED A DOCTOR.

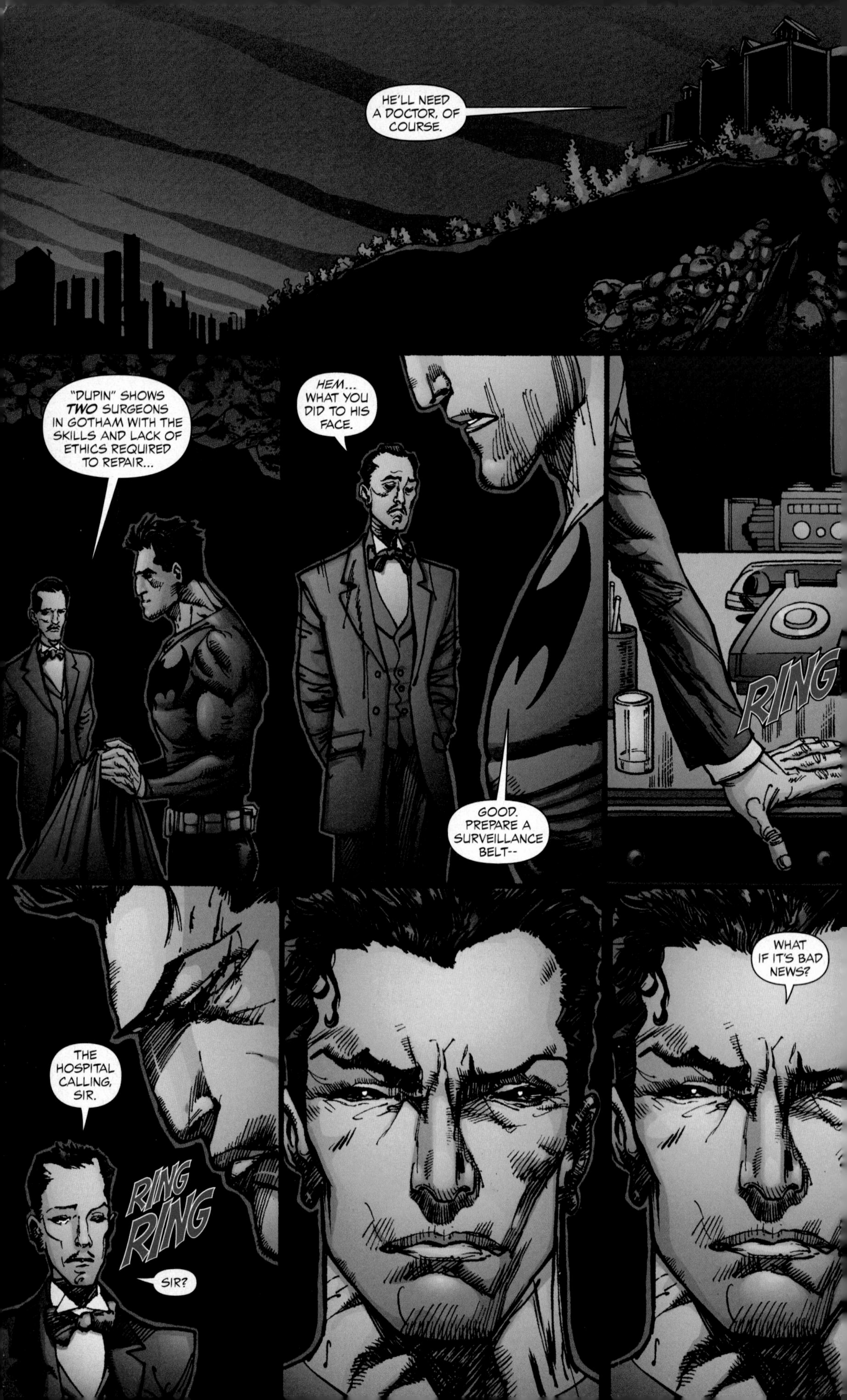
HE'LL NEED A DOCTOR, OF COURSE.
"DUPIN" SHOWS TWO SURGEONS IN GOTHAM WITH THE SKILLS AND LACK OF ETHICS REQUIRED TO REPAIR...
HEM... WHAT YOU DID TO HIS FACE.
GOOD. PREPARE A SURVEILLANCE BELT--
RING
THE HOSPITAL CALLING, SIR.
RING RING
SIR?
WHAT IF IT'S BAD NEWS?

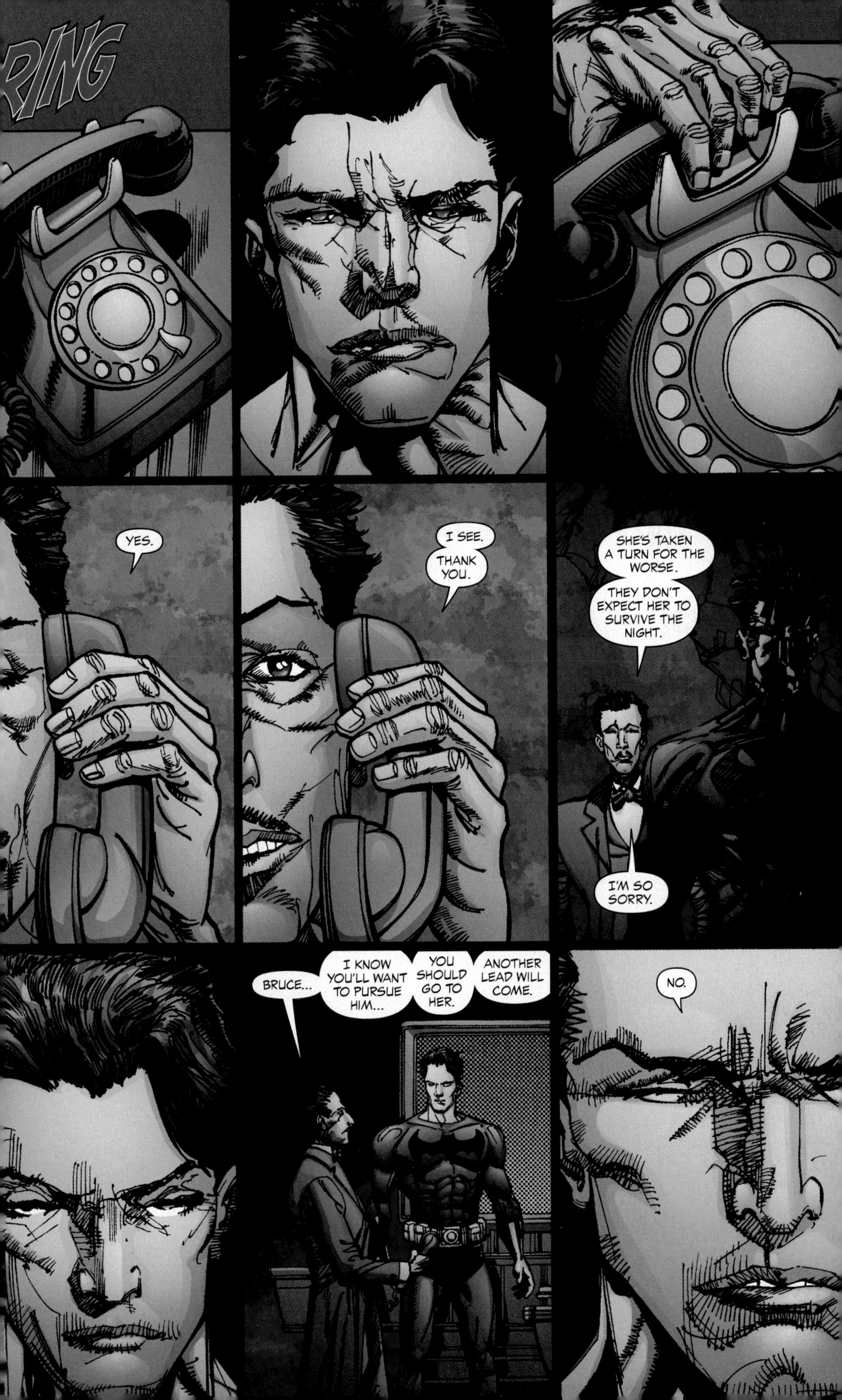
RING
YES.
I SEE.
THANK YOU.
SHE'S TAKEN A TURN FOR THE WORSE.
THEY DON'T EXPECT HER TO SURVIVE THE NIGHT.
I'M SO SORRY.
BRUCE...
I KNOW YOU'LL WANT TO PURSUE HIM...
YOU SHOULD GO TO HER.
ANOTHER LEAD WILL COME.
NO.

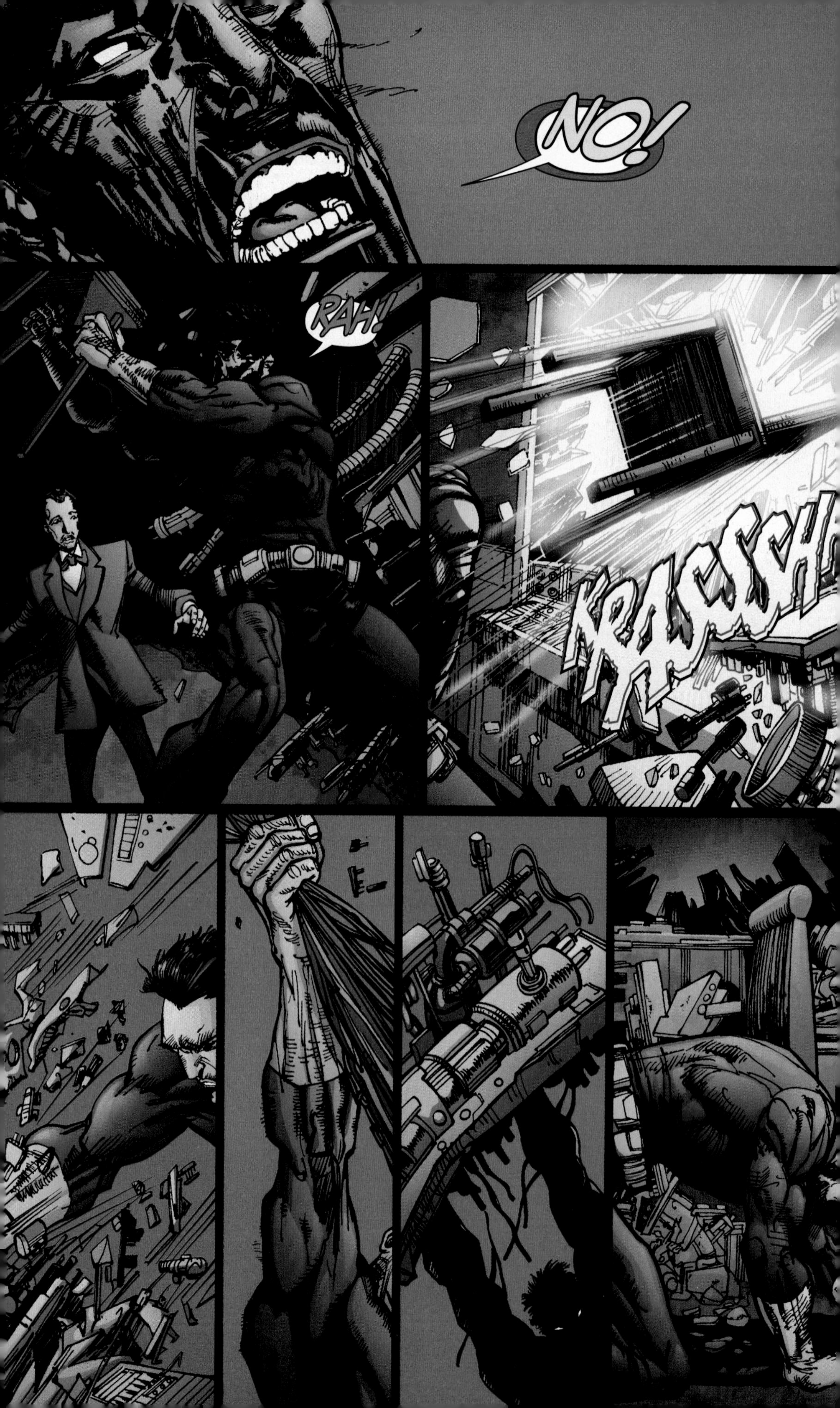

NO!
RAH!
KRASCH

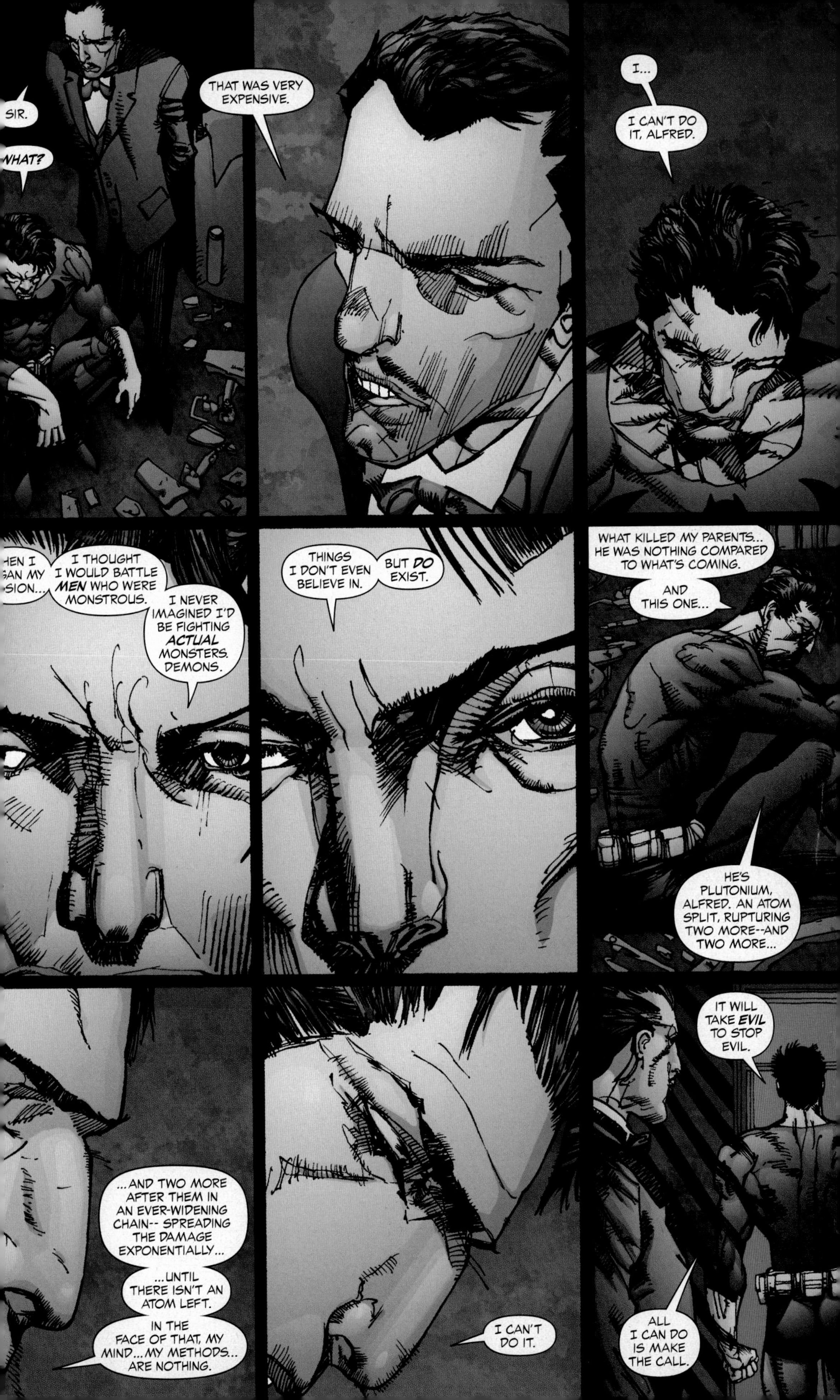

SIR.
WHAT?
THAT WAS VERY EXPENSIVE.
I...
I CAN'T DO IT, ALFRED.
HEN I GAN MY SION...
I THOUGHT I WOULD BATTLE MEN WHO WERE MONSTROUS.
I NEVER IMAGINED I'D BE FIGHTING ACTUAL MONSTERS. DEMONS.
THINGS I DON'T EVEN BELIEVE IN.
BUT DO EXIST.
WHAT KILLED MY PARENTS... HE WAS NOTHING COMPARED TO WHAT'S COMING.
AND THIS ONE...
HE'S PLUTONIUM, ALFRED. AN ATOM SPLIT, RUPTURING TWO MORE--AND TWO MORE...
...AND TWO MORE AFTER THEM IN AN EVER-WIDENING CHAIN-- SPREADING THE DAMAGE EXPONENTIALLY...
...UNTIL THERE ISN'T AN ATOM LEFT.
IN THE FACE OF THAT, MY MIND... MY METHODS... ARE NOTHING.
I CAN'T DO IT.
IT WILL TAKE EVIL TO STOP EVIL.
ALL I CAN DO IS MAKE THE CALL.

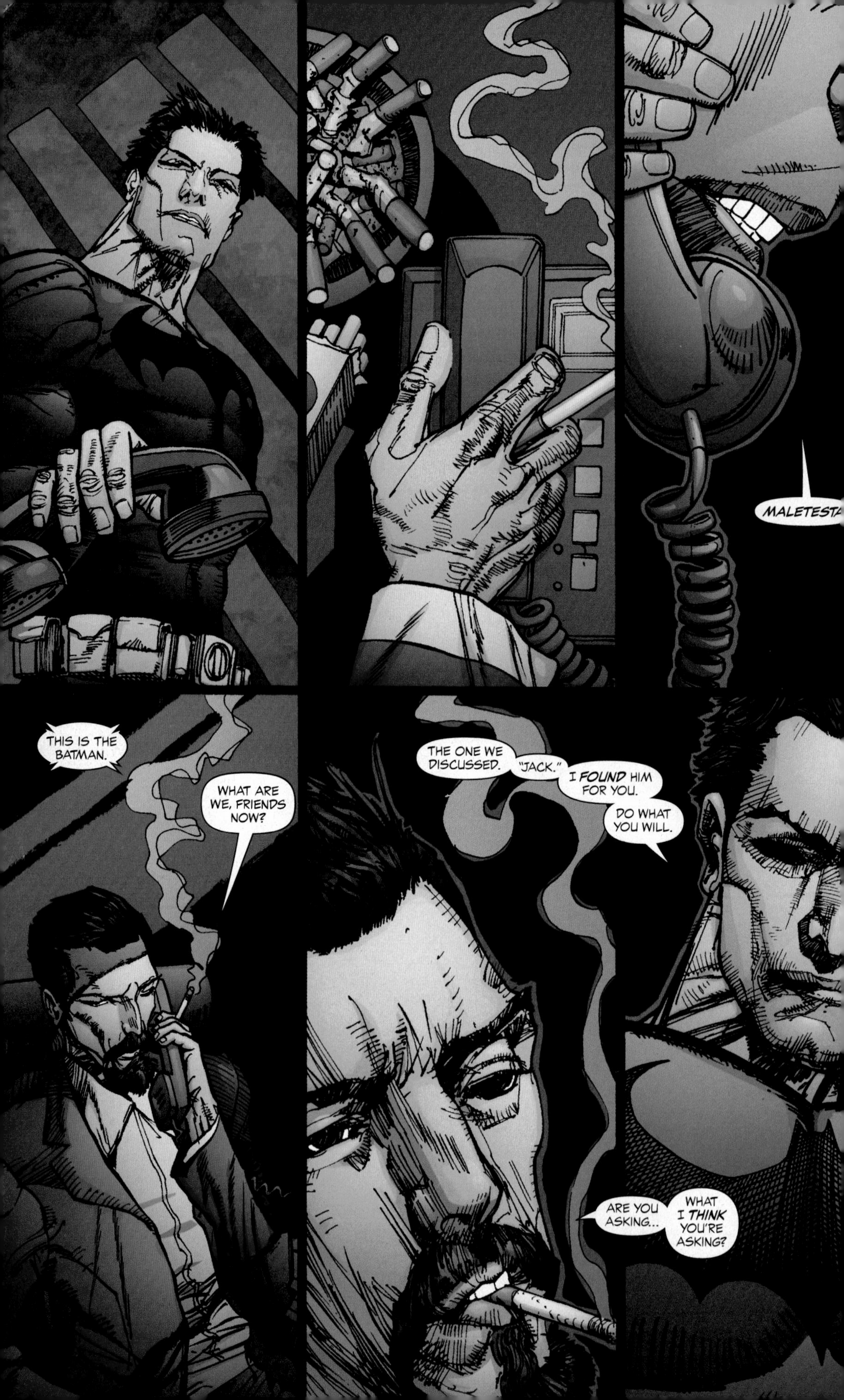

MALETESTA
THIS IS THE BATMAN.
WHAT ARE WE, FRIENDS NOW?
THE ONE WE DISCUSSED.
"JACK."
I FOUND HIM FOR YOU.
DO WHAT YOU WILL.
ARE YOU ASKING...
WHAT I THINK YOU'RE ASKING?

chapter four **LAUGHING MATTERS**

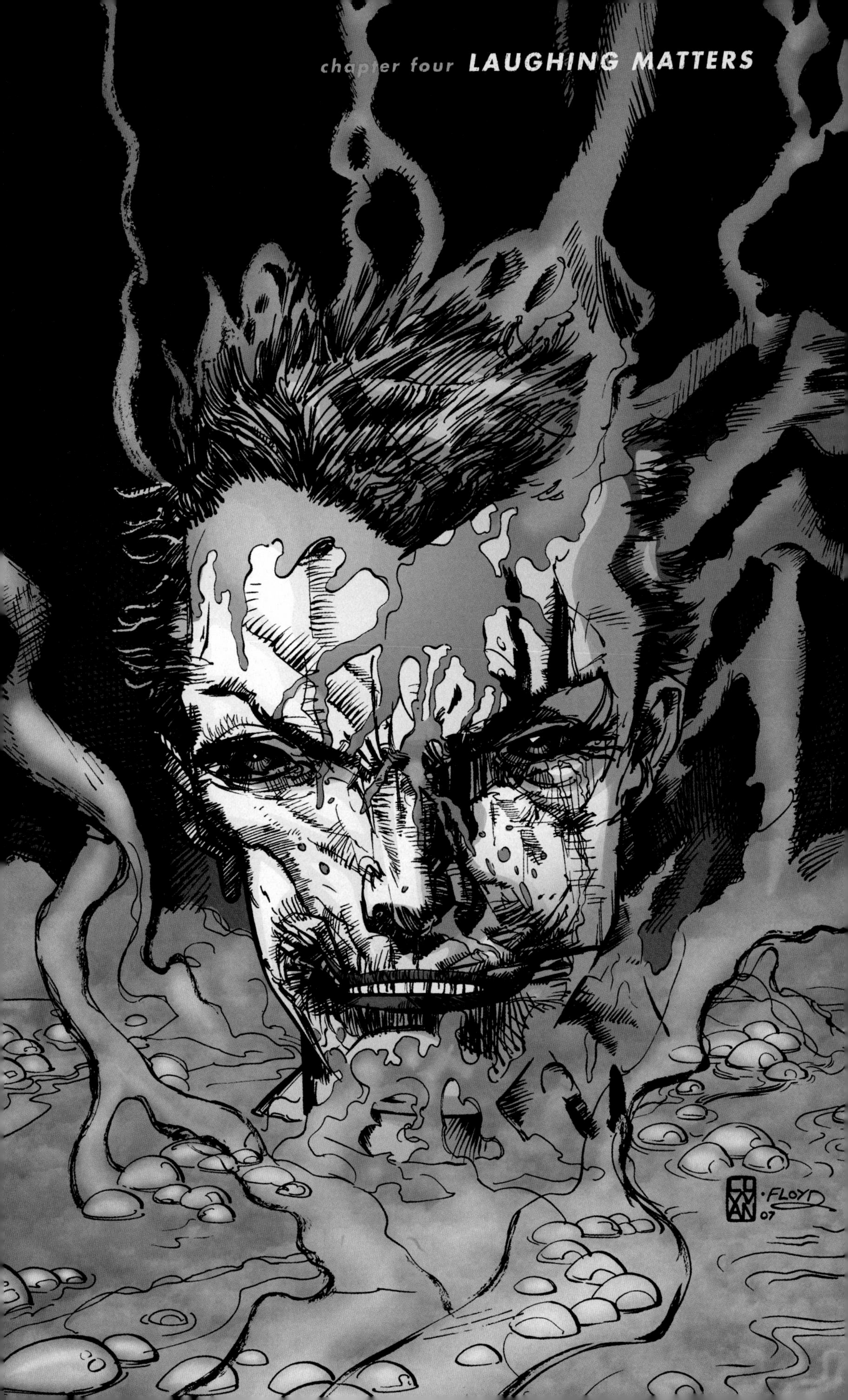
·FLOYD
07

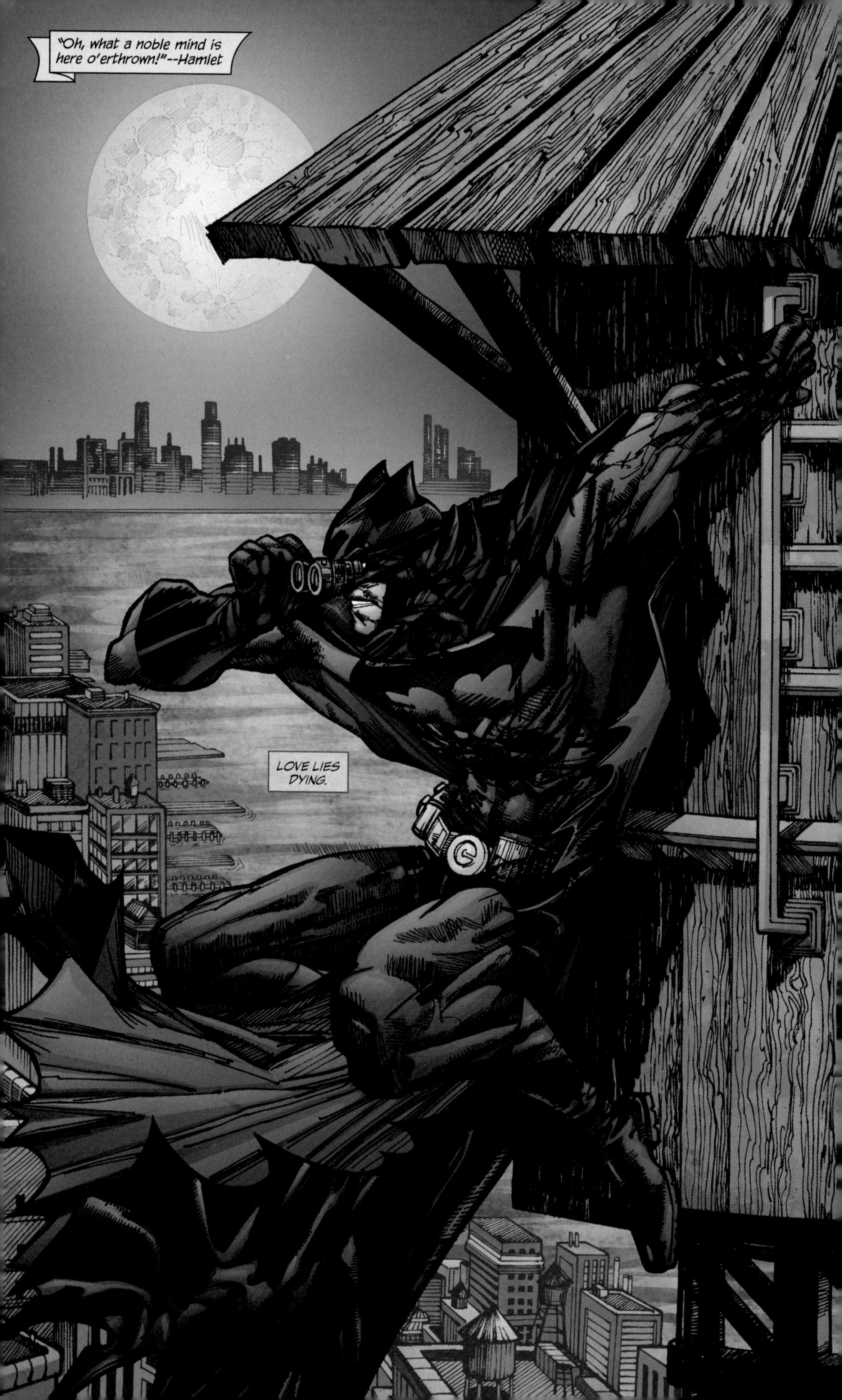
"Oh, what a noble mind is here o'erthrown!"--Hamlet
LOVE LIES DYING.

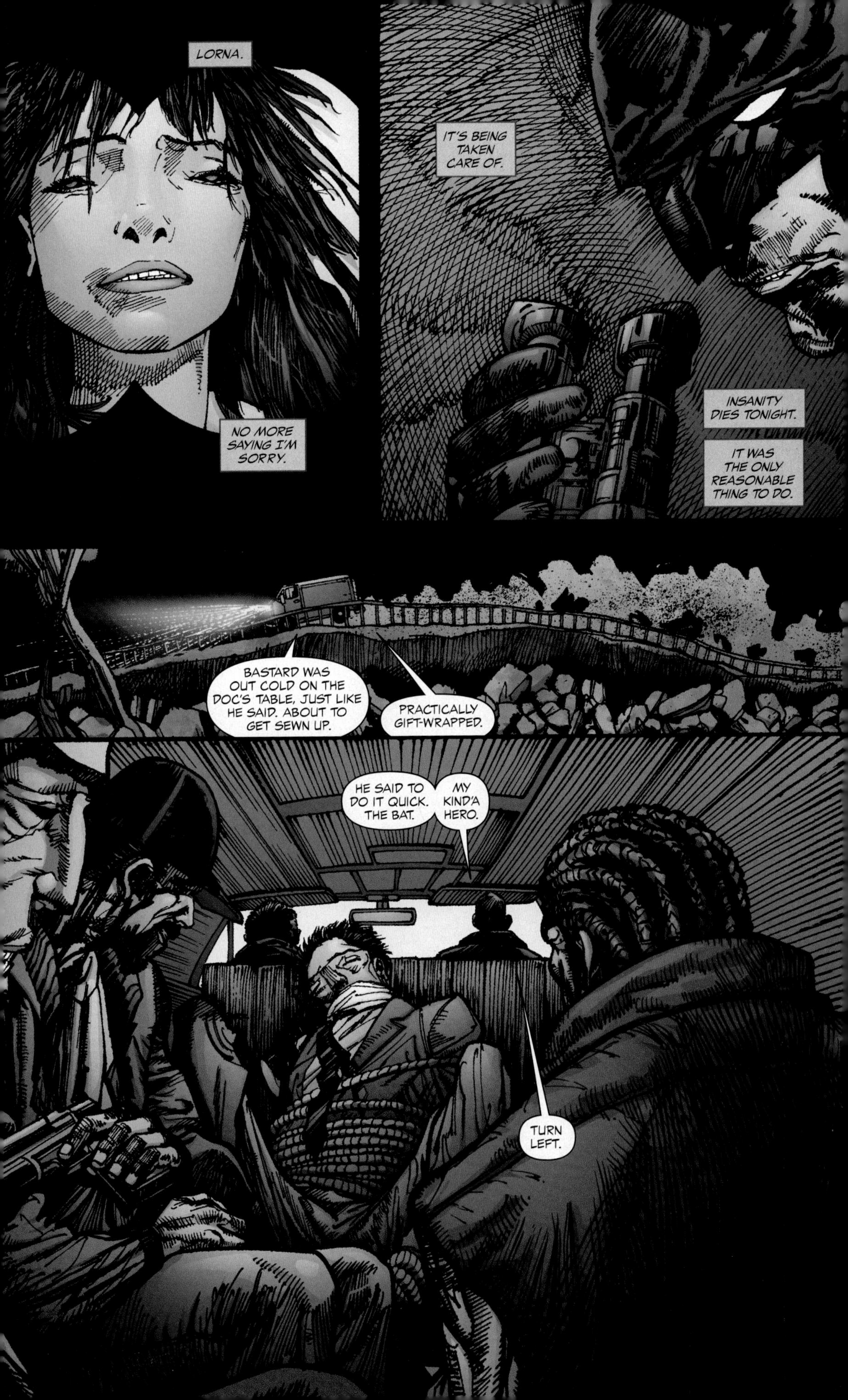
LORNA.
NO MORE SAYING I'M SORRY.
IT'S BEING TAKEN CARE OF.
INSANITY DIES TONIGHT.
IT WAS THE ONLY REASONABLE THING TO DO.
BASTARD WAS OUT COLD ON THE DOC'S TABLE, JUST LIKE HE SAID. ABOUT TO GET SEWN UP.
PRACTICALLY GIFT-WRAPPED.
HE SAID TO DO IT QUICK. THE BAT.
MY KIND'A HERO.
TURN LEFT.

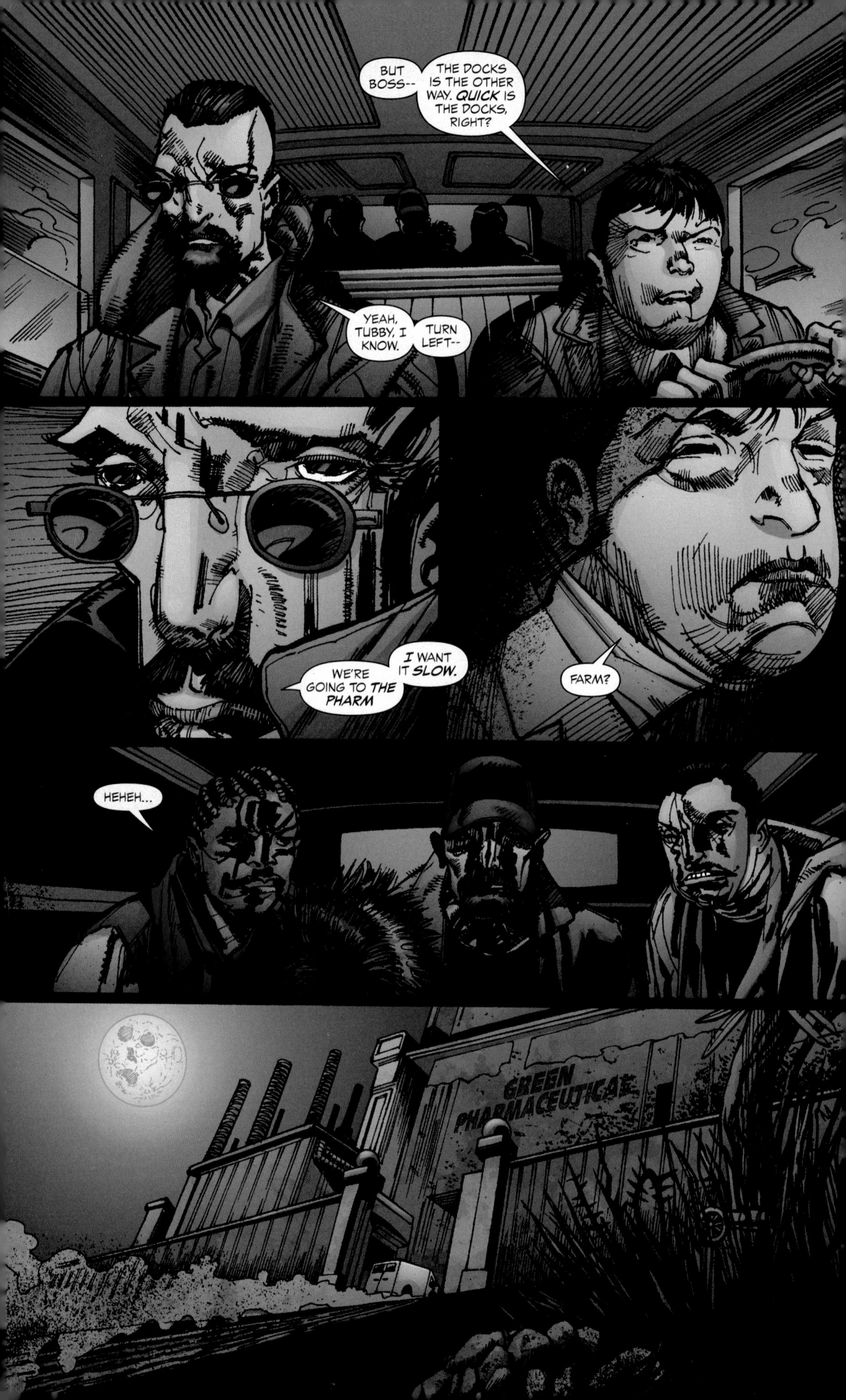
BUT BOSS--
THE DOCKS IS THE OTHER WAY. QUICK IS THE DOCKS, RIGHT?
YEAH, TUBBY, I KNOW.
TURN LEFT--
WE'RE GOING TO THE PHARM
I WANT IT SLOW.
FARM?
HEHEH...
GREEN PHARMACEUTICAL

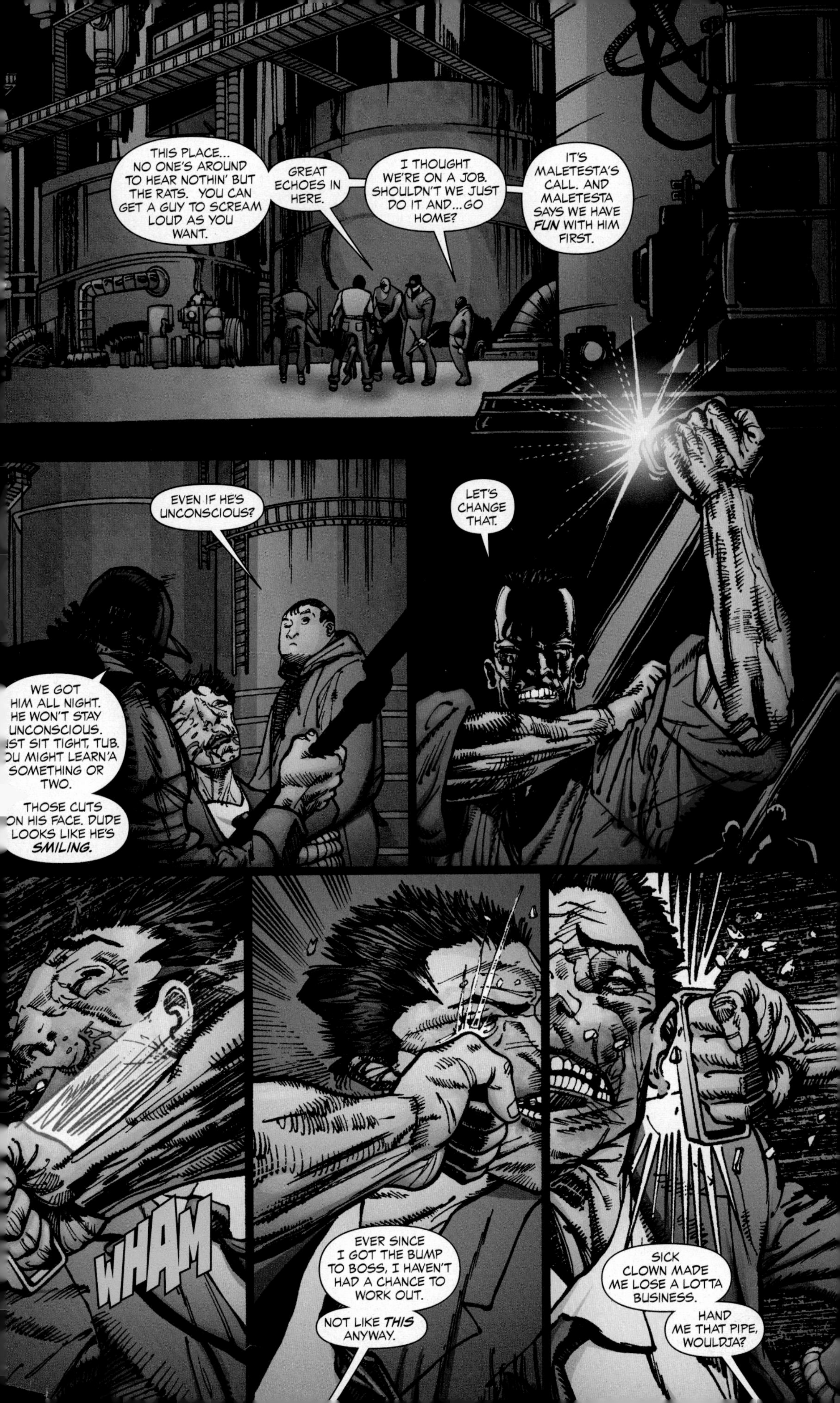
THIS PLACE... NO ONE'S AROUND TO HEAR NOTHIN' BUT THE RATS. YOU CAN GET A GUY TO SCREAM LOUD AS YOU WANT.
GREAT ECHOES IN HERE.
I THOUGHT WE'RE ON A JOB. SHOULDN'T WE JUST DO IT AND...GO HOME?
IT'S MALETESTA'S CALL. AND MALETESTA SAYS WE HAVE FUN WITH HIM FIRST.
EVEN IF HE'S UNCONSCIOUS?
WE GOT HIM ALL NIGHT. HE WON'T STAY UNCONSCIOUS. JST SIT TIGHT, TUB. OU MIGHT LEARN'A SOMETHING OR TWO.
THOSE CUTS ON HIS FACE. DUDE LOOKS LIKE HE'S SMILING.
LET'S CHANGE THAT.
WHAM
EVER SINCE I GOT THE BUMP TO BOSS, I HAVEN'T HAD A CHANCE TO WORK OUT.
NOT LIKE THIS ANYWAY.
SICK CLOWN MADE ME LOSE A LOTTA BUSINESS.
HAND ME THAT PIPE, WOULDJA?

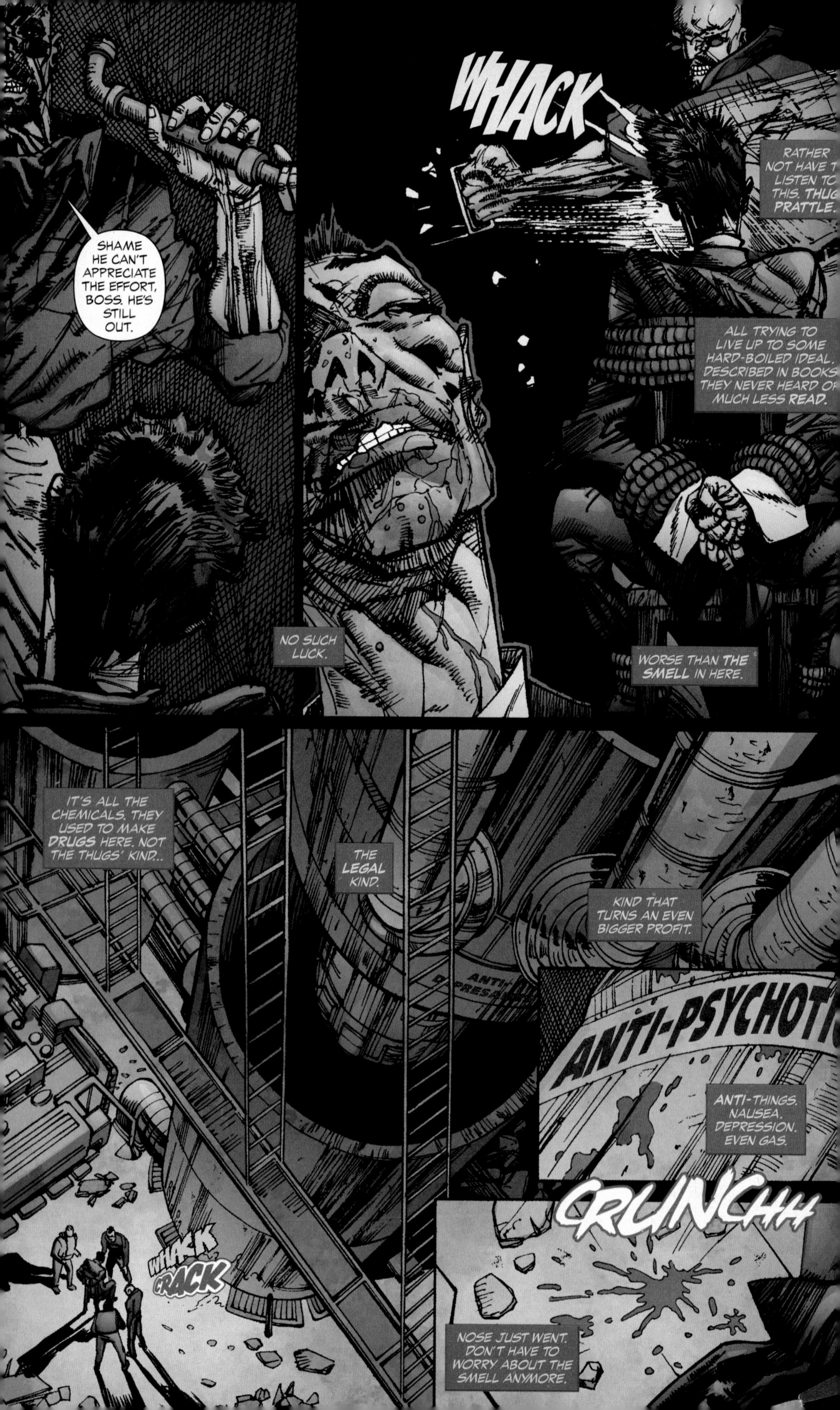

SHAME HE CAN'T APPRECIATE THE EFFORT, BOSS. HE'S STILL OUT.
WHACK
NO SUCH LUCK.
RATHER NOT HAVE T LISTEN TO THIS. THUG PRATTLE.
ALL TRYING TO LIVE UP TO SOME HARD-BOILED IDEAL. DESCRIBED IN BOOKS THEY NEVER HEARD OF MUCH LESS READ.
WORSE THAN THE SMELL IN HERE.
IT'S ALL THE CHEMICALS. THEY USED TO MAKE DRUGS HERE. NOT THE THUGS' KIND..
THE LEGAL KIND.
KIND THAT TURNS AN EVEN BIGGER PROFIT.
ANTI-PSYCHOTI
ANTI-THINGS. NAUSEA. DEPRESSION. EVEN GAS.
CRACK
CRUNCHH
NOSE JUST WENT. DON'T HAVE TO WORRY ABOUT THE SMELL ANYMORE.

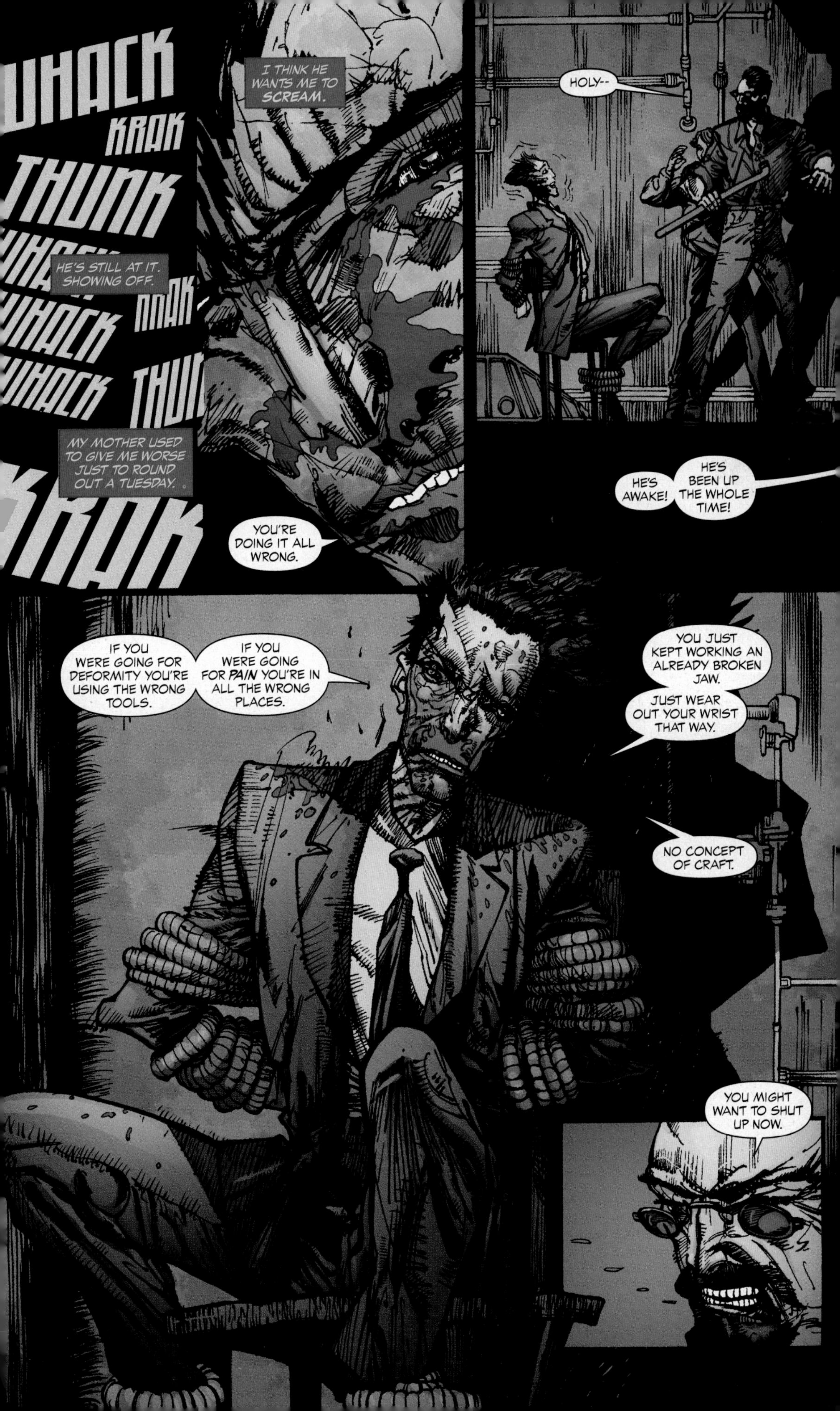
WHACK
KRAK
THUNK
I THINK HE WANTS ME TO SCREAM.
HE'S STILL AT IT. SHOWING OFF.
WHACK
WHACK
MY MOTHER USED TO GIVE ME WORSE JUST TO ROUND OUT A TUESDAY.
KRAK
YOU'RE DOING IT ALL WRONG.
HOLY--
HE'S AWAKE!
HE'S BEEN UP THE WHOLE TIME!
IF YOU WERE GOING FOR DEFORMITY YOU'RE USING THE WRONG TOOLS.
IF YOU WERE GOING FOR PAIN YOU'RE IN ALL THE WRONG PLACES.
YOU JUST KEPT WORKING AN ALREADY BROKEN JAW.
JUST WEAR OUT YOUR WRIST THAT WAY.
NO CONCEPT OF CRAFT.
YOU MIGHT WANT TO SHUT UP NOW.

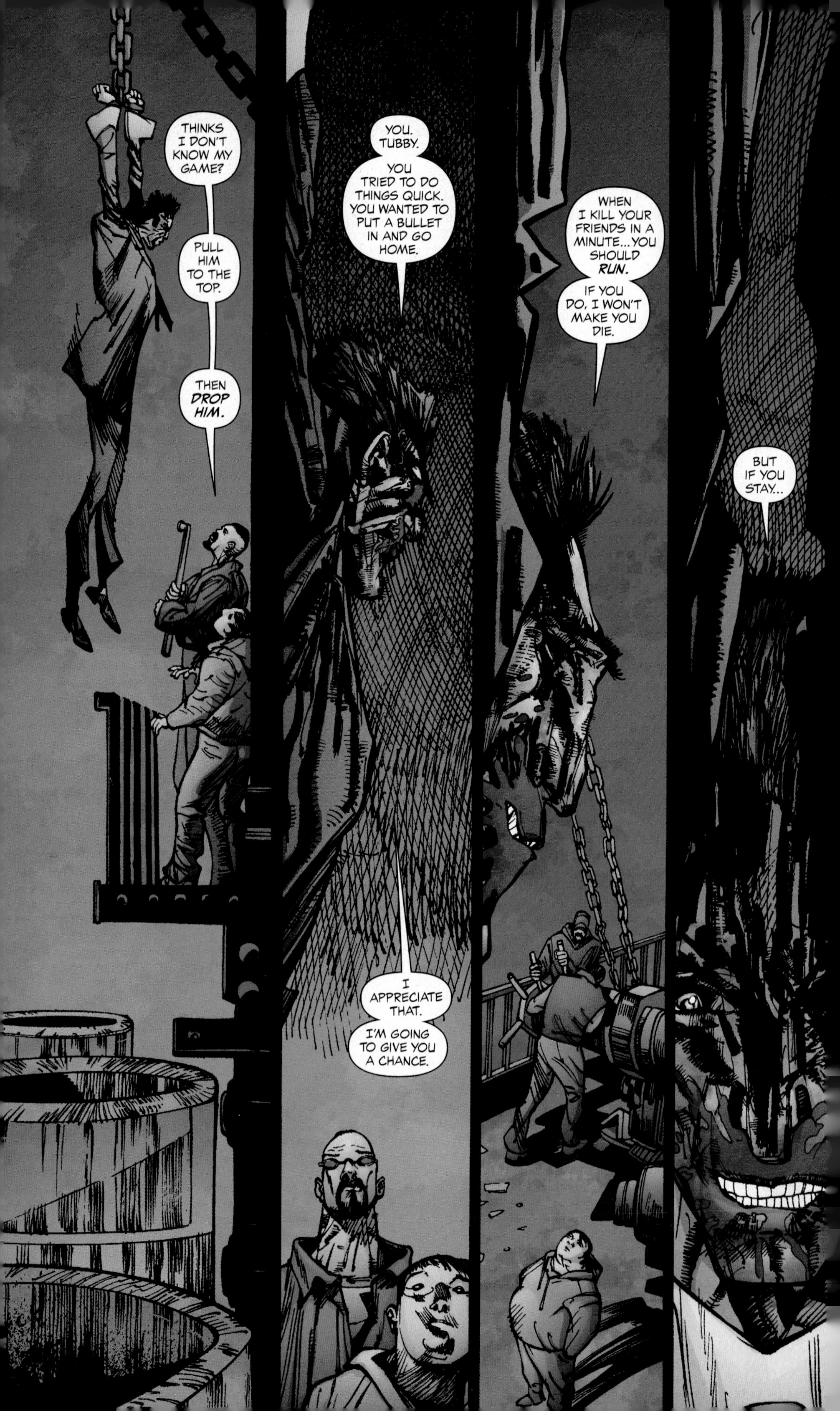
THINKS I DON'T KNOW MY GAME?
PULL HIM TO THE TOP.
THEN DROP HIM.
YOU. TUBBY.
YOU TRIED TO DO THINGS QUICK. YOU WANTED TO PUT A BULLET IN AND GO HOME.
I APPRECIATE THAT.
I'M GOING TO GIVE YOU A CHANCE.
WHEN I KILL YOUR FRIENDS IN A MINUTE... YOU SHOULD RUN.
IF YOU DO, I WON'T MAKE YOU DIE.
BUT IF YOU STAY...

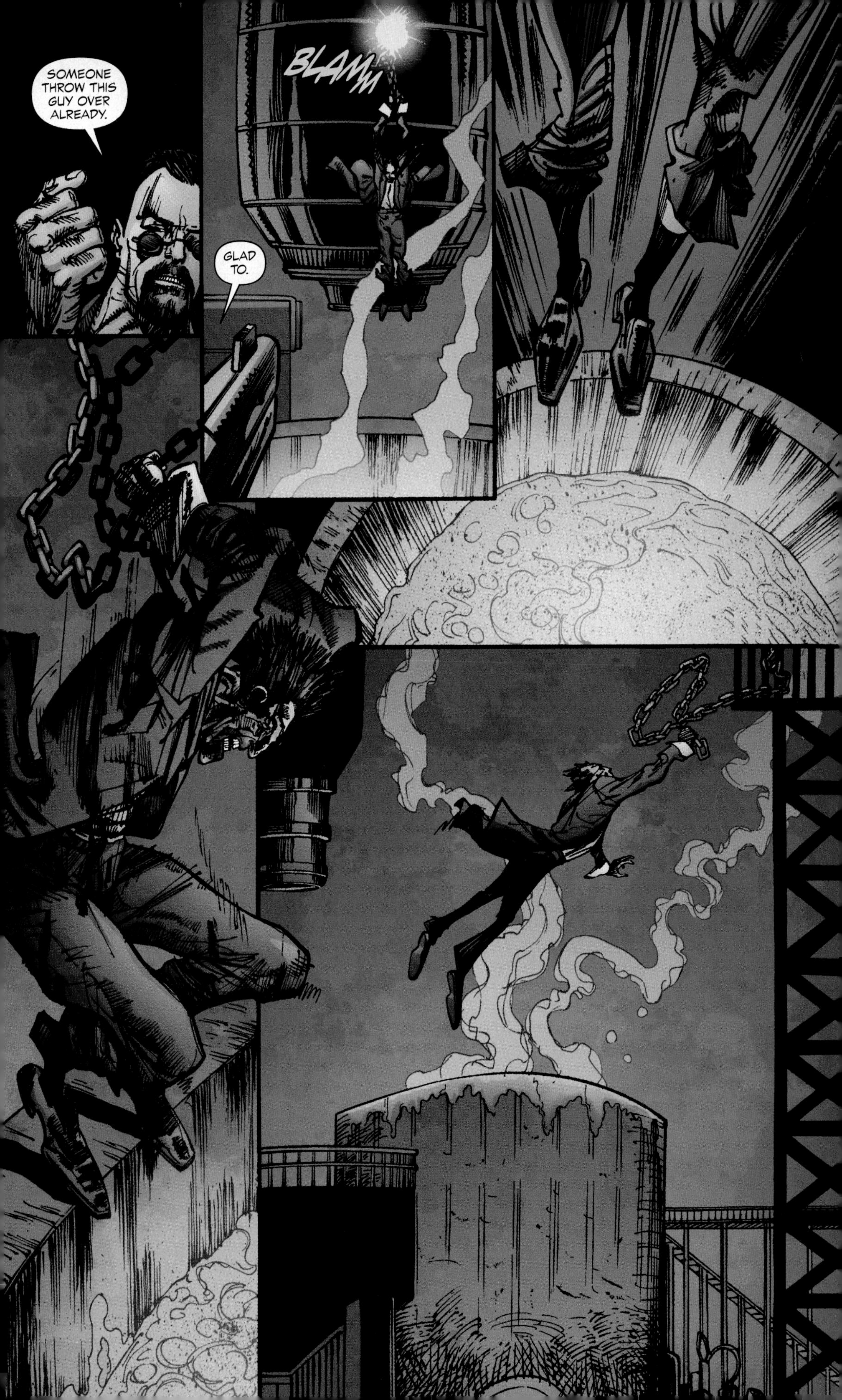

SOMEONE THROW THIS GUY OVER ALREADY.
GLAD TO.
BLAMM

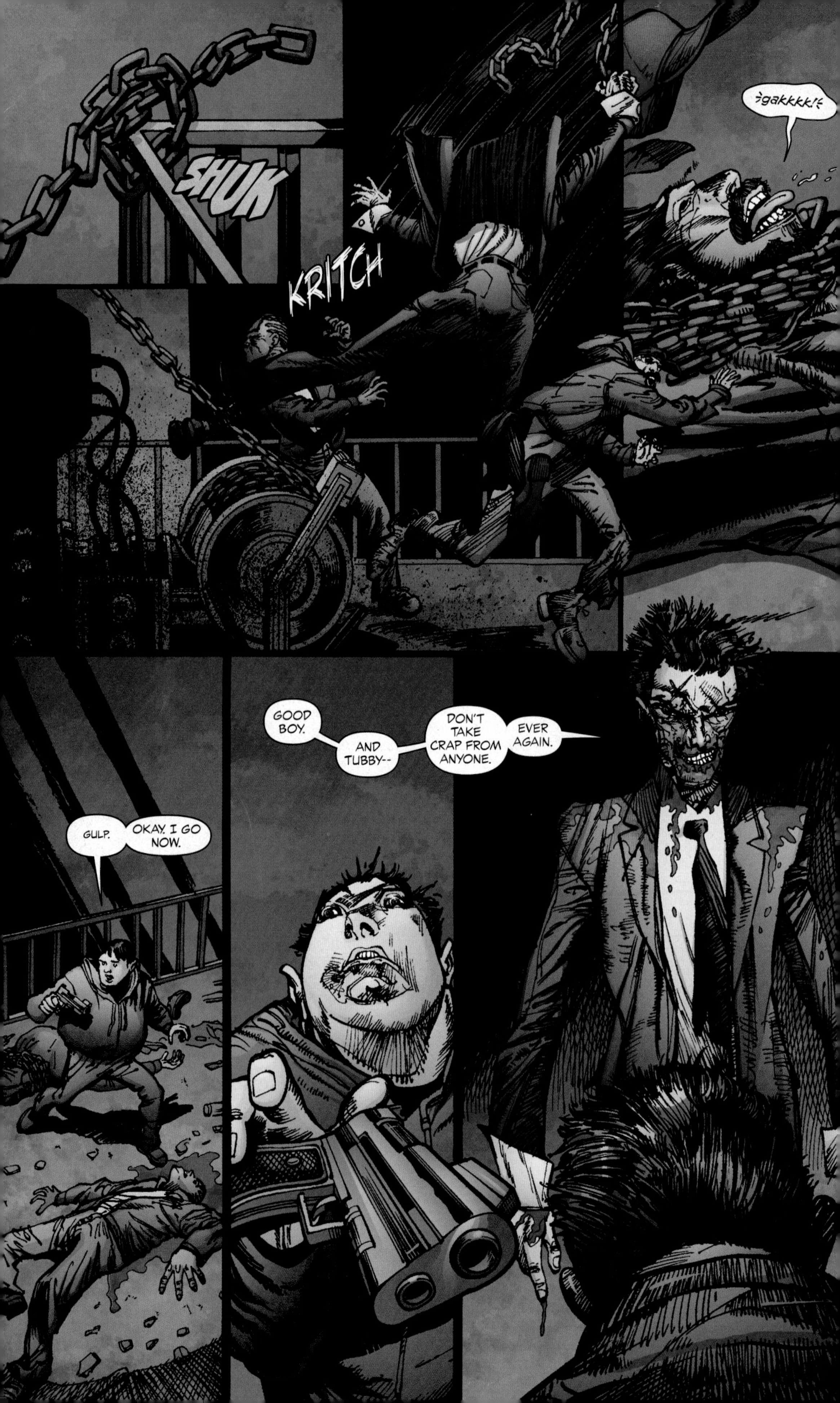
SHUK
KRITCH
gakkkk!
GULP.
OKAY. I GO NOW.
GOOD BOY.
AND TUBBY--
DON'T TAKE CRAP FROM ANYONE.
EVER AGAIN.

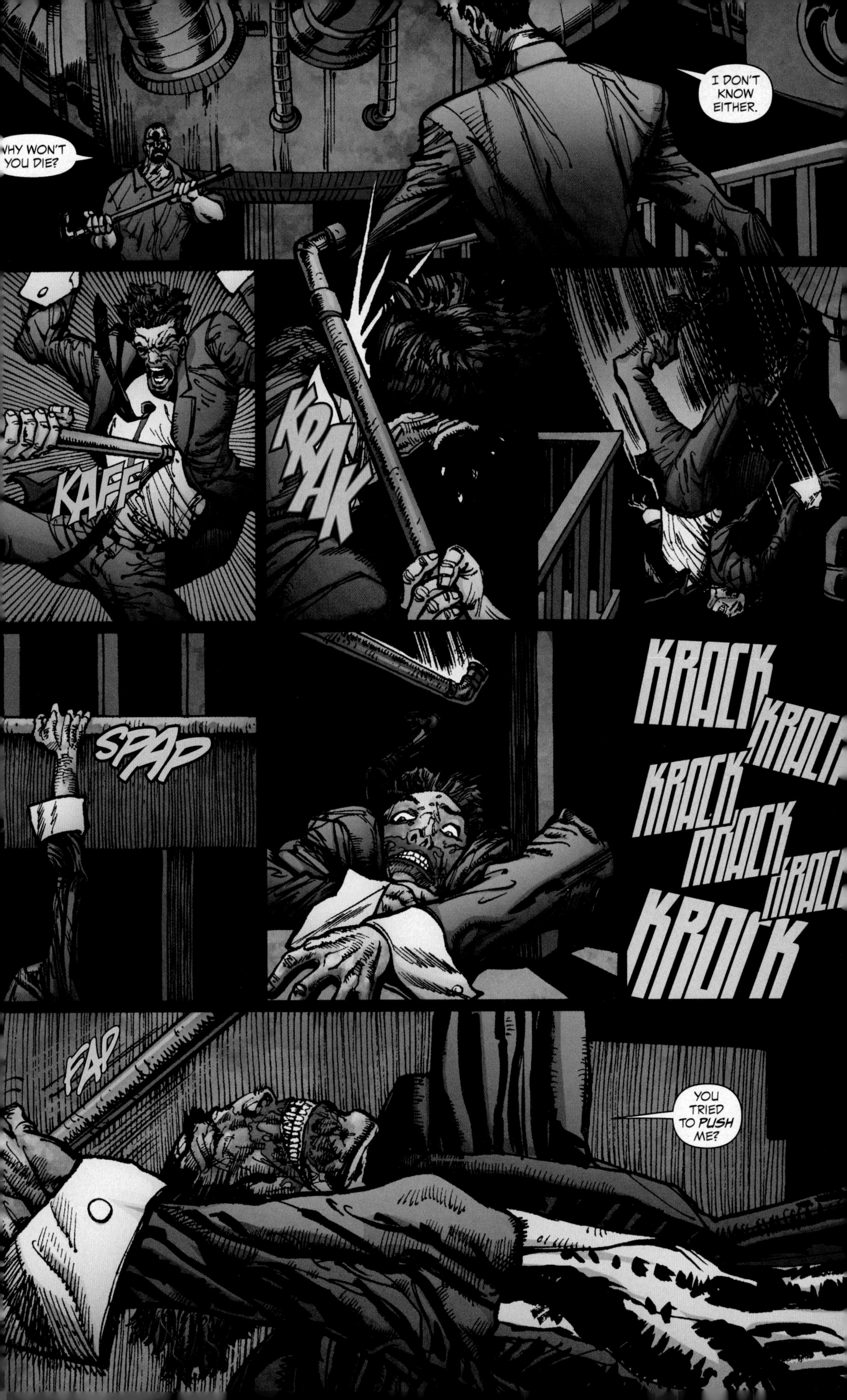
WHY WON'T YOU DIE?
I DON'T KNOW EITHER.
KAFF
KRAK
SPAP
KRACK KRACK
KRACK KRACK KRACK
KROCK
FAP
YOU TRIED TO *PUSH* ME?

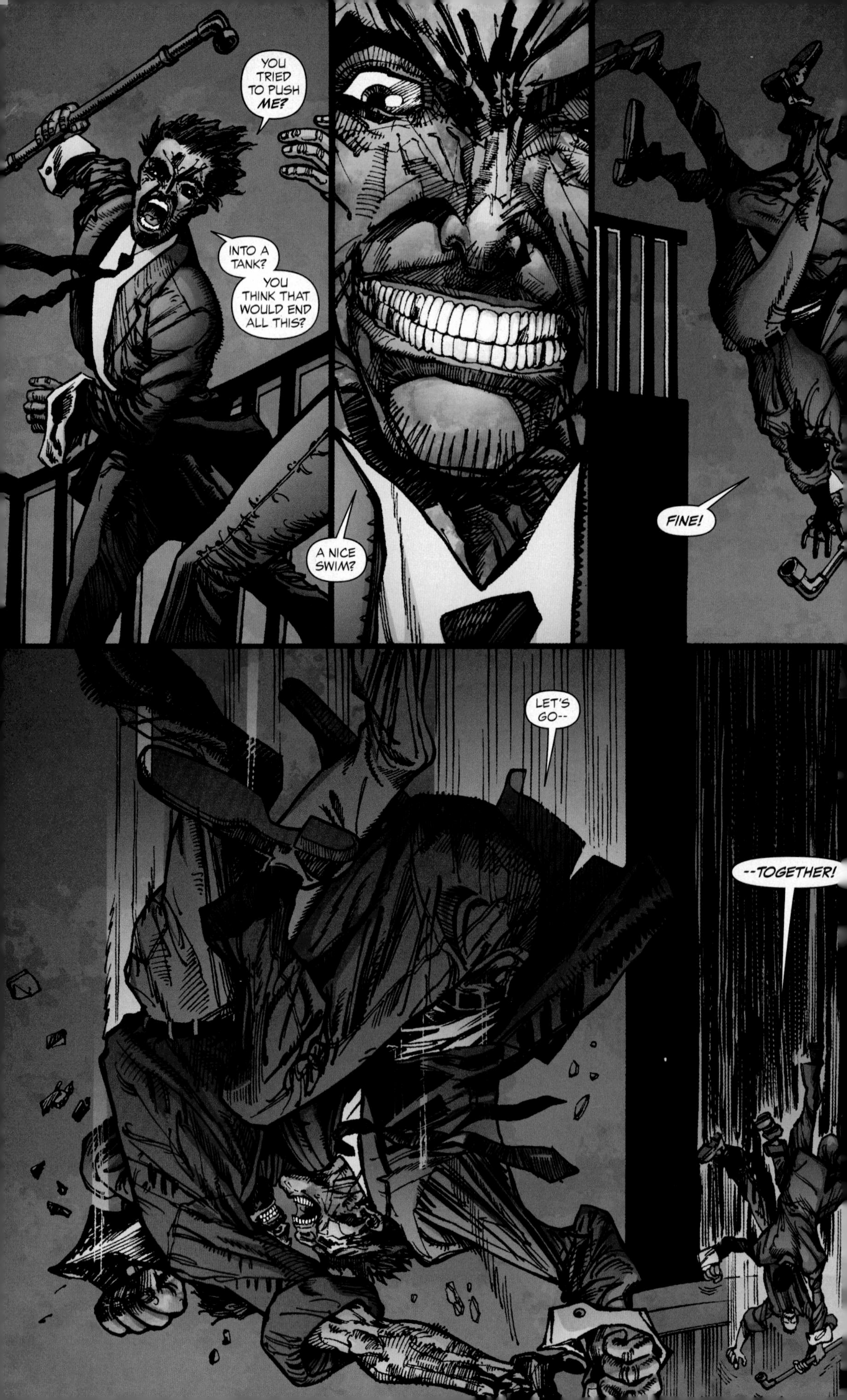
YOU TRIED TO PUSH *ME?*
INTO A TANK?
YOU THINK THAT WOULD END ALL THIS?
A NICE SWIM?
FINE!
LET'S GO--
--TOGETHER!

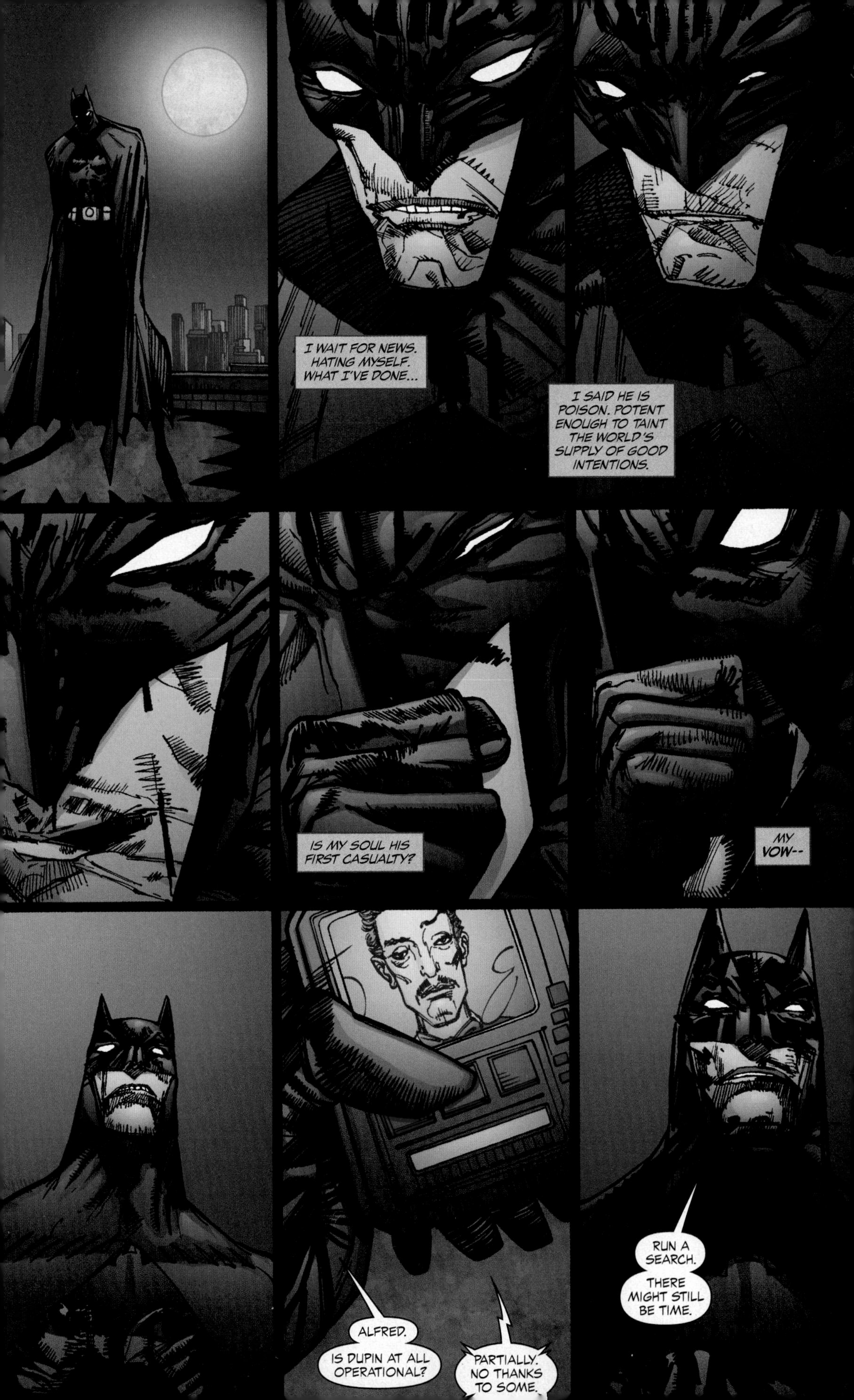
I WAIT FOR NEWS. HATING MYSELF. WHAT I'VE DONE...
I SAID HE IS POISON. POTENT ENOUGH TO TAINT THE WORLD'S SUPPLY OF GOOD INTENTIONS.
IS MY SOUL HIS FIRST CASUALTY?
MY VOW--
ALFRED.
IS DUPIN AT ALL OPERATIONAL?
PARTIALLY. NO THANKS TO SOME.
RUN A SEARCH.
THERE MIGHT STILL BE TIME.

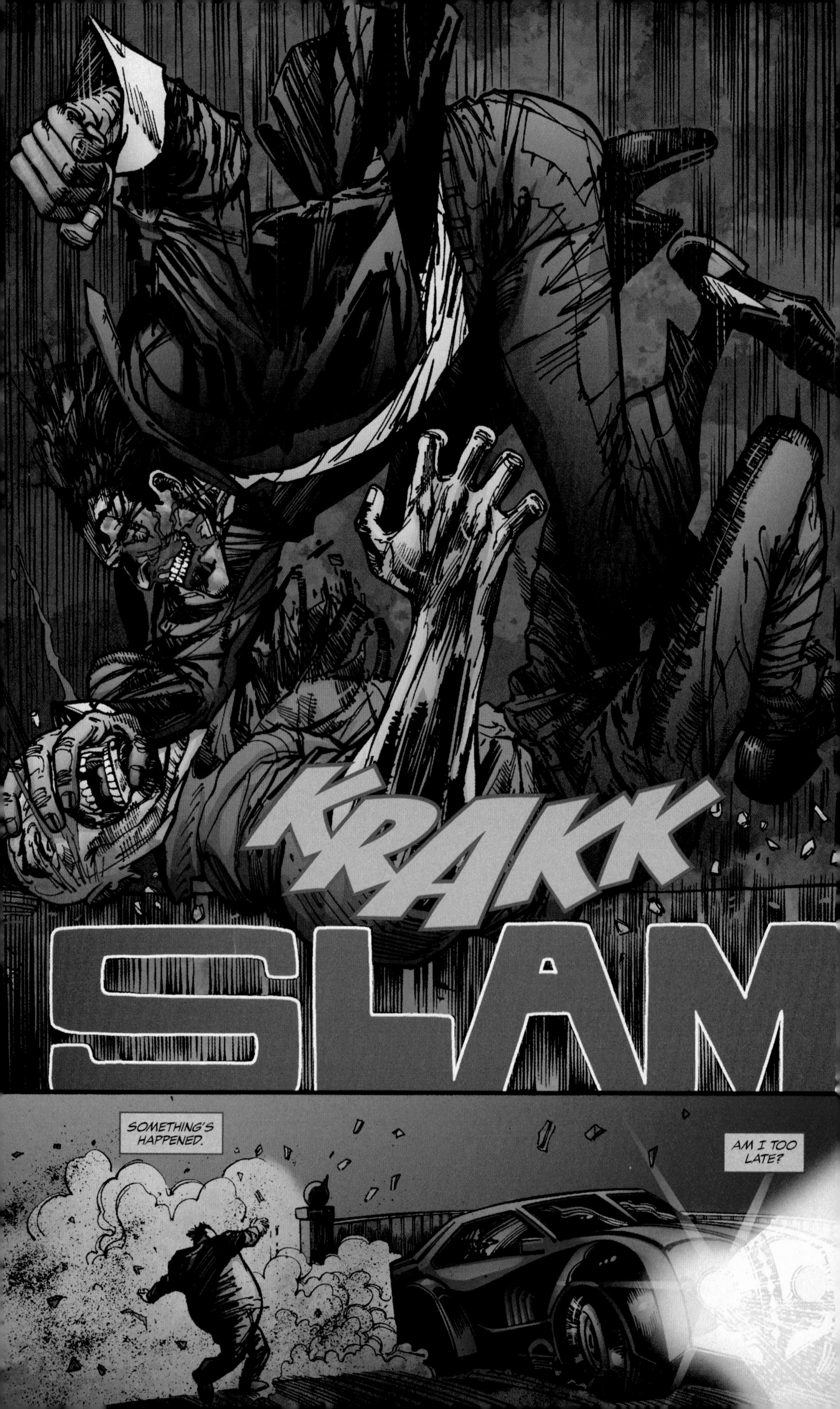
KRAKK
SLAM
SOMETHING'S HAPPENED.
AM I TOO LATE?

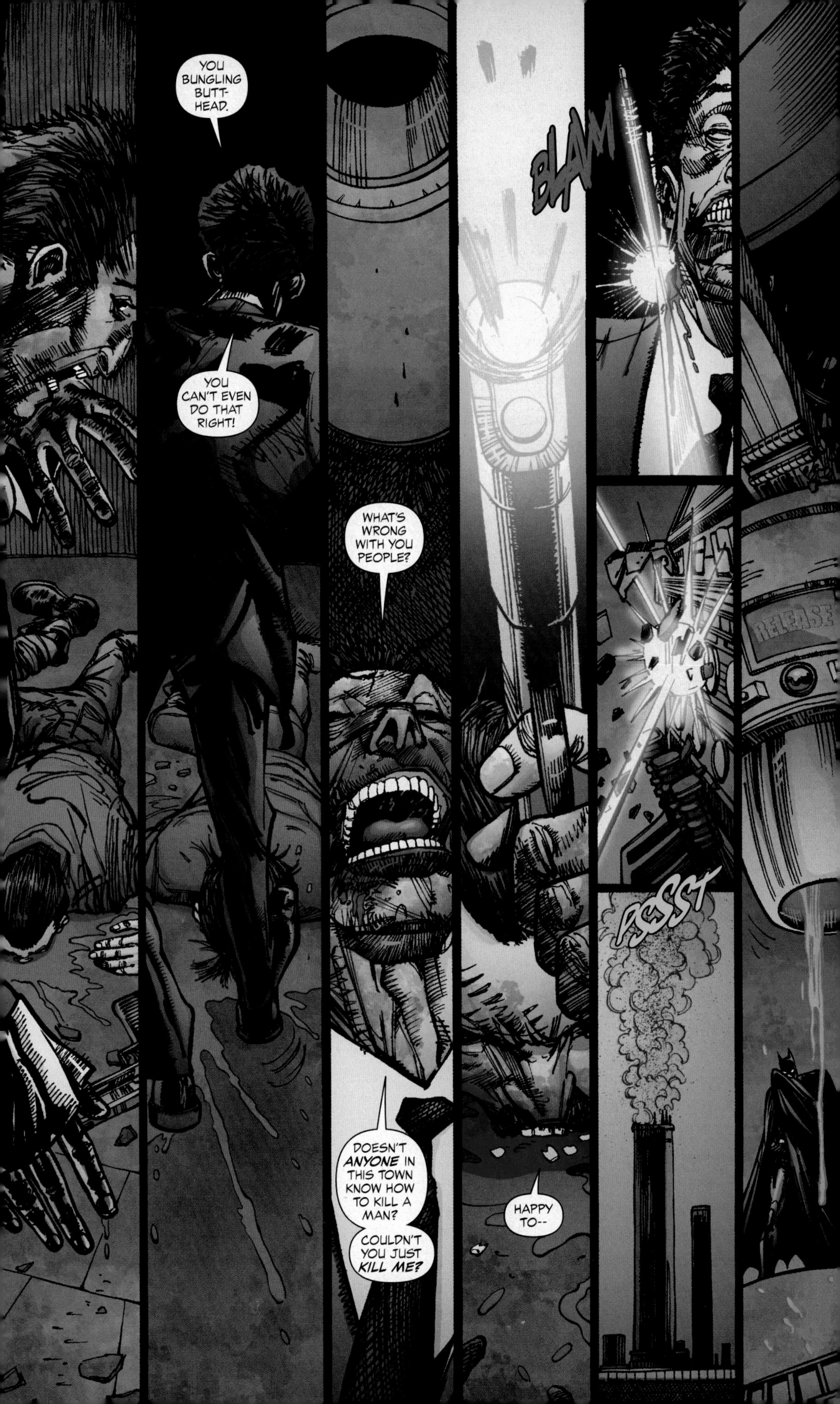

YOU BUNGLING BUTT-HEAD.
YOU CAN'T EVEN DO THAT RIGHT!
WHAT'S WRONG WITH YOU PEOPLE?
DOESN'T *ANYONE* IN THIS TOWN KNOW HOW TO KILL A MAN?
COULDN'T YOU JUST *KILL ME?*
BLAM
HAPPY TO--
RELEASE
PSSST

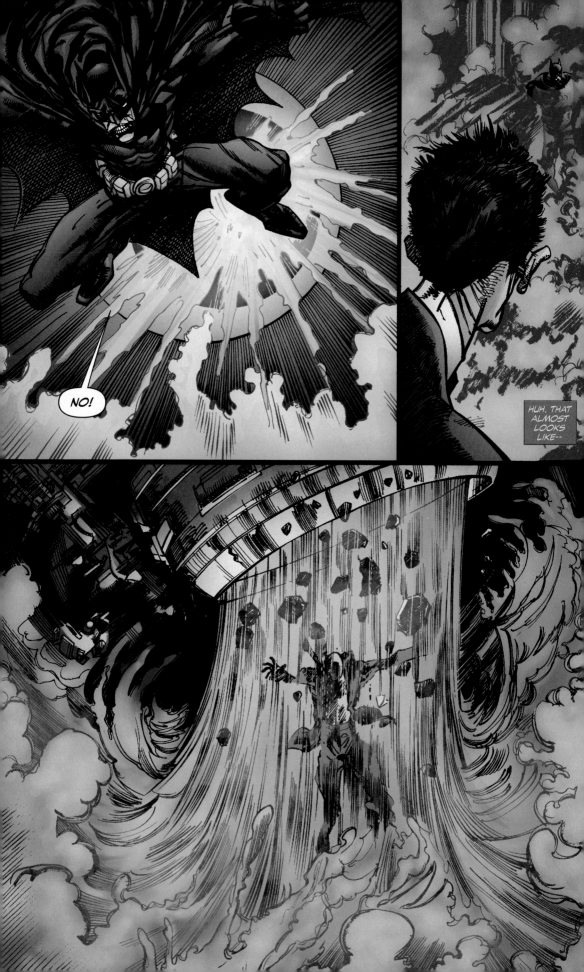

NO!

HUH. THAT ALMOST LOOKS LIKE--

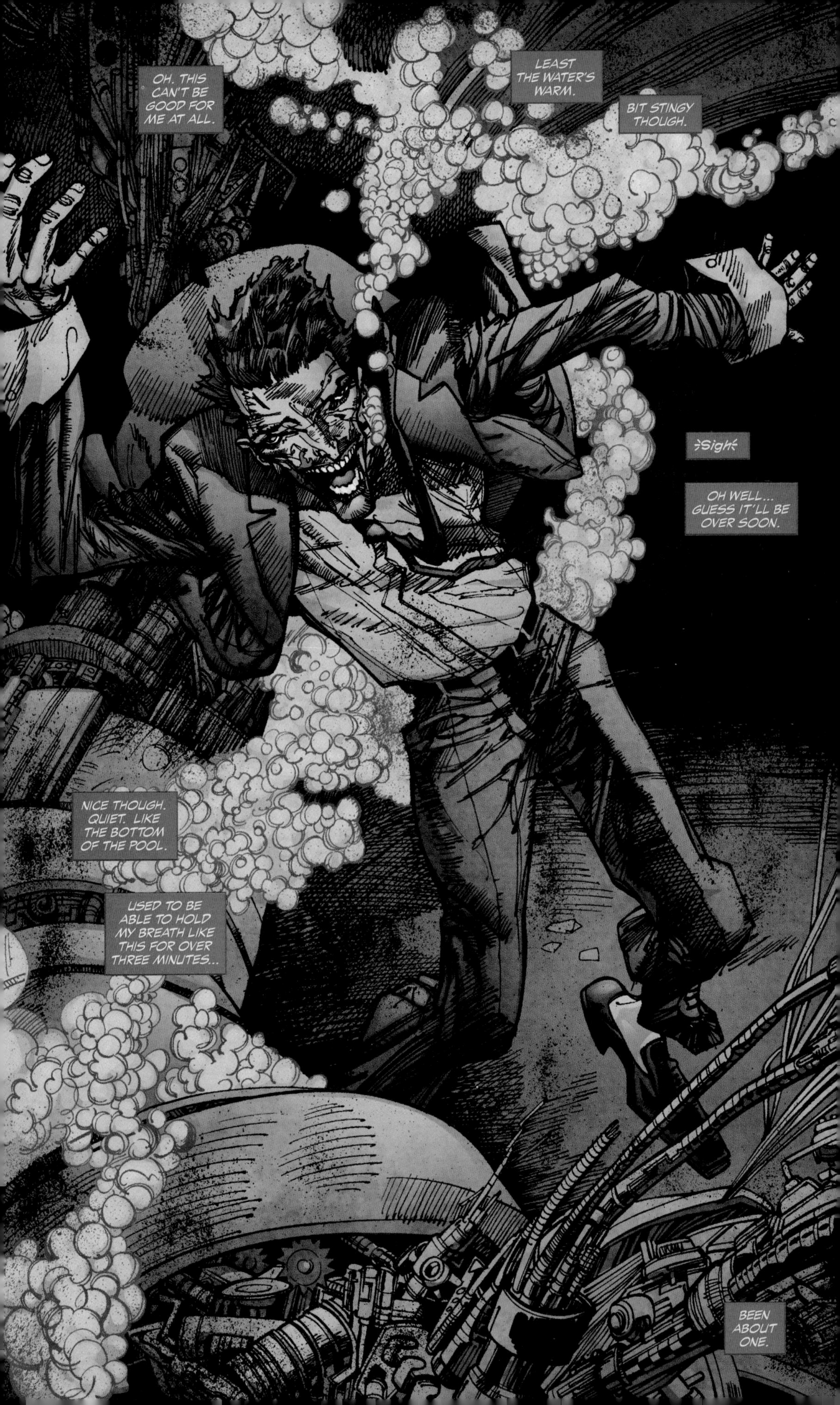
OH. THIS CAN'T BE GOOD FOR ME AT ALL.
LEAST THE WATER'S WARM.
BIT STINGY THOUGH.
Sigh
OH WELL... GUESS IT'LL BE OVER SOON.
NICE THOUGH. QUIET. LIKE THE BOTTOM OF THE POOL.
USED TO BE ABLE TO HOLD MY BREATH LIKE THIS FOR OVER THREE MINUTES...
BEEN ABOUT ONE.

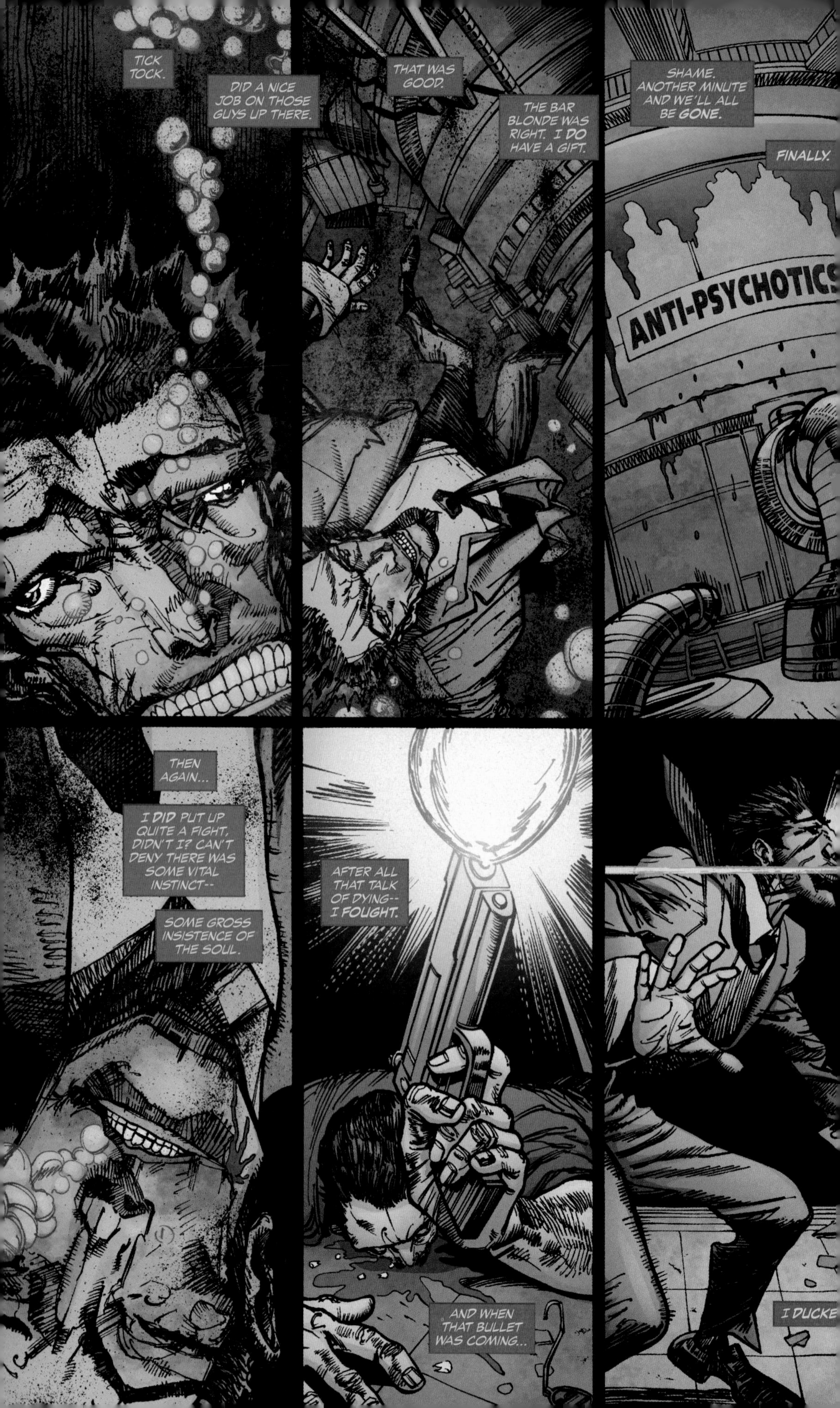
TICK TOCK.
DID A NICE JOB ON THOSE GUYS UP THERE.
THAT WAS GOOD.
THE BAR BLONDE WAS RIGHT. I DO HAVE A GIFT.
SHAME. ANOTHER MINUTE AND WE'LL ALL BE GONE.
FINALLY.
ANTI-PSYCHOTICS
THEN AGAIN...
I DID PUT UP QUITE A FIGHT, DIDN'T I? CAN'T DENY THERE WAS SOME VITAL INSTINCT--
SOME GROSS INSISTENCE OF THE SOUL.
AFTER ALL THAT TALK OF DYING-- I FOUGHT.
AND WHEN THAT BULLET WAS COMING...
I DUCKE

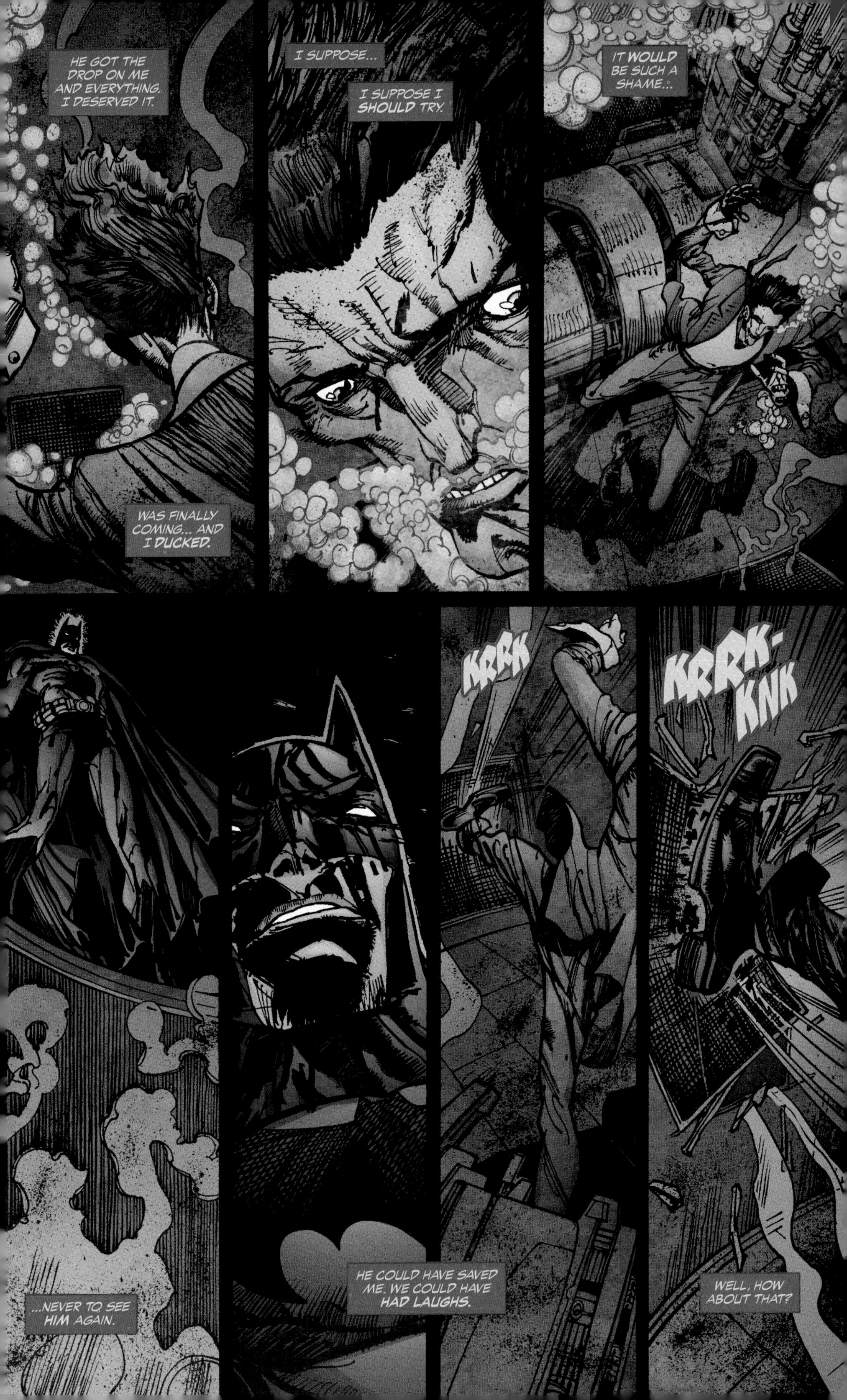
HE GOT THE DROP ON ME AND EVERYTHING. I DESERVED IT.
WAS FINALLY COMING... AND I DUCKED.
I SUPPOSE...
I SUPPOSE I SHOULD TRY.
IT WOULD BE SUCH A SHAME...
...NEVER TO SEE HIM AGAIN.
HE COULD HAVE SAVED ME. WE COULD HAVE HAD LAUGHS.
KRRK
KRRK-KNK
WELL, HOW ABOUT THAT?

IT WOULD HAVE BEEN SO MUCH EASIER IF THAT DIDN'T JUST HAPPEN.

OH WELL.

FOUR MINUTES NOW. NOTHING LEFT IN MY LUNGS BUT BLOOD AND CHEMICALS.

DON'T KNOW HOW MUCH MORE I CAN--

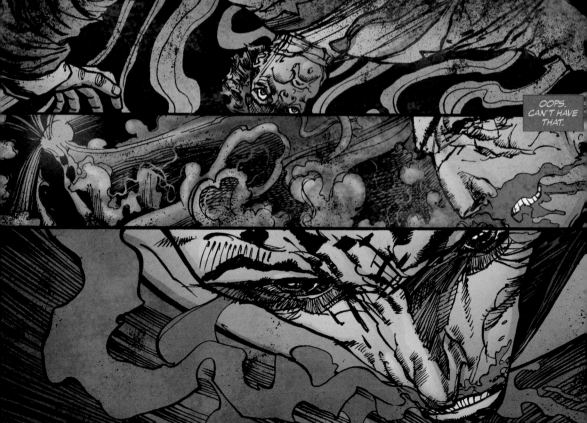

OOPS. CAN'T HAVE THAT.

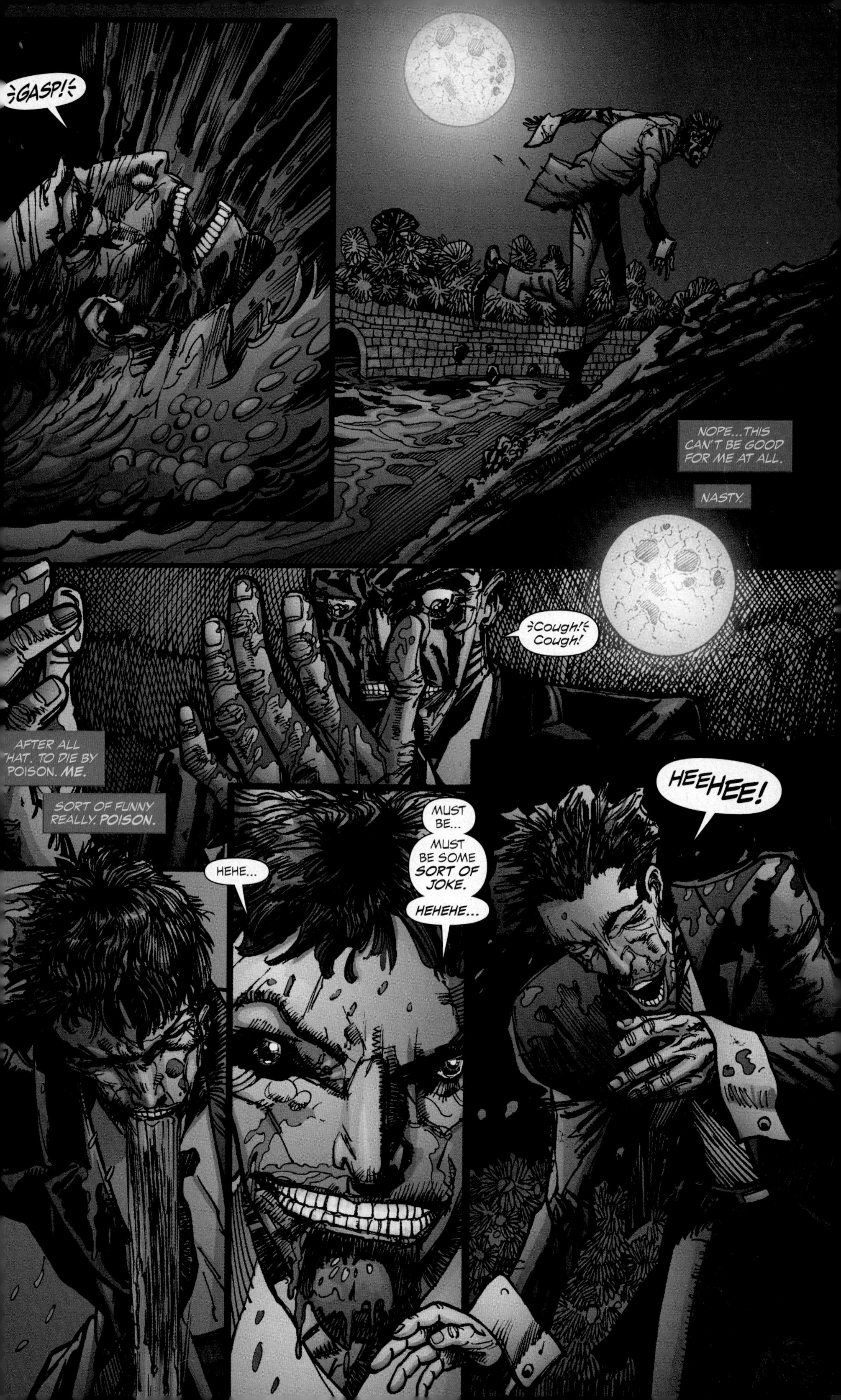
GASP!
NOPE...THIS CAN'T BE GOOD FOR ME AT ALL.
NASTY.
Cough! Cough!
AFTER ALL THAT. TO DIE BY POISON. ME.
SORT OF FUNNY REALLY. POISON.
HEHE...
MUST BE...
MUST BE SOME SORT OF JOKE.
HEHEHE...
HEEHEE!

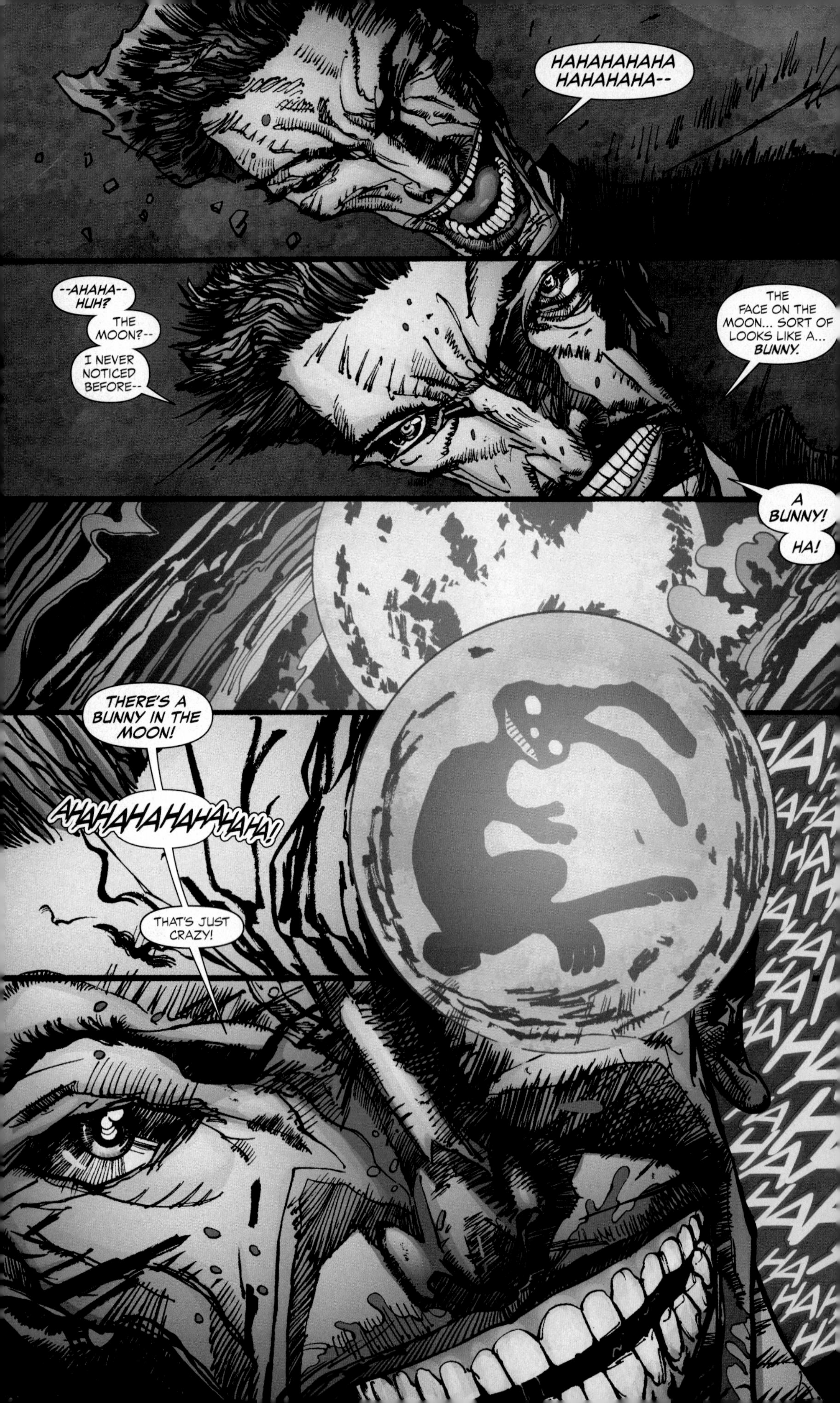
HAHAHAHAHA HAHAHAHA--
--AHAHA-- HUH?
THE MOON?--
I NEVER NOTICED BEFORE--
THE FACE ON THE MOON... SORT OF LOOKS LIKE A... BUNNY.
A BUNNY!
HA!
THERE'S A BUNNY IN THE MOON!
AHAHAHAHAHAHAHA!
THAT'S JUST CRAZY!
HAHAHAHAHAHAHAHAHAHAHAHAHAHAHA

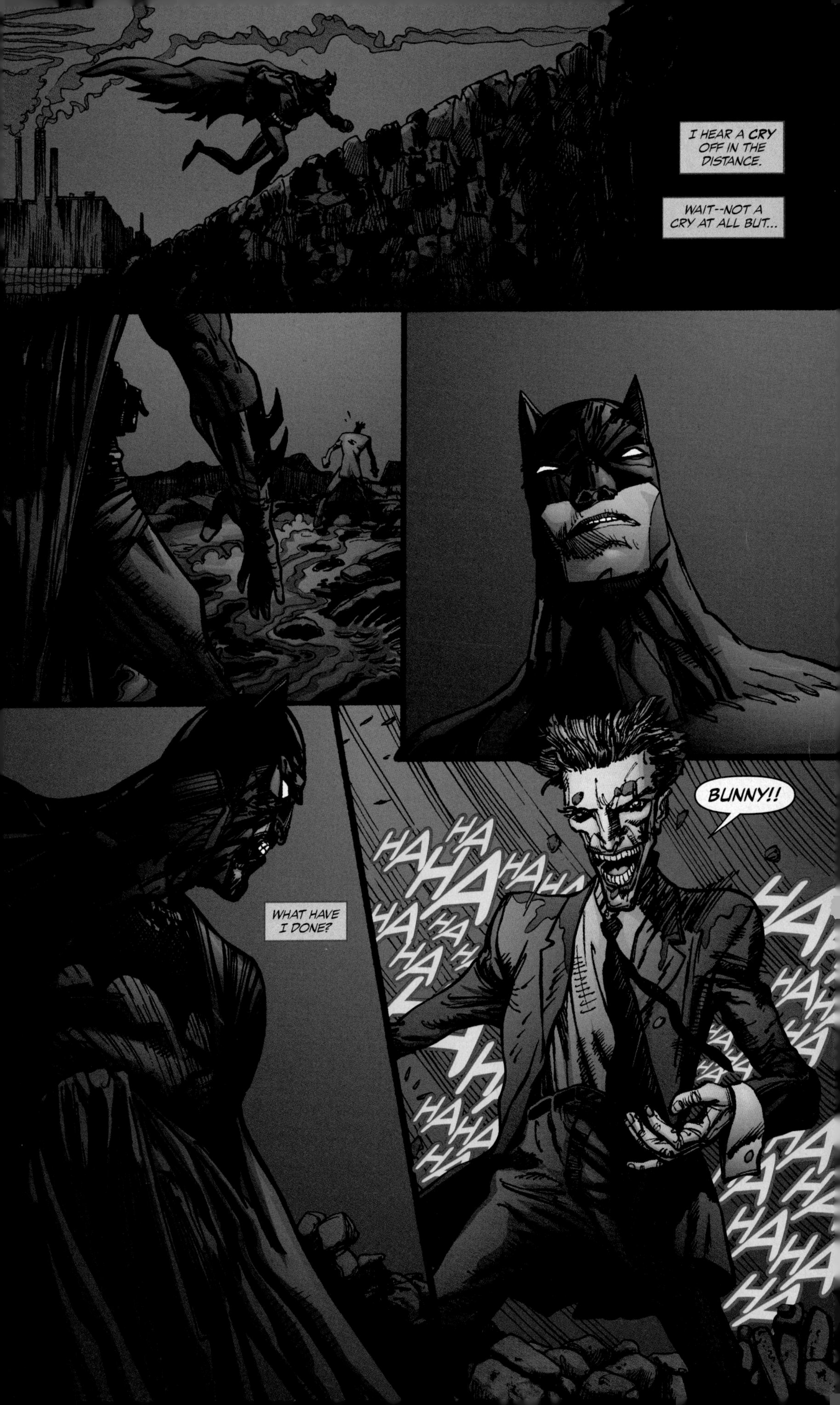
I HEAR A CRY OFF IN THE DISTANCE.
WAIT--NOT A CRY AT ALL BUT...
BUNNY!!
WHAT HAVE I DONE?
HA HA HA HA HA HA HA HA HA HA HA HA HA HA HA HA HA HA HA HA

chapter five **THIS APPARITION COME**

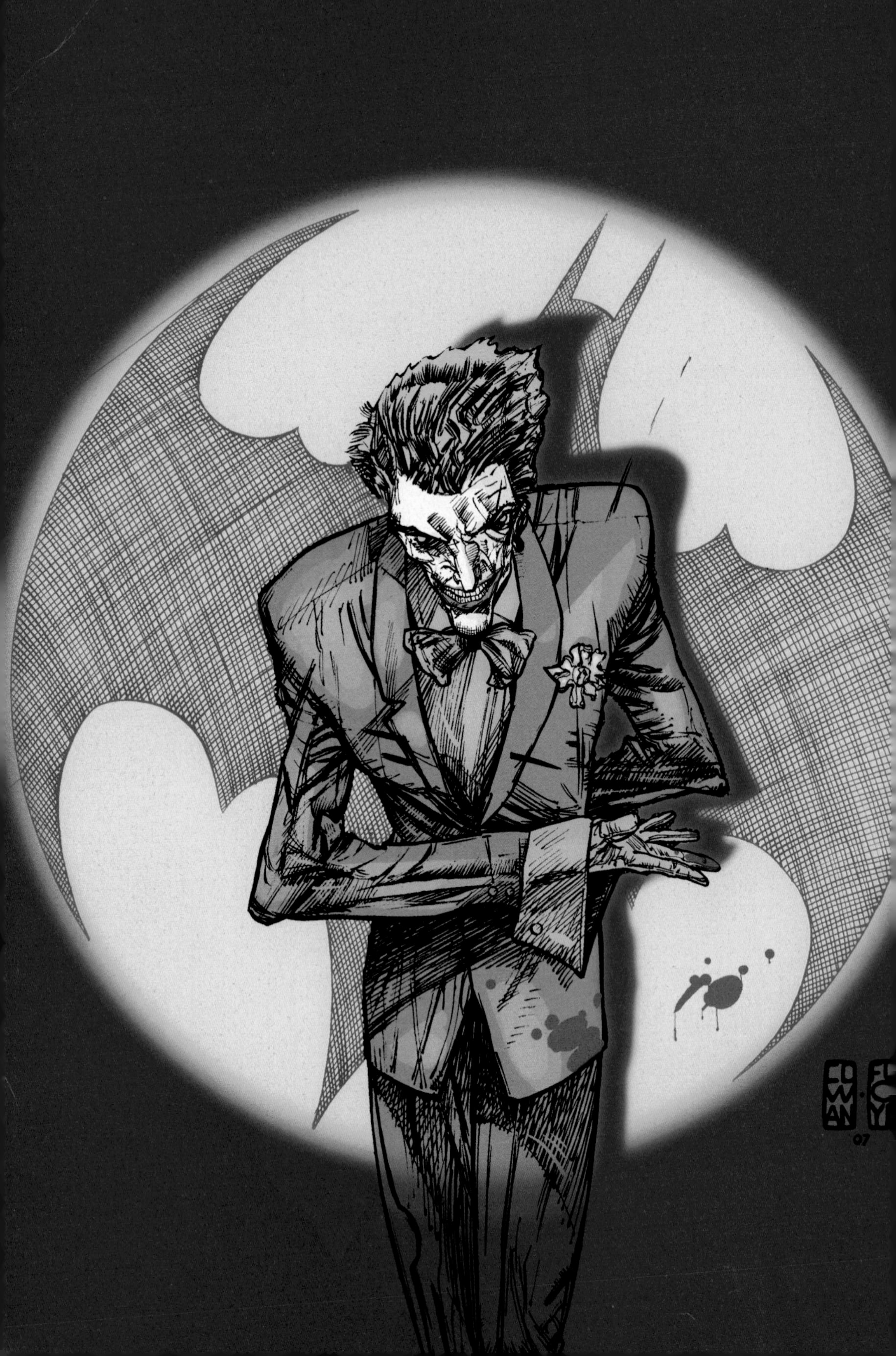

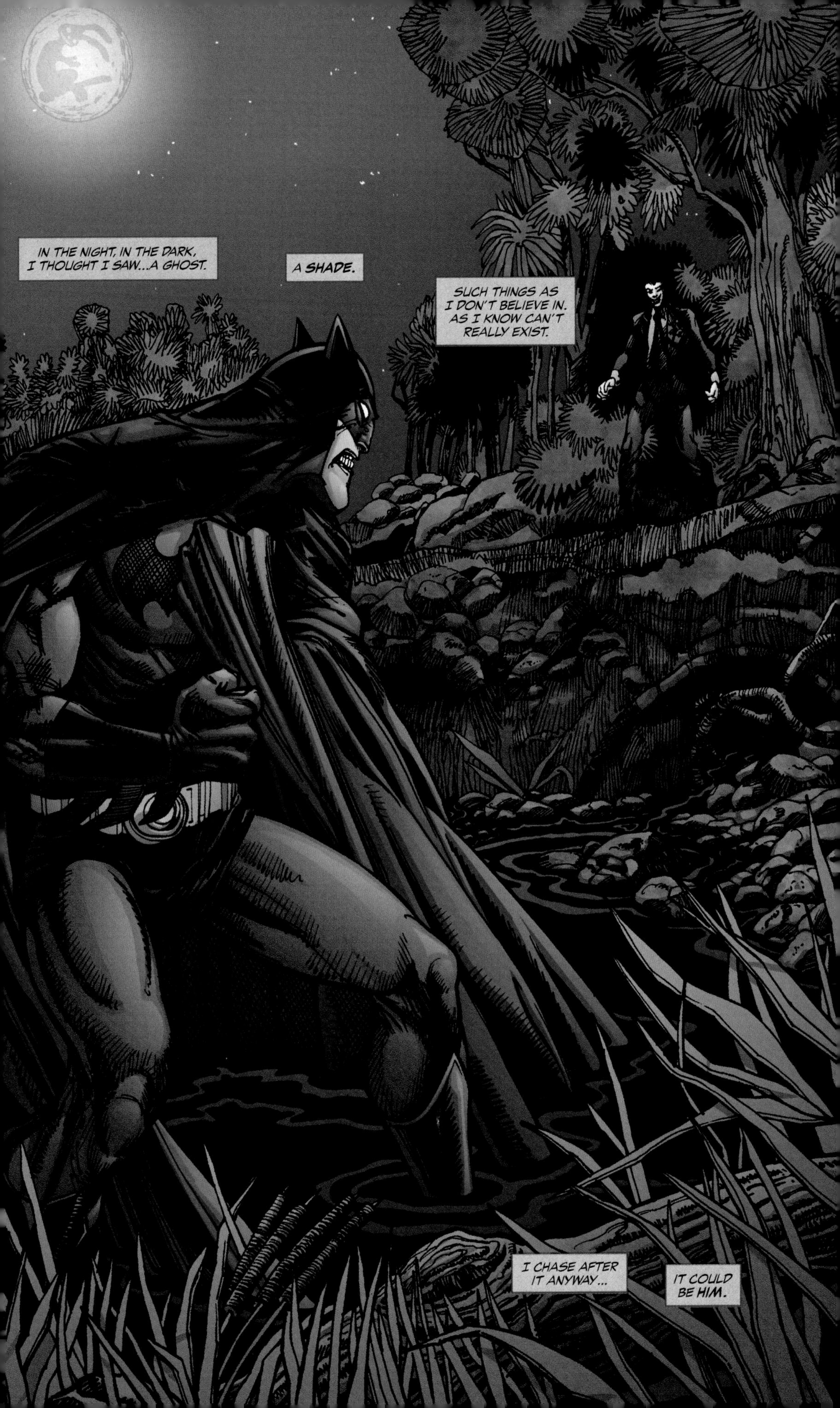
IN THE NIGHT, IN THE DARK, I THOUGHT I SAW...A GHOST.
A SHADE.
SUCH THINGS AS I DON'T BELIEVE IN. AS I KNOW CAN'T REALLY EXIST.
I CHASE AFTER IT ANYWAY...
IT COULD BE HIM.

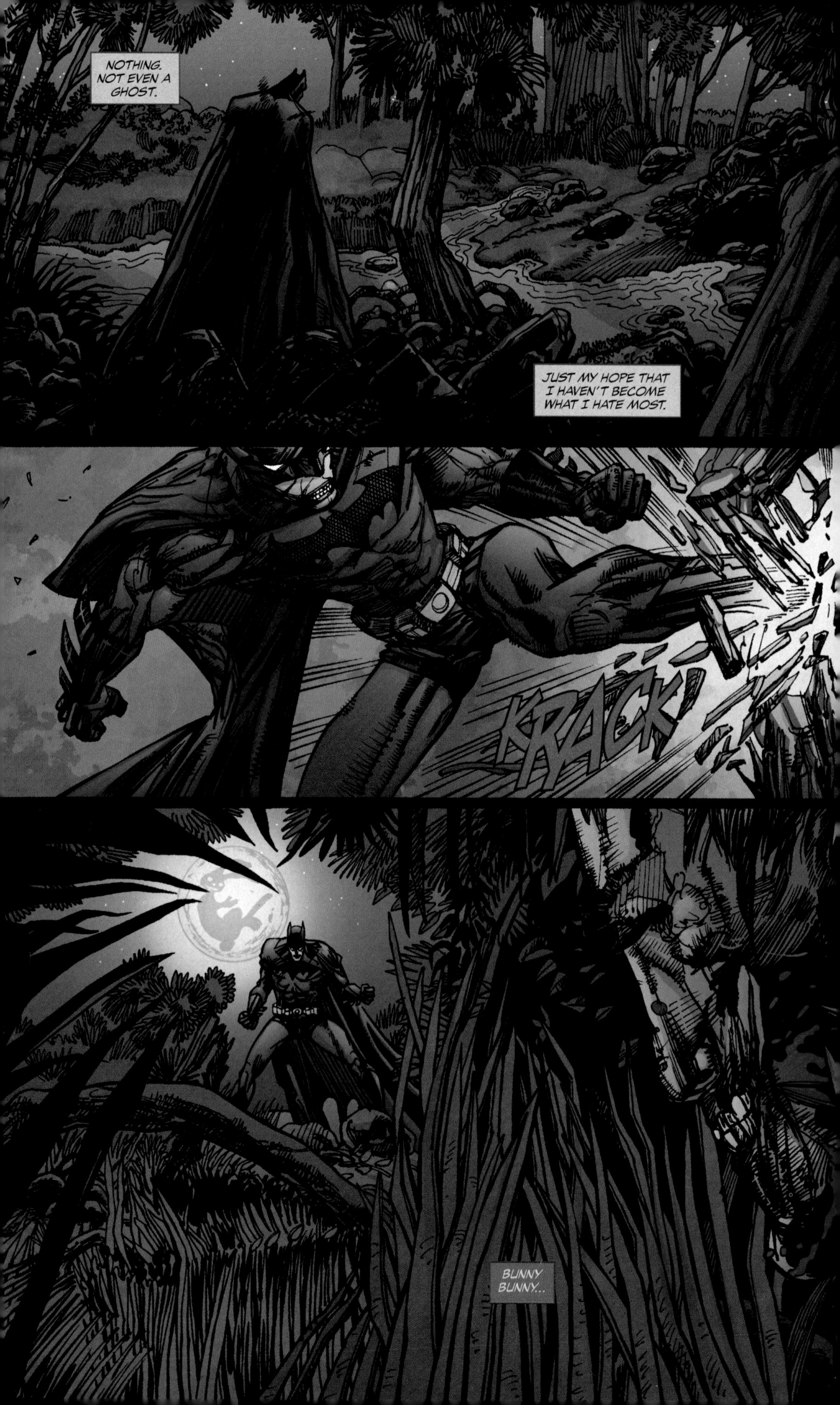
NOTHING. NOT EVEN A GHOST.
JUST MY HOPE THAT I HAVEN'T BECOME WHAT I HATE MOST.
KRACK
BUNNY BUNNY...

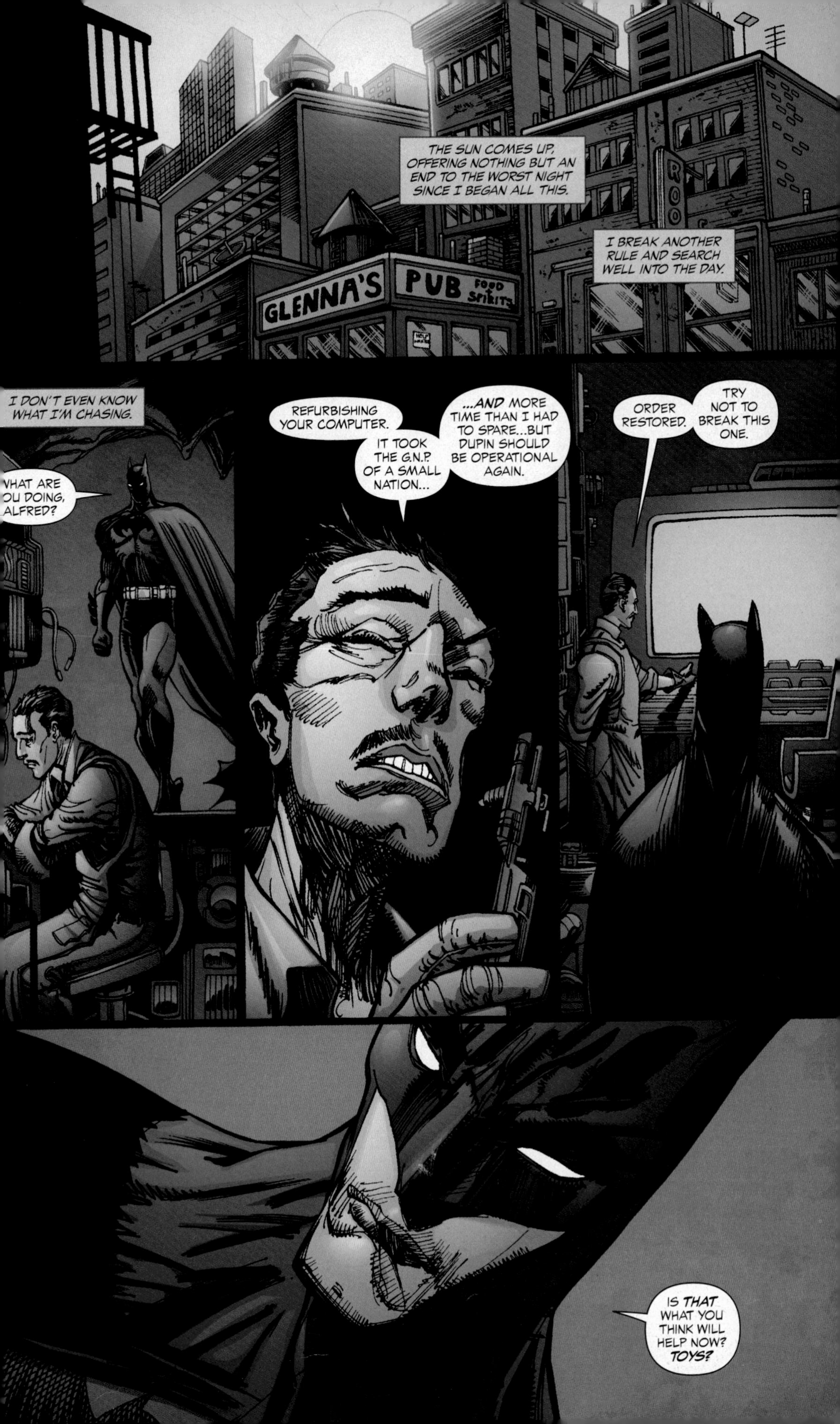

THE SUN COMES UP, OFFERING NOTHING BUT AN END TO THE WORST NIGHT SINCE I BEGAN ALL THIS.
I BREAK ANOTHER RULE AND SEARCH WELL INTO THE DAY.
GLENNA'S PUB FOOD + SPIRITS
I DON'T EVEN KNOW WHAT I'M CHASING.
WHAT ARE OU DOING, ALFRED?
REFURBISHING YOUR COMPUTER.
IT TOOK THE G.N.P. OF A SMALL NATION...
...AND MORE TIME THAN I HAD TO SPARE...BUT DUPIN SHOULD BE OPERATIONAL AGAIN.
ORDER RESTORED.
TRY NOT TO BREAK THIS ONE.
IS THAT WHAT YOU THINK WILL HELP NOW? TOYS?

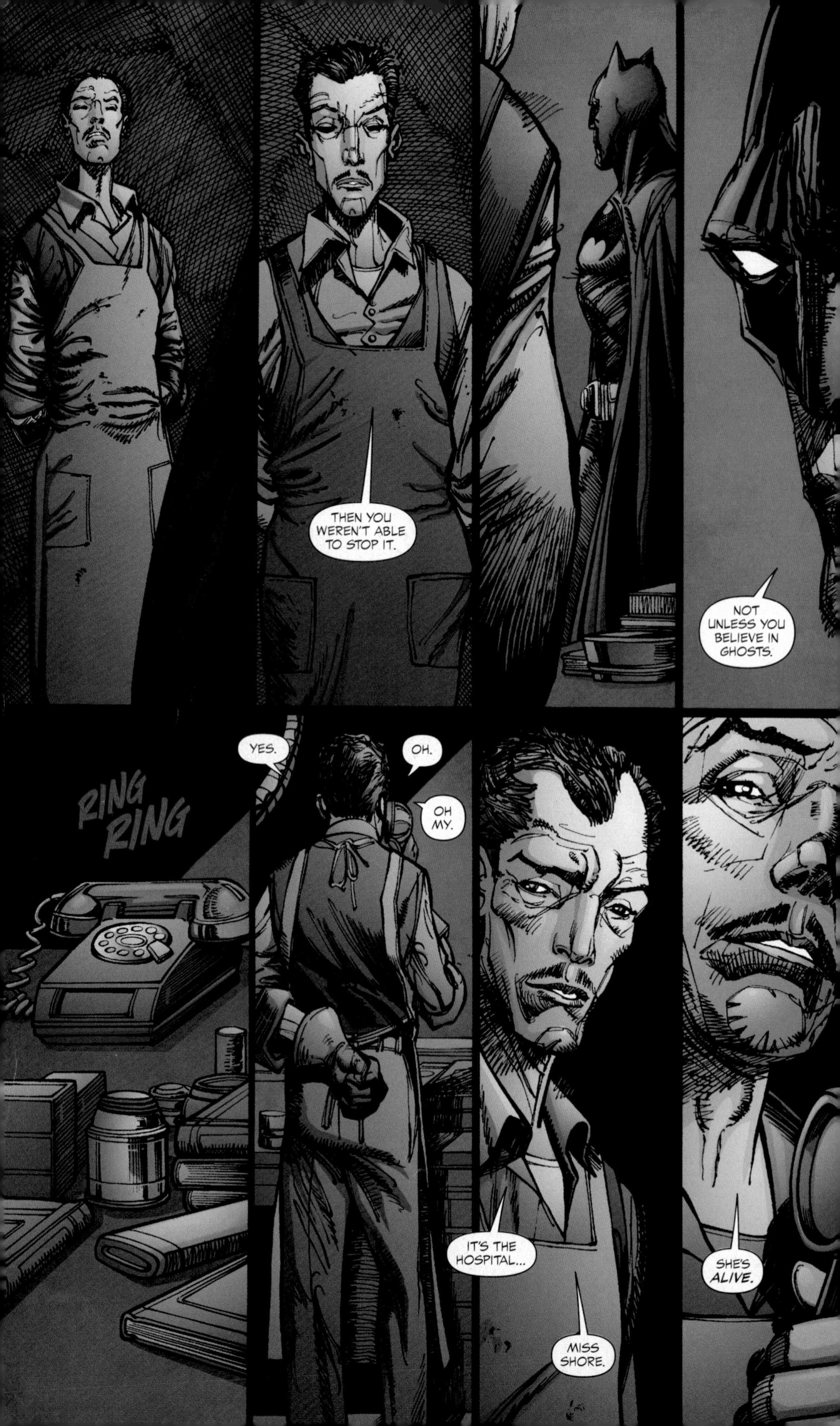
THEN YOU WEREN'T ABLE TO STOP IT.
NOT UNLESS YOU BELIEVE IN GHOSTS.
RING RING
YES.
OH.
OH MY.
IT'S THE HOSPITAL...
MISS SHORE.
SHE'S *ALIVE.*

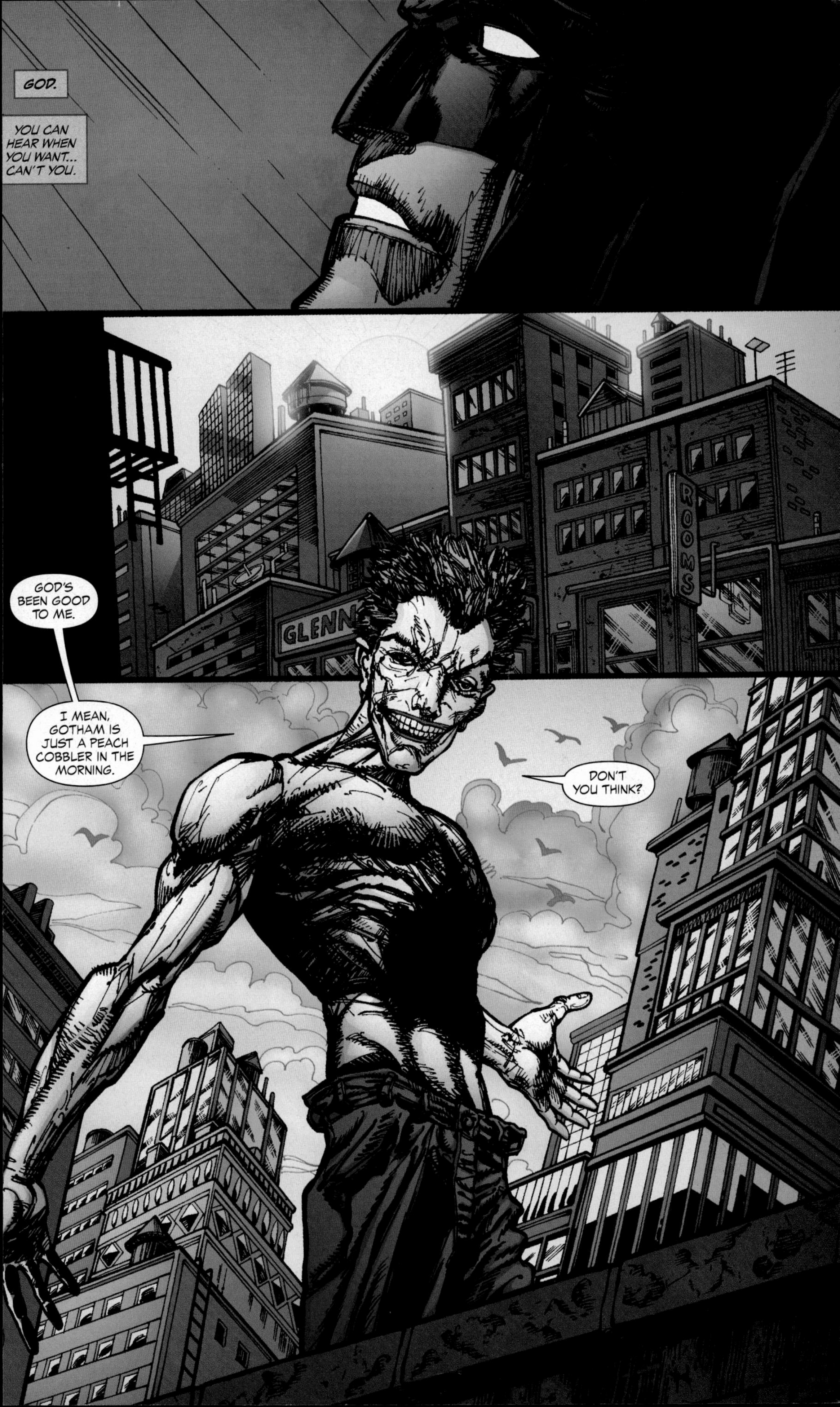
GOD.
YOU CAN HEAR WHEN YOU WANT... CAN'T YOU.
ROOMS
GLENN
GOD'S BEEN GOOD TO ME.
I MEAN, GOTHAM IS JUST A PEACH COBBLER IN THE MORNING.
DON'T YOU THINK?

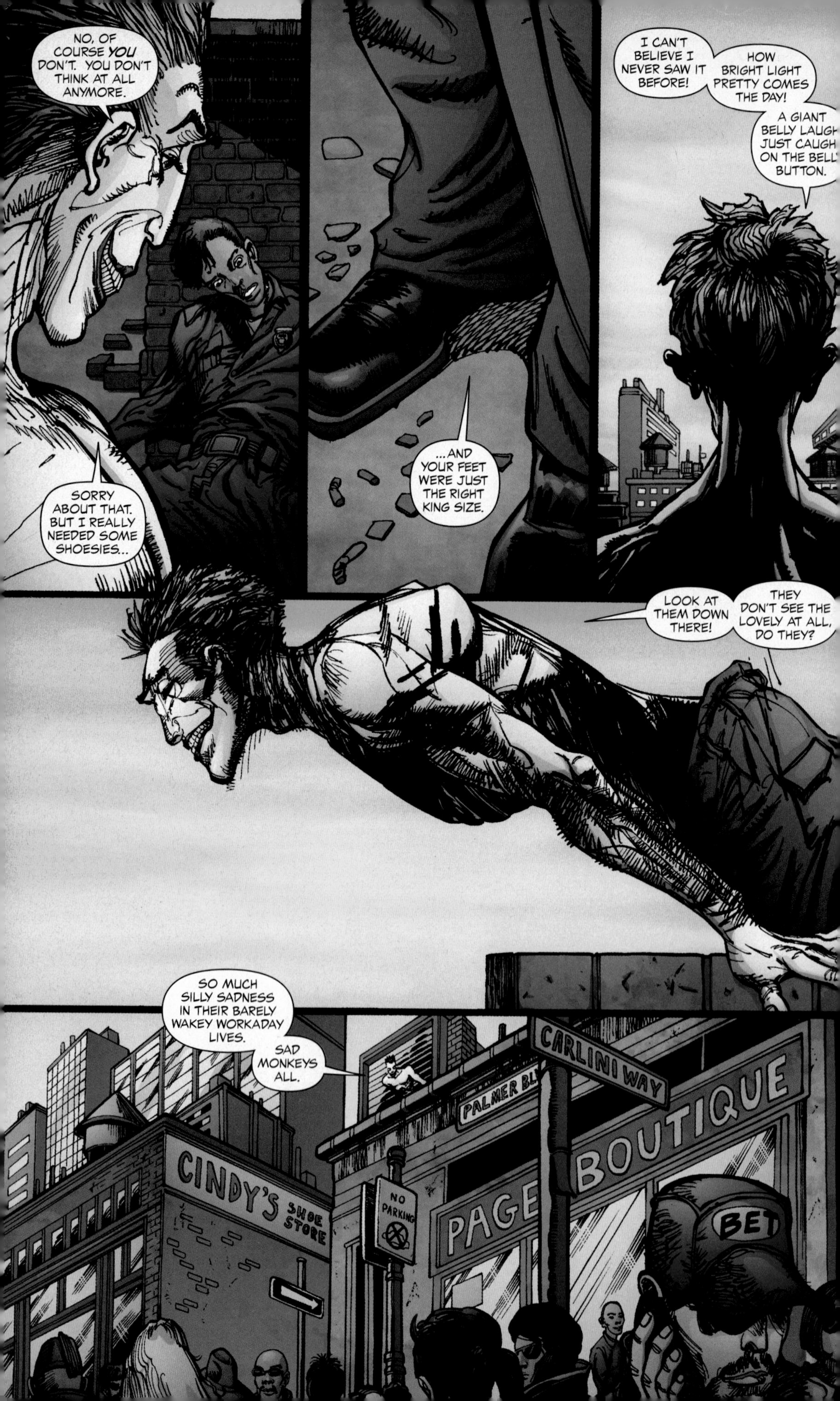
NO, OF COURSE YOU DON'T. YOU DON'T THINK AT ALL ANYMORE.
SORRY ABOUT THAT. BUT I REALLY NEEDED SOME SHOESIES...
...AND YOUR FEET WERE JUST THE RIGHT KING SIZE.
I CAN'T BELIEVE I NEVER SAW IT BEFORE!
HOW BRIGHT LIGHT PRETTY COMES THE DAY!
A GIANT BELLY LAUGH JUST CAUGHT ON THE BELLY BUTTON.
LOOK AT THEM DOWN THERE!
THEY DON'T SEE THE LOVELY AT ALL, DO THEY?
SO MUCH SILLY SADNESS IN THEIR BARELY WAKEY WORKADAY LIVES.
SAD MONKEYS ALL.
CARLINI WAY
PALMER BL
BOUTIQUE
CINDY'S SHOE STORE
NO PARKING
PAGE
BET

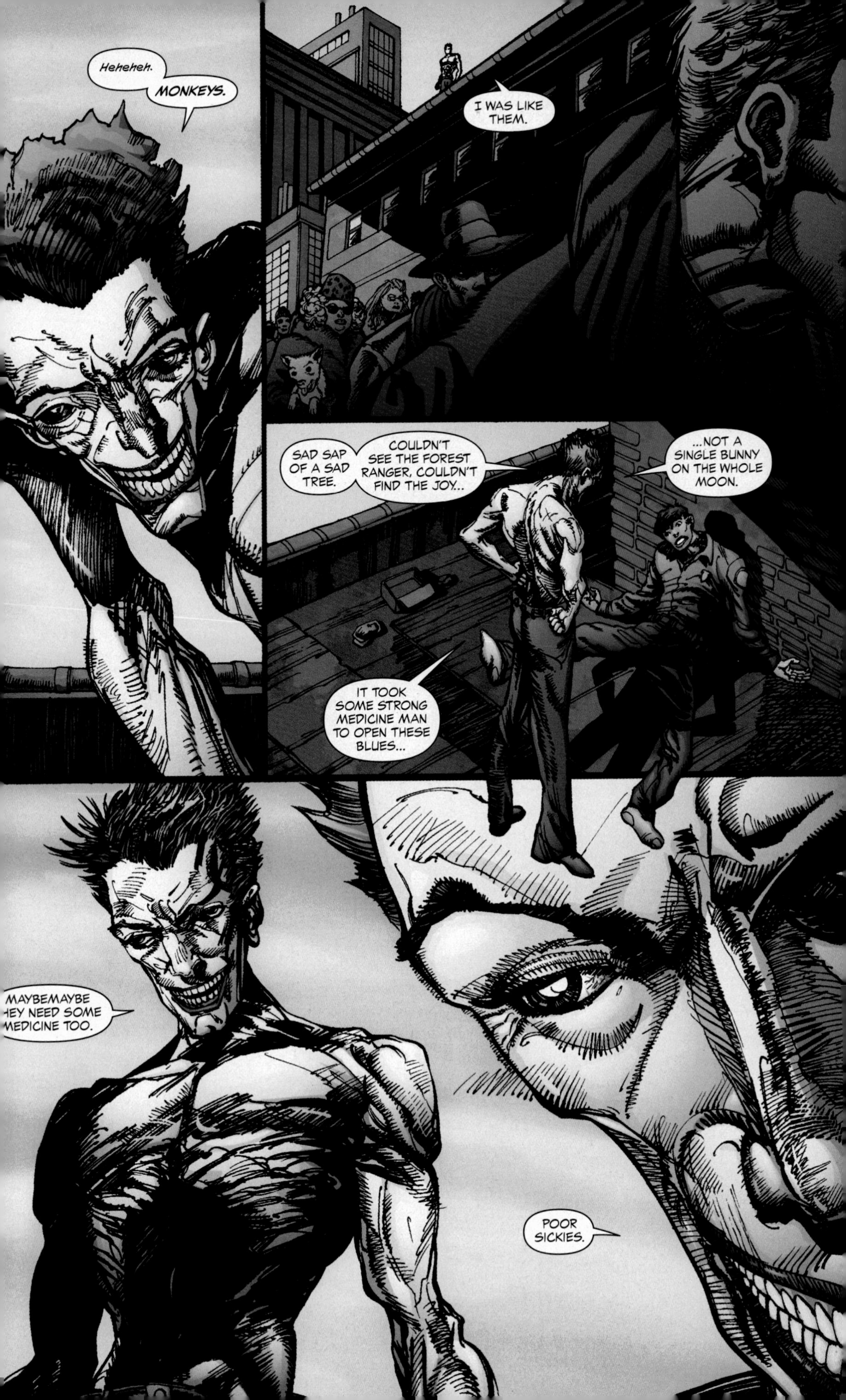
Heheheh.
MONKEYS.
I WAS LIKE THEM.
SAD SAP OF A SAD TREE.
COULDN'T SEE THE FOREST RANGER, COULDN'T FIND THE JOY...
...NOT A SINGLE BUNNY ON THE WHOLE MOON.
IT TOOK SOME STRONG MEDICINE MAN TO OPEN THESE BLUES...
MAYBEMAYBE HEY NEED SOME MEDICINE TOO.
POOR SICKIES.

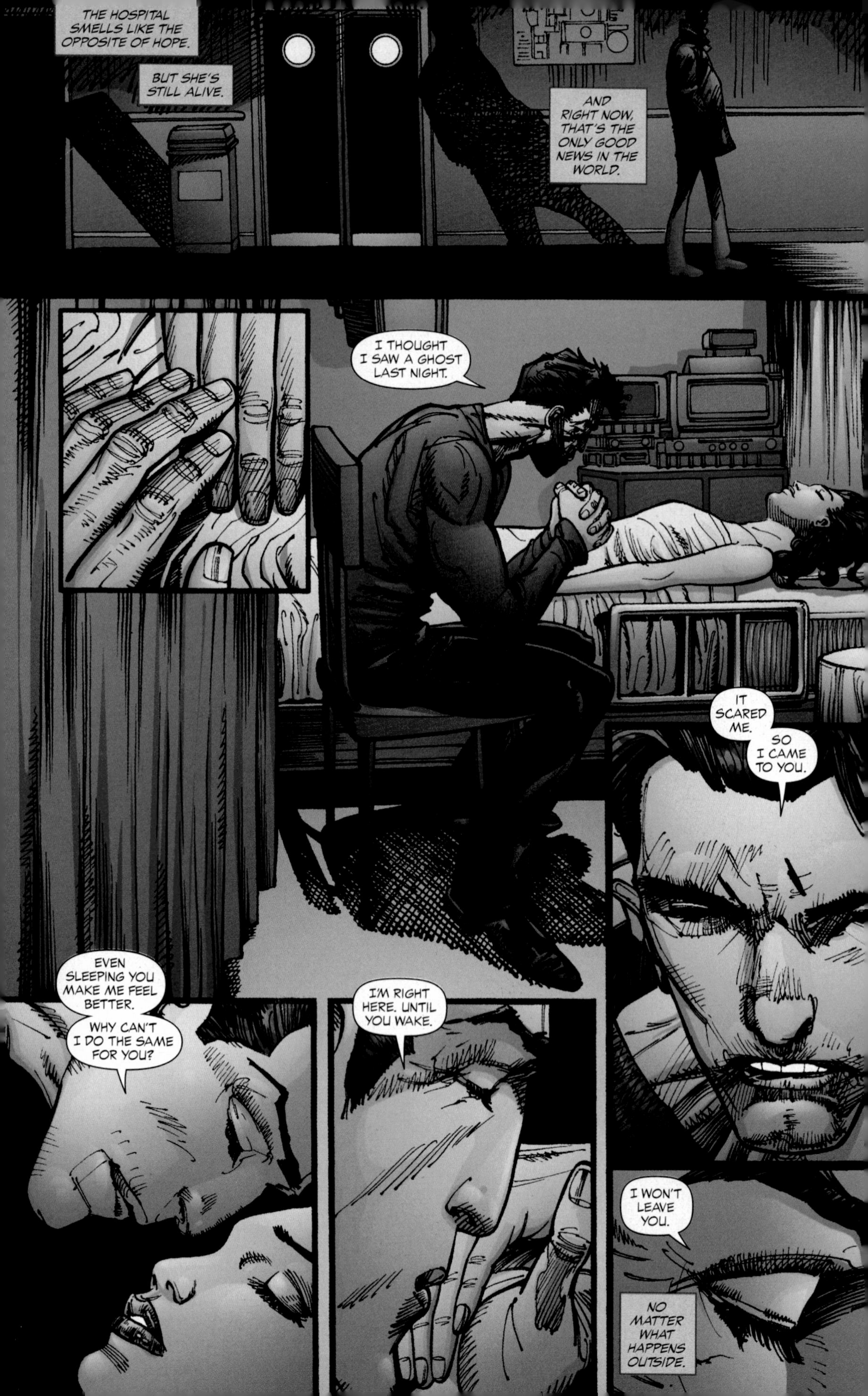
THE HOSPITAL SMELLS LIKE THE OPPOSITE OF HOPE.
BUT SHE'S STILL ALIVE.
AND RIGHT NOW, THAT'S THE ONLY GOOD NEWS IN THE WORLD.
I THOUGHT I SAW A GHOST LAST NIGHT.
IT SCARED ME.
SO I CAME TO YOU.
EVEN SLEEPING YOU MAKE ME FEEL BETTER.
WHY CAN'T I DO THE SAME FOR YOU?
I'M RIGHT HERE. UNTIL YOU WAKE.
I WON'T LEAVE YOU.
NO MATTER WHAT HAPPENS OUTSIDE.

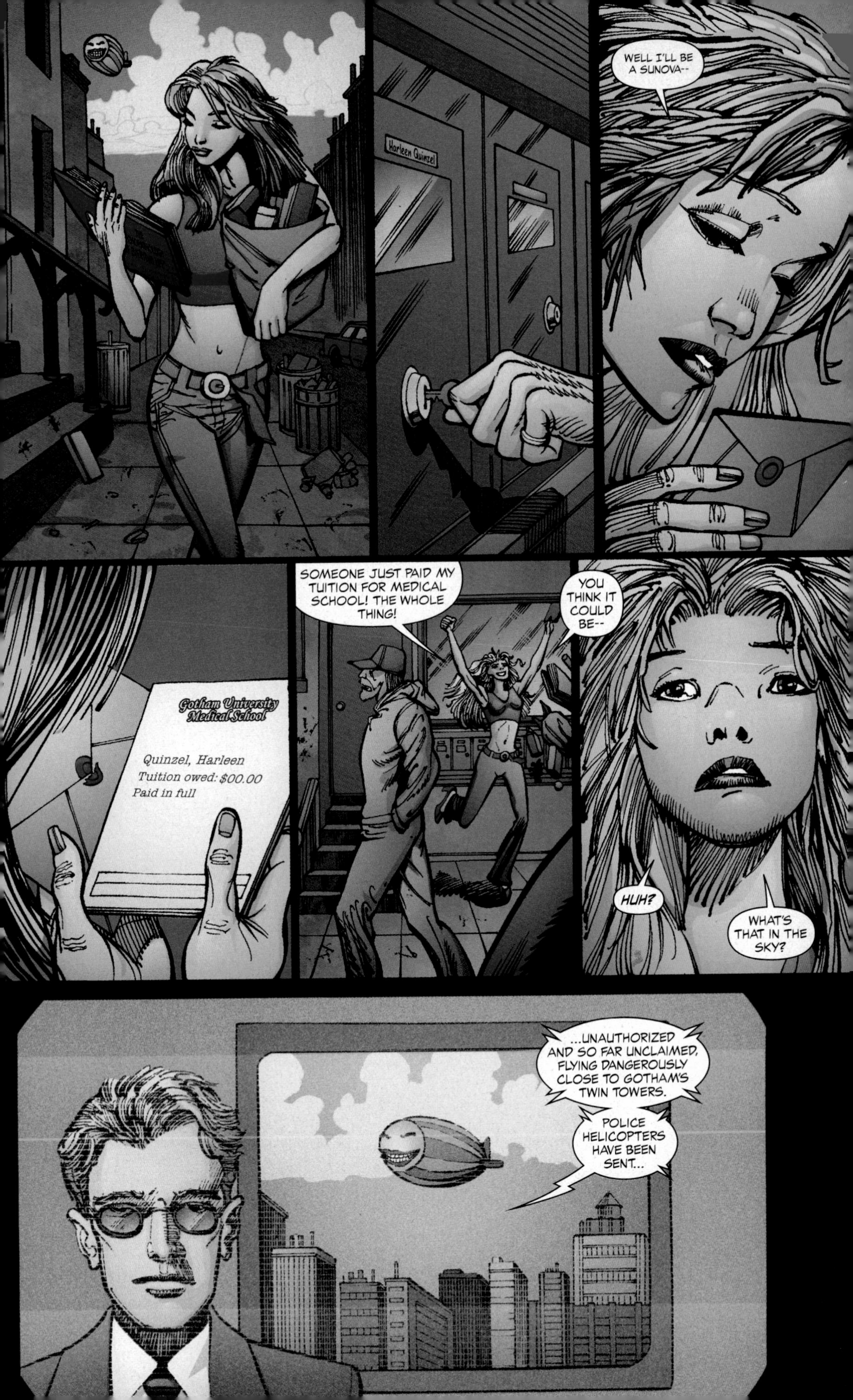

Harleen Quinzel
WELL I'LL BE A SUNOVA--
Gotham University Medical School
Quinzel, Harleen
Tuition owed: $00.00
Paid in full
SOMEONE JUST PAID MY TUITION FOR MEDICAL SCHOOL! THE WHOLE THING!
YOU THINK IT COULD BE--
HUH?
WHAT'S THAT IN THE SKY?
...UNAUTHORIZED AND SO FAR UNCLAIMED, FLYING DANGEROUSLY CLOSE TO GOTHAM'S TWIN TOWERS.
POLICE HELICOPTERS HAVE BEEN SENT...

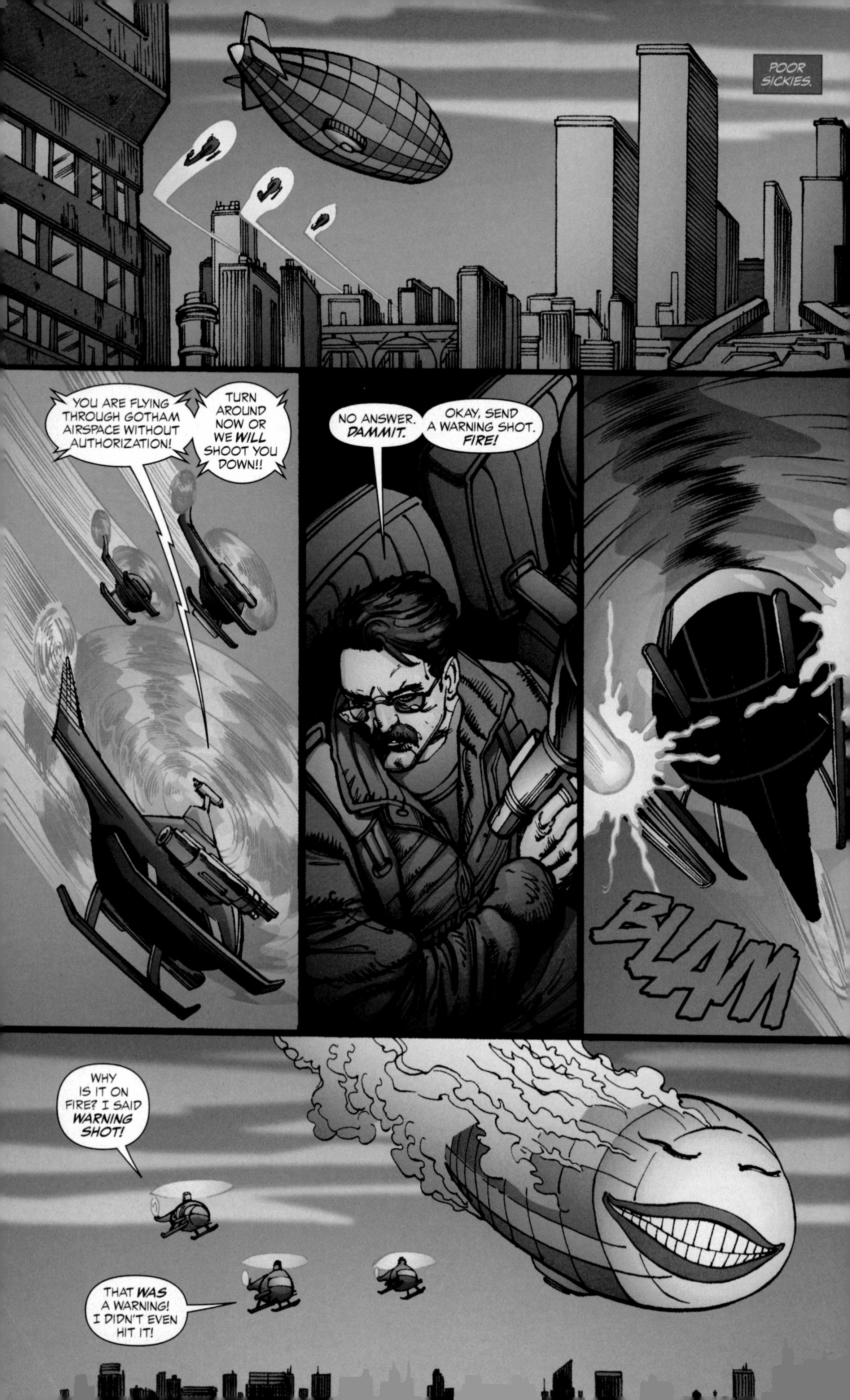

POOR SICKIES.
YOU ARE FLYING THROUGH GOTHAM AIRSPACE WITHOUT AUTHORIZATION!
TURN AROUND NOW OR WE WILL SHOOT YOU DOWN!!
NO ANSWER. DAMMIT.
OKAY, SEND A WARNING SHOT. FIRE!
BLAM
WHY IS IT ON FIRE? I SAID WARNING SHOT!
THAT WAS A WARNING! I DIDN'T EVEN HIT IT!

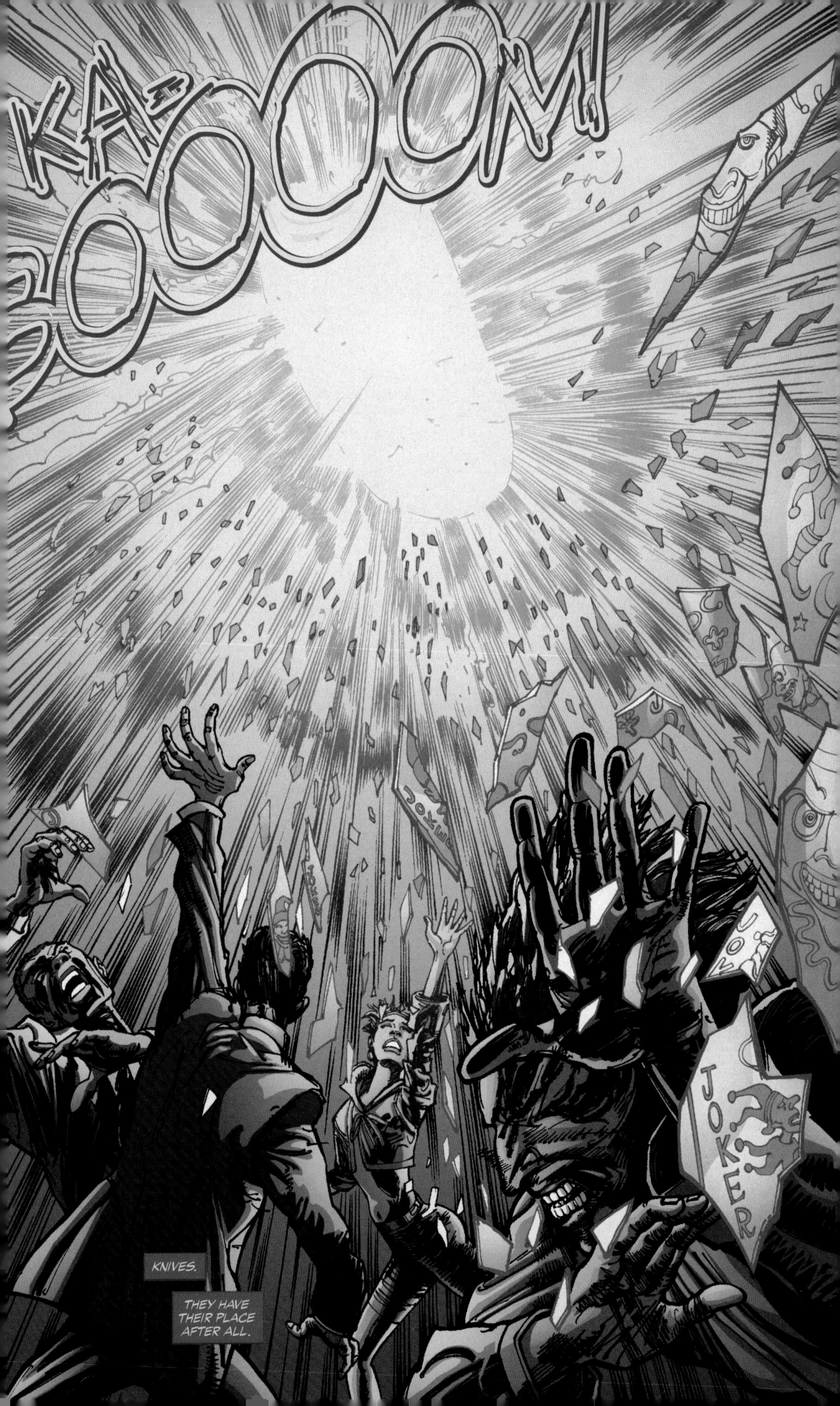
KA-BOOOOOM!
KNIVES.
THEY HAVE THEIR PLACE AFTER ALL.

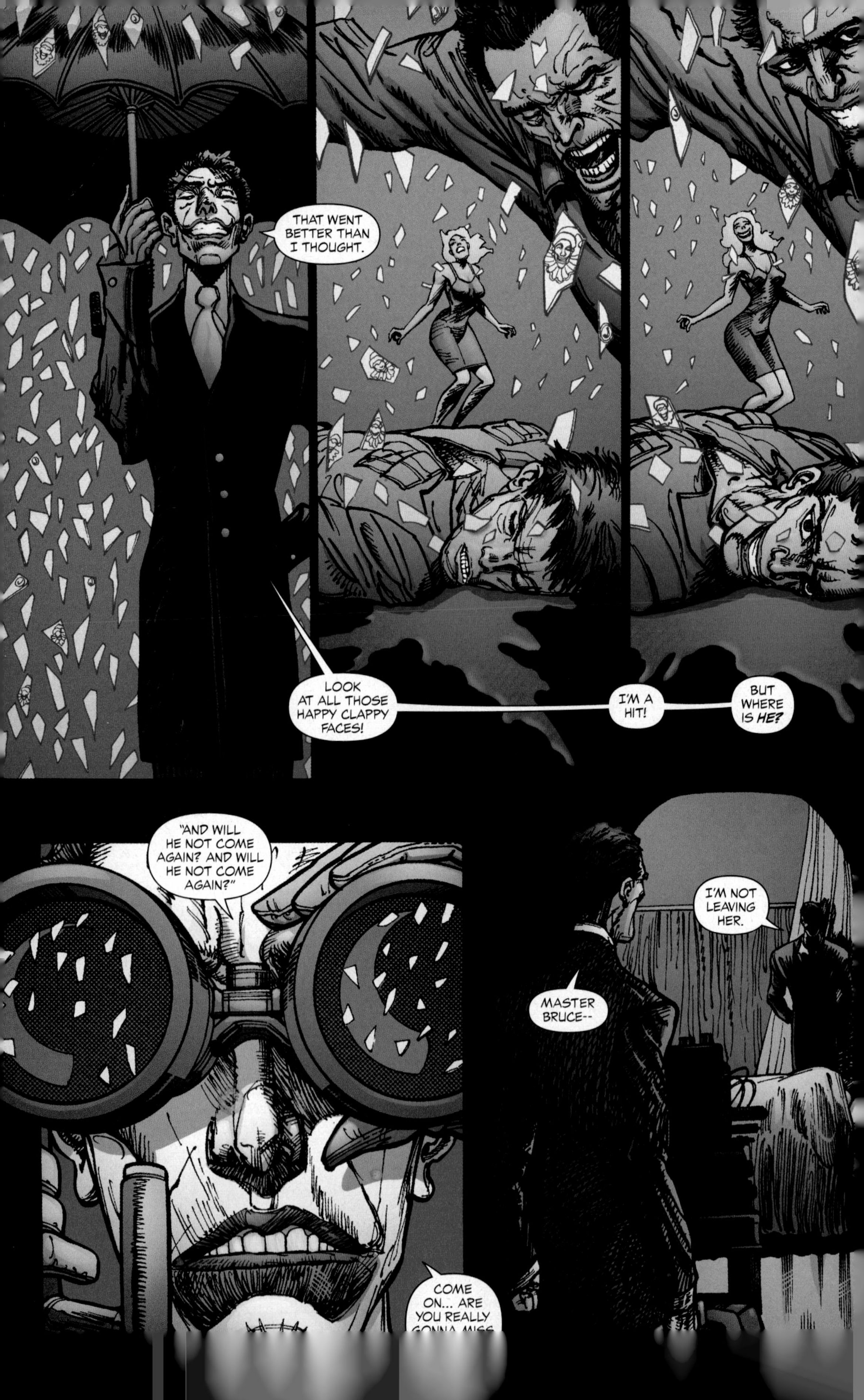
THAT WENT BETTER THAN I THOUGHT.
LOOK AT ALL THOSE HAPPY CLAPPY FACES!
I'M A HIT!
BUT WHERE IS *HE?*
"AND WILL HE NOT COME AGAIN? AND WILL HE NOT COME AGAIN?"
COME ON... ARE YOU REALLY
I'M NOT LEAVING HER.
MASTER BRUCE--

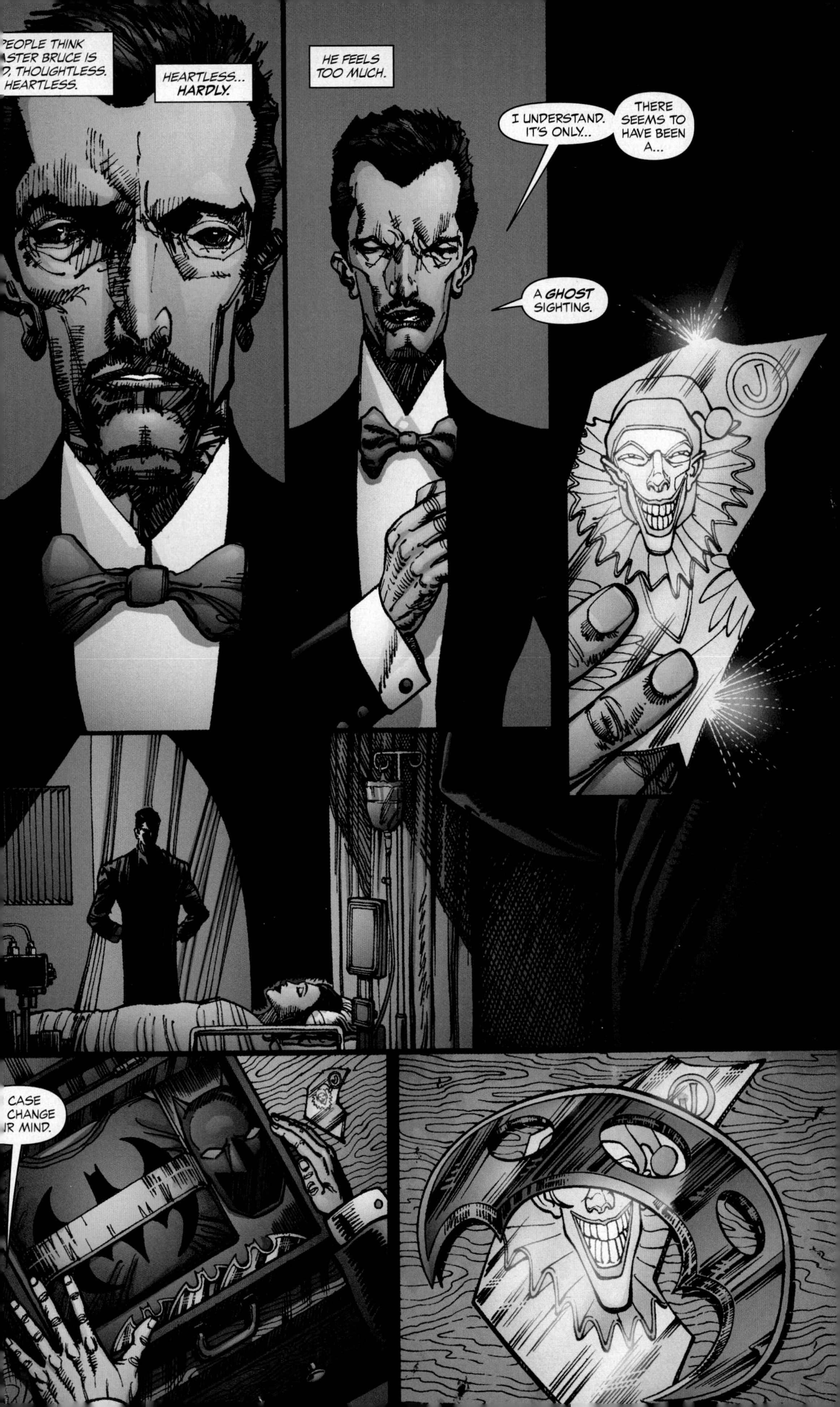

PEOPLE THINK
ASTER BRUCE IS
D, THOUGHTLESS.
HEARTLESS.
HEARTLESS... HARDLY.
HE FEELS TOO MUCH.
I UNDERSTAND. IT'S ONLY...
THERE SEEMS TO HAVE BEEN A...
A GHOST SIGHTING.
CASE
CHANGE
R MIND.

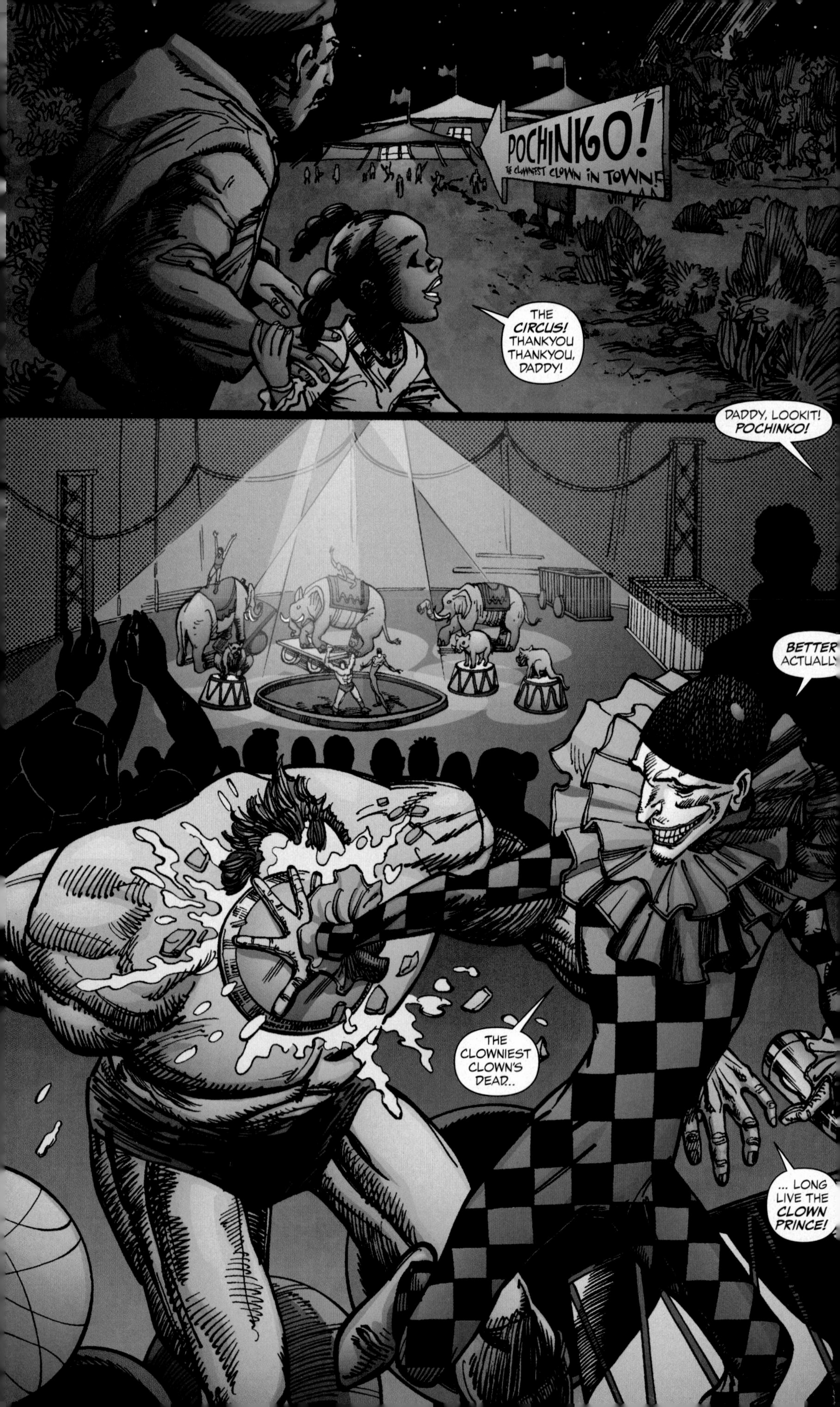
POCHINKO!
THE CLOWNIEST CLOWN IN TOWN!
THE *CIRCUS!* THANKYOU THANKYOU, DADDY!
DADDY, LOOKIT! *POCHINKO!*
BETTER ACTUALLY
THE CLOWNIEST CLOWN'S DEAD..
... LONG LIVE THE *CLOWN PRINCE!*

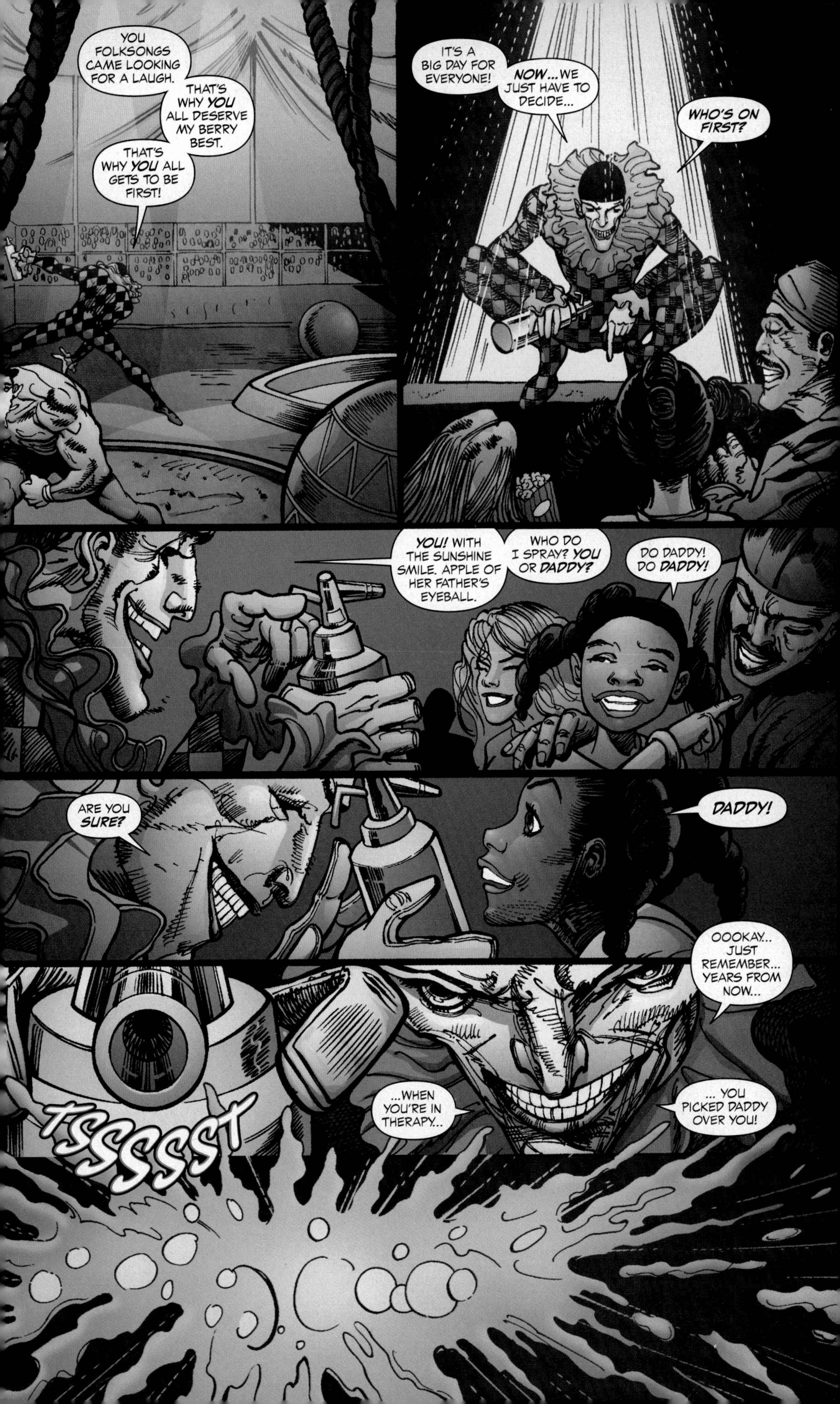
YOU FOLKSONGS CAME LOOKING FOR A LAUGH.
THAT'S WHY YOU ALL DESERVE MY BERRY BEST.
THAT'S WHY YOU ALL GETS TO BE FIRST!
IT'S A BIG DAY FOR EVERYONE!
NOW... WE JUST HAVE TO DECIDE...
WHO'S ON FIRST?
YOU! WITH THE SUNSHINE SMILE. APPLE OF HER FATHER'S EYEBALL.
WHO DO I SPRAY? YOU OR DADDY?
DO DADDY! DO DADDY!
ARE YOU SURE?
DADDY!
OOOKAY... JUST REMEMBER... YEARS FROM NOW...
...WHEN YOU'RE IN THERAPY...
... YOU PICKED DADDY OVER YOU!
TSSSSST

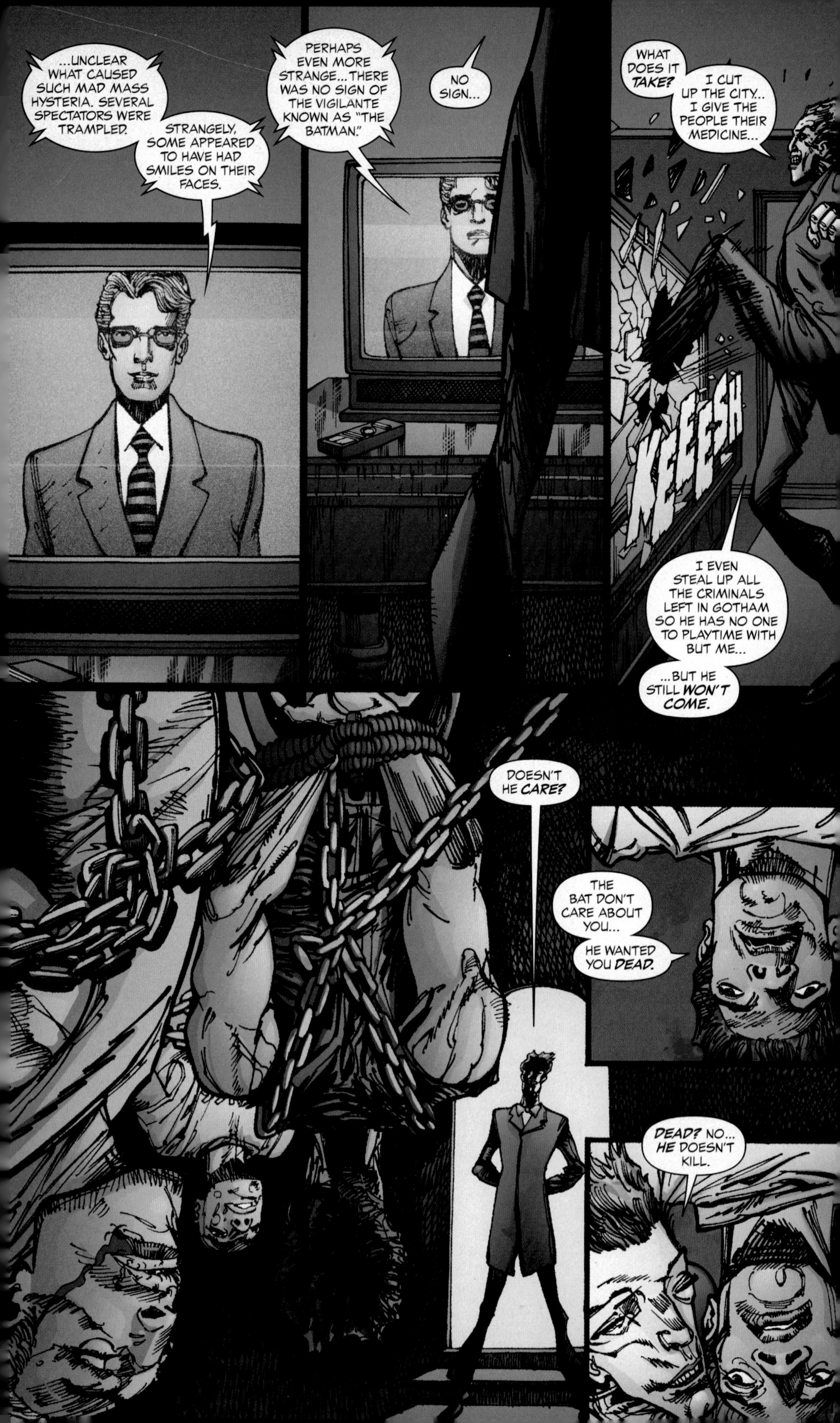

...UNCLEAR WHAT CAUSED SUCH MAD MASS HYSTERIA. SEVERAL SPECTATORS WERE TRAMPLED.
STRANGELY, SOME APPEARED TO HAVE HAD SMILES ON THEIR FACES.
PERHAPS EVEN MORE STRANGE... THERE WAS NO SIGN OF THE VIGILANTE KNOWN AS "THE BATMAN."
NO SIGN...
WHAT DOES IT TAKE?
I CUT UP THE CITY... I GIVE THE PEOPLE THEIR MEDICINE...
KEEESH
I EVEN STEAL UP ALL THE CRIMINALS LEFT IN GOTHAM SO HE HAS NO ONE TO PLAYTIME WITH BUT ME...
...BUT HE STILL WON'T COME.
DOESN'T HE CARE?
THE BAT DON'T CARE ABOUT YOU...
HE WANTED YOU DEAD.
DEAD? NO... HE DOESN'T KILL.

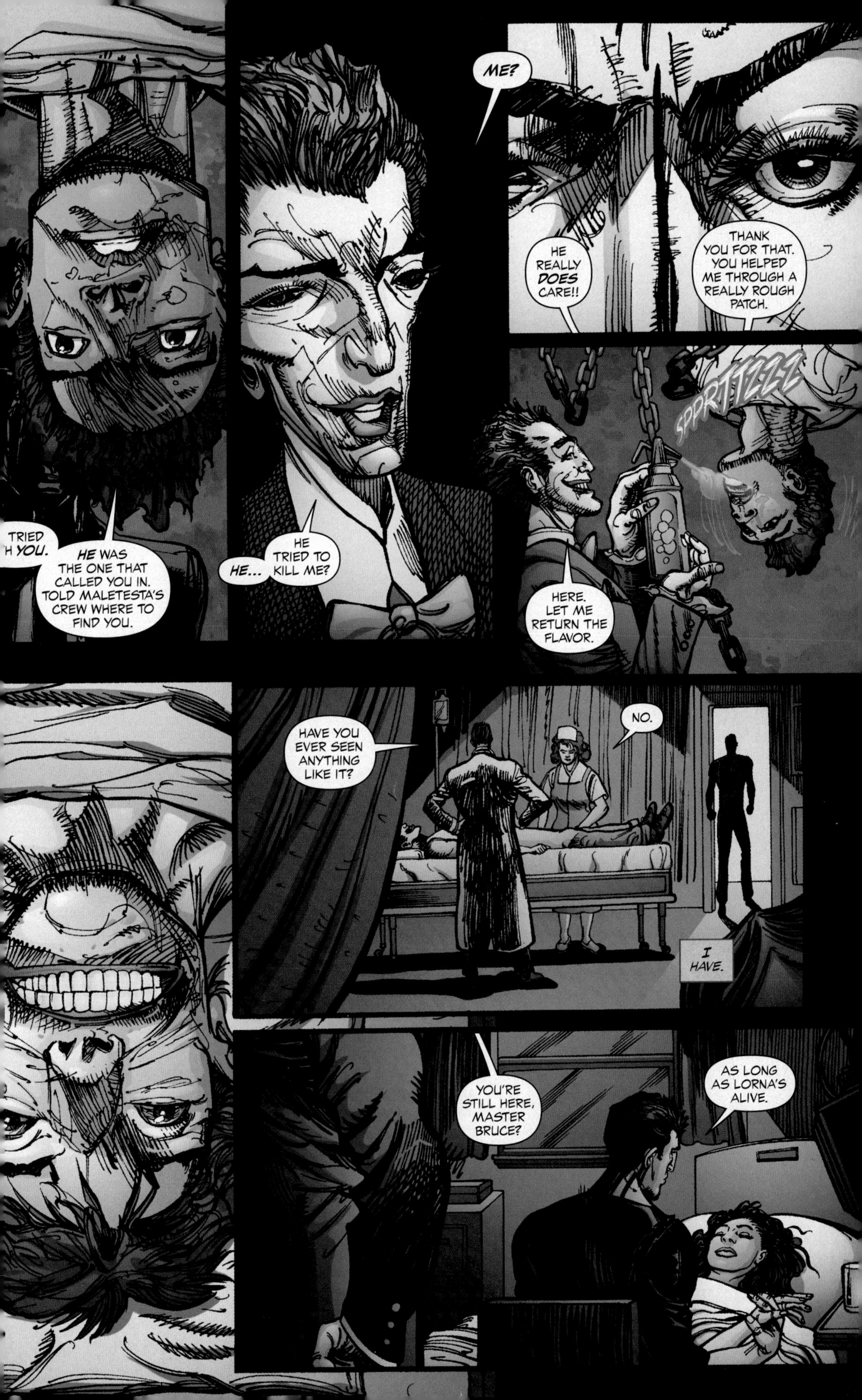
TRIED
H YOU.
HE WAS THE ONE THAT CALLED YOU IN. TOLD MALETESTA'S CREW WHERE TO FIND YOU.
HE...
HE TRIED TO KILL ME?
ME?
HE REALLY DOES CARE!!
THANK YOU FOR THAT. YOU HELPED ME THROUGH A REALLY ROUGH PATCH.
SPPRTTZZZ
HERE. LET ME RETURN THE FLAVOR.
HAVE YOU EVER SEEN ANYTHING LIKE IT?
NO.
I HAVE.
YOU'RE STILL HERE, MASTER BRUCE?
AS LONG AS LORNA'S ALIVE.

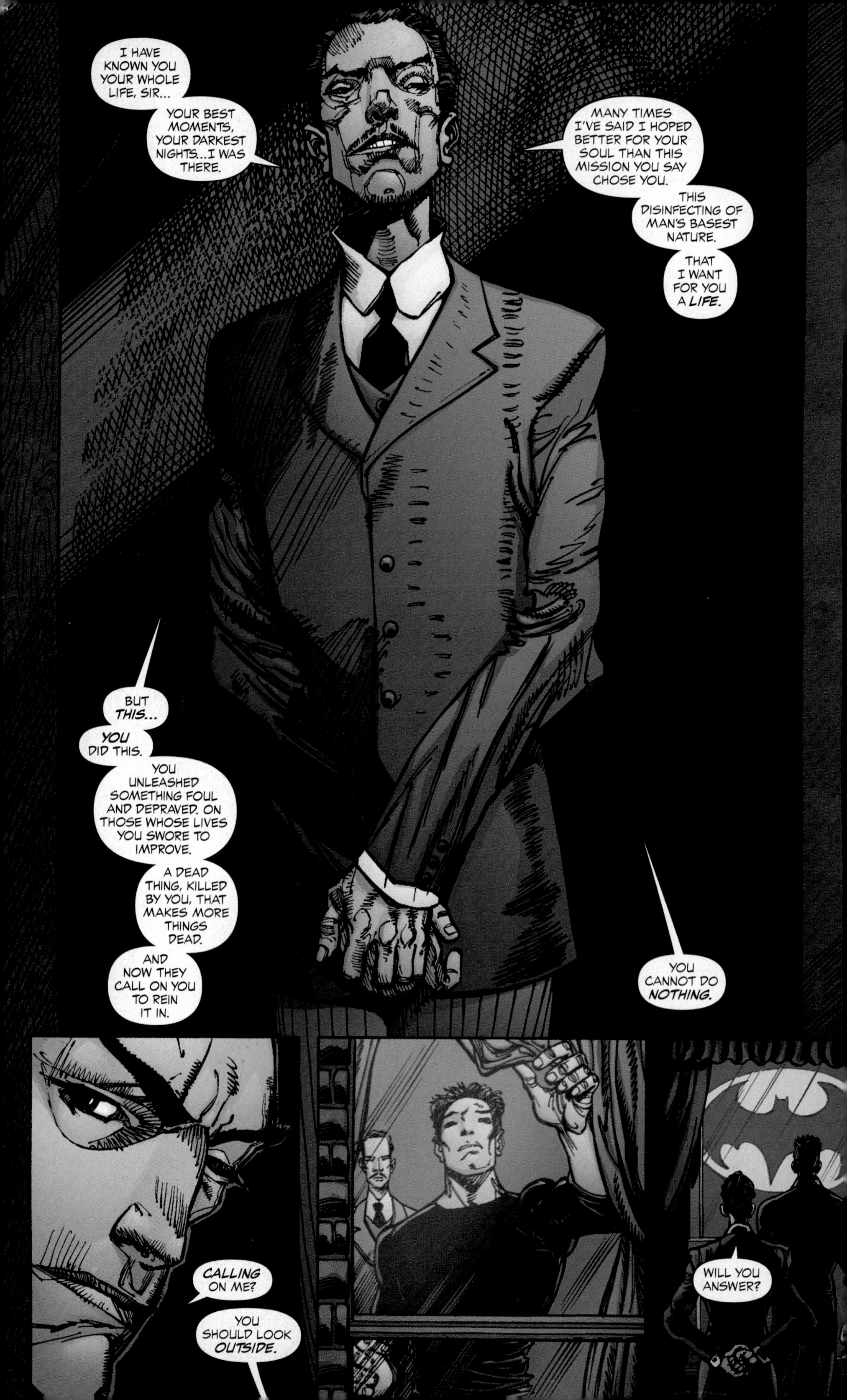
I HAVE KNOWN YOU YOUR WHOLE LIFE, SIR...
YOUR BEST MOMENTS, YOUR DARKEST NIGHTS...I WAS THERE.
MANY TIMES I'VE SAID I HOPED BETTER FOR YOUR SOUL THAN THIS MISSION YOU SAY CHOSE YOU.
THIS DISINFECTING OF MAN'S BASEST NATURE.
THAT I WANT FOR YOU A *LIFE*.
BUT *THIS...*
YOU DID THIS.
YOU UNLEASHED SOMETHING FOUL AND DEPRAVED. ON THOSE WHOSE LIVES YOU SWORE TO IMPROVE.
A DEAD THING, KILLED BY YOU, THAT MAKES MORE THINGS DEAD.
AND NOW THEY CALL ON YOU TO REIN IT IN.
YOU CANNOT DO *NOTHING*.
CALLING ON ME?
YOU SHOULD LOOK *OUTSIDE*.
WILL YOU ANSWER?

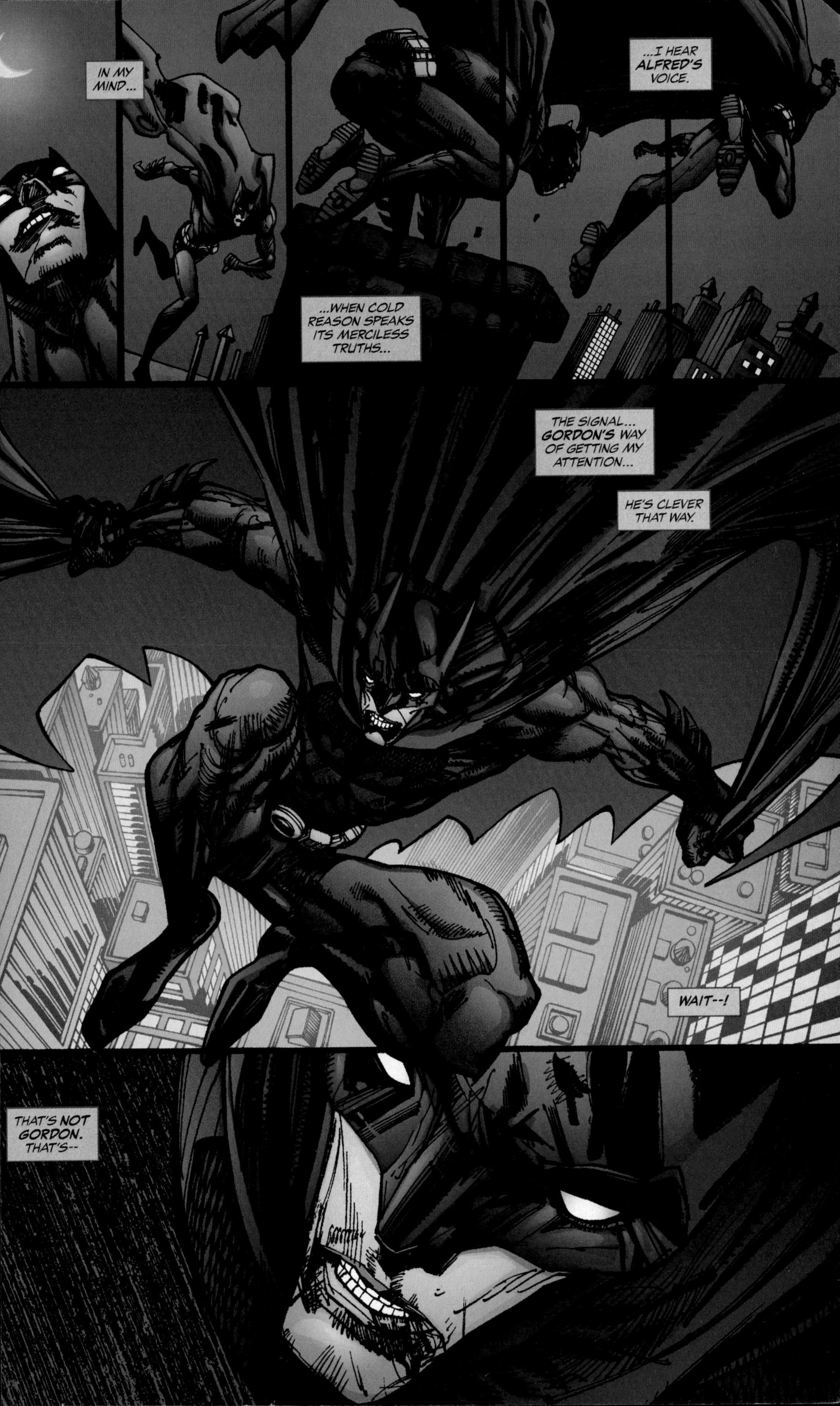
IN MY MIND...
...I HEAR ALFRED'S VOICE.
...WHEN COLD REASON SPEAKS ITS MERCILESS TRUTHS...
THE SIGNAL... GORDON'S WAY OF GETTING MY ATTENTION...
HE'S CLEVER THAT WAY.
WAIT--!
THAT'S NOT GORDON. THAT'S--

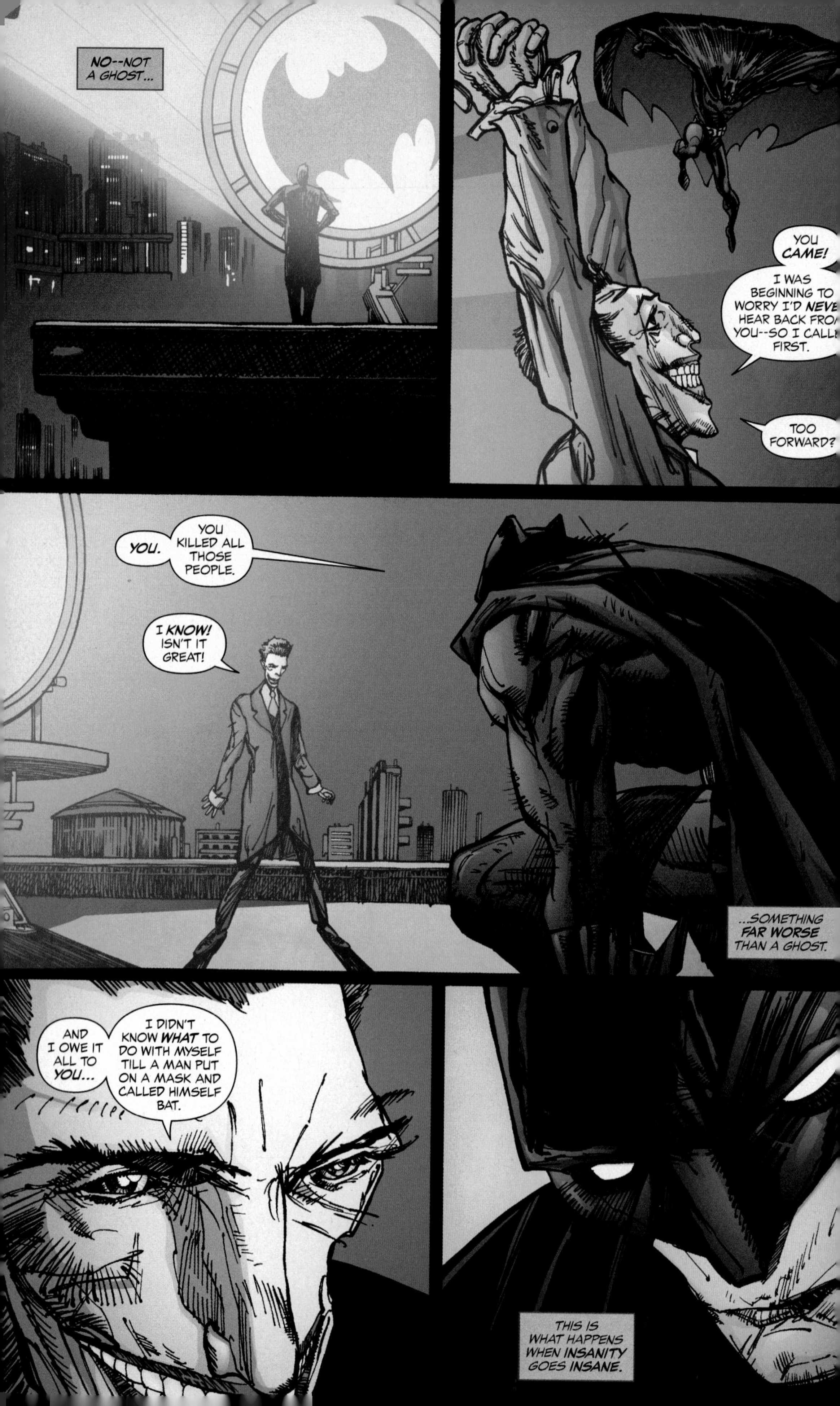
NO--NOT A GHOST...
YOU CAME!
I WAS BEGINNING TO WORRY I'D NEVE HEAR BACK FRO YOU--SO I CALL FIRST.
TOO FORWARD?
YOU.
YOU KILLED ALL THOSE PEOPLE.
I KNOW! ISN'T IT GREAT!
...SOMETHING FAR WORSE THAN A GHOST.
AND I OWE IT ALL TO YOU...
I DIDN'T KNOW WHAT TO DO WITH MYSELF TILL A MAN PUT ON A MASK AND CALLED HIMSELF BAT.
THIS IS WHAT HAPPENS WHEN INSANITY GOES INSANE.

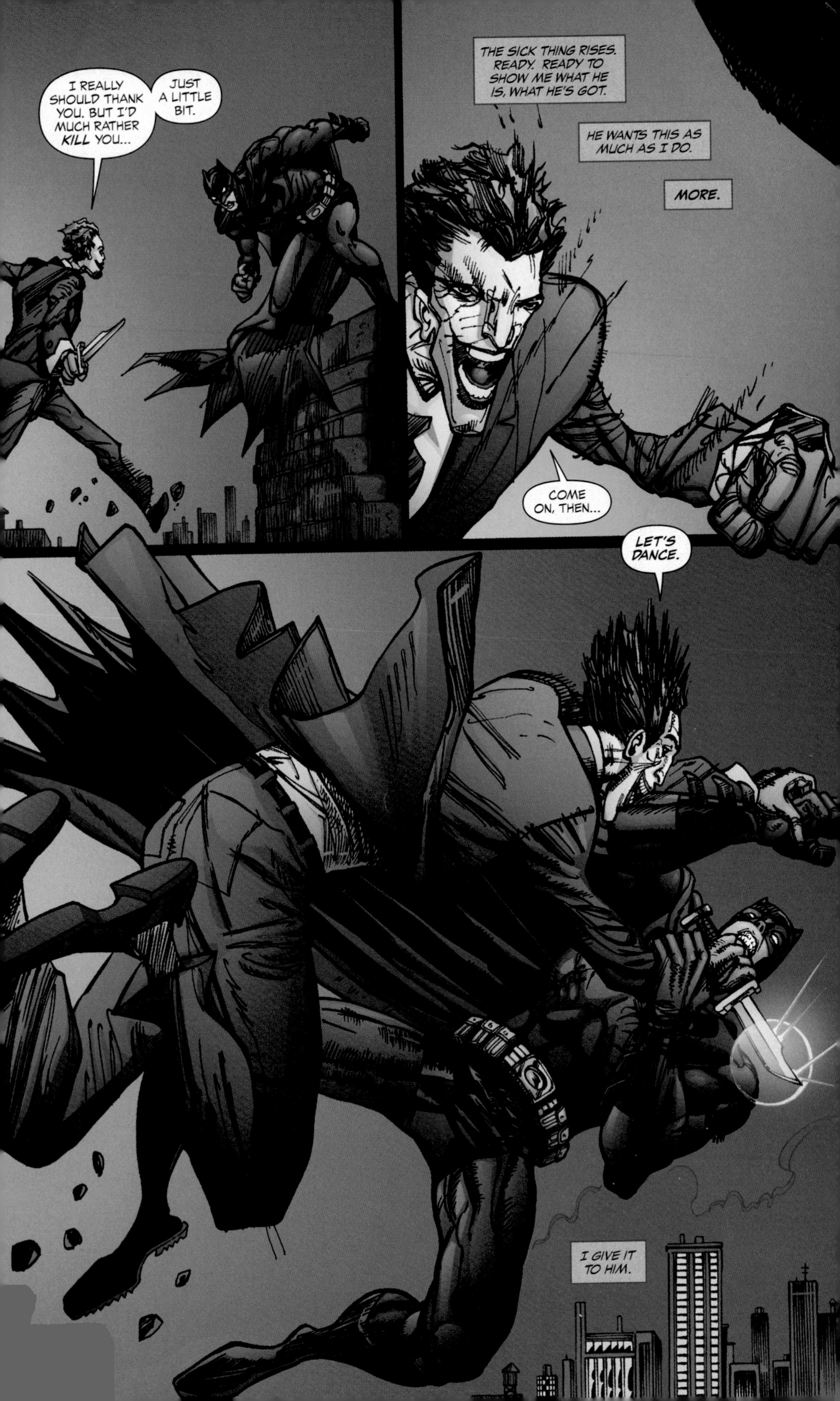

I REALLY SHOULD THANK YOU. BUT I'D MUCH RATHER **KILL** YOU...
JUST A LITTLE BIT.
THE SICK THING RISES. READY. READY TO SHOW ME WHAT HE IS, WHAT HE'S GOT.
HE WANTS THIS AS MUCH AS I DO.
MORE.
COME ON, THEN...
LET'S DANCE.
I GIVE IT TO HIM.

chapter six **PUNCH LINE**

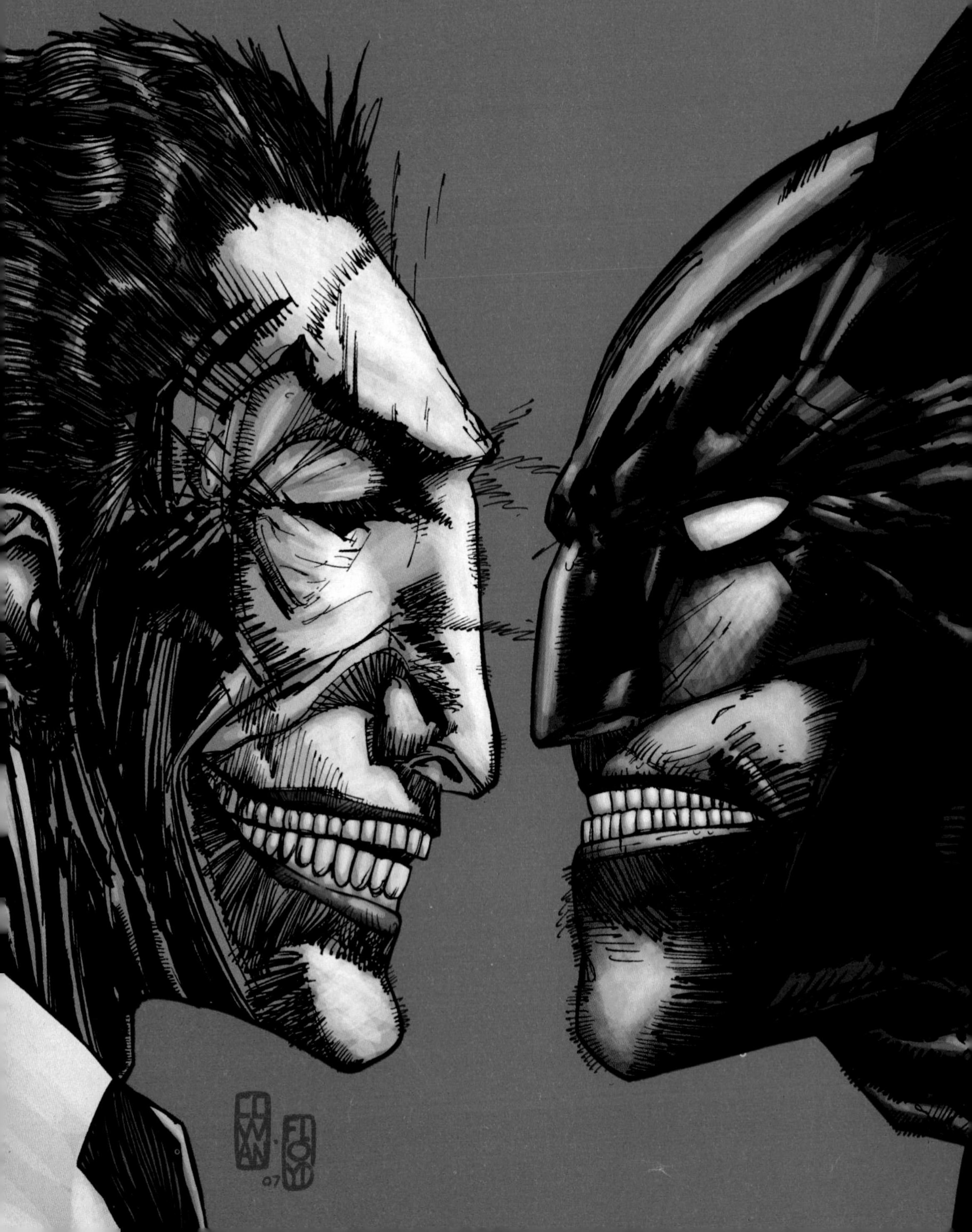

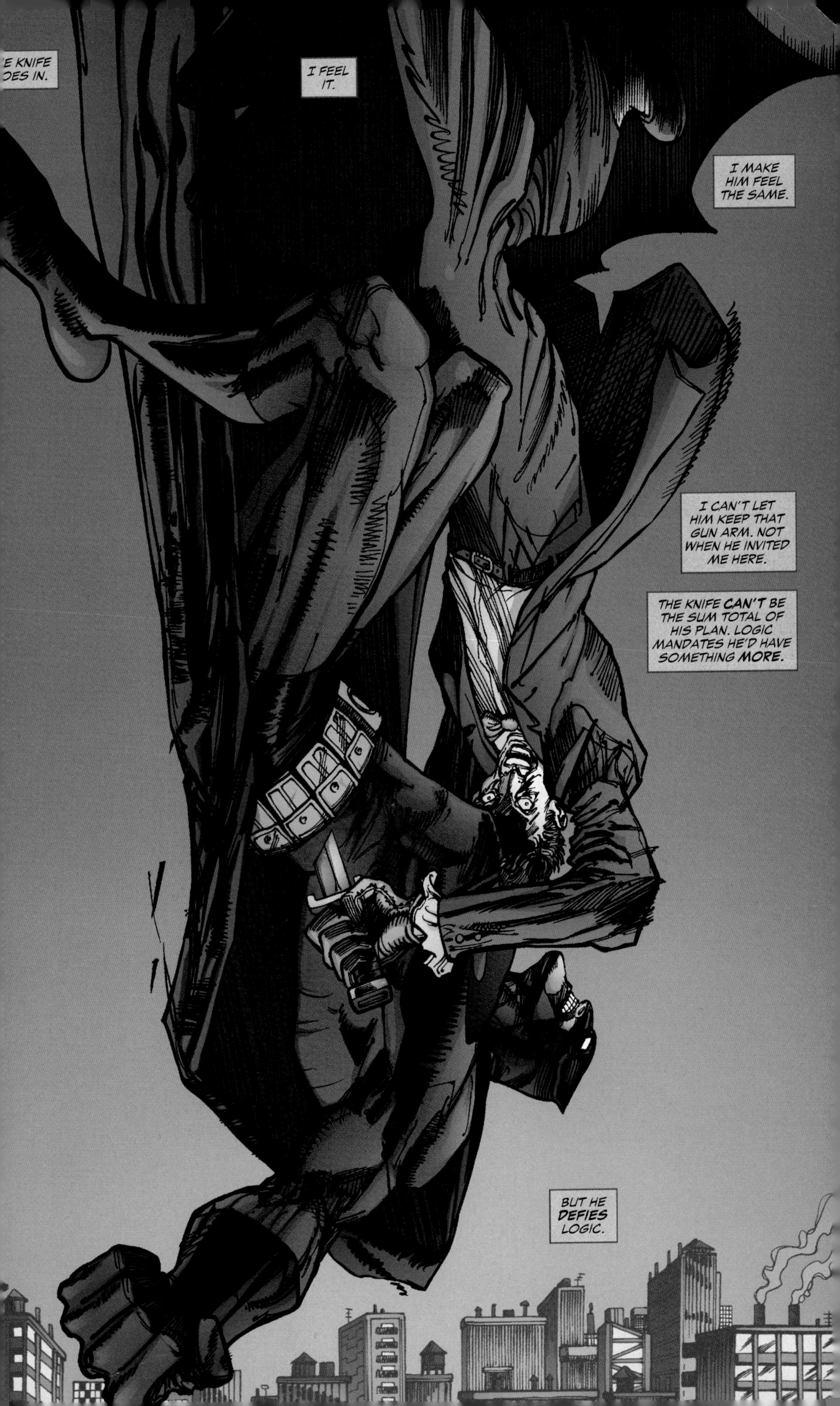
E KNIFE
OES IN.
I FEEL IT.
I MAKE HIM FEEL THE SAME.
I CAN'T LET HIM KEEP THAT GUN ARM. NOT WHEN HE INVITED ME HERE.
THE KNIFE CAN'T BE THE SUM TOTAL OF HIS PLAN. LOGIC MANDATES HE'D HAVE SOMETHING MORE.
BUT HE DEFIES LOGIC.

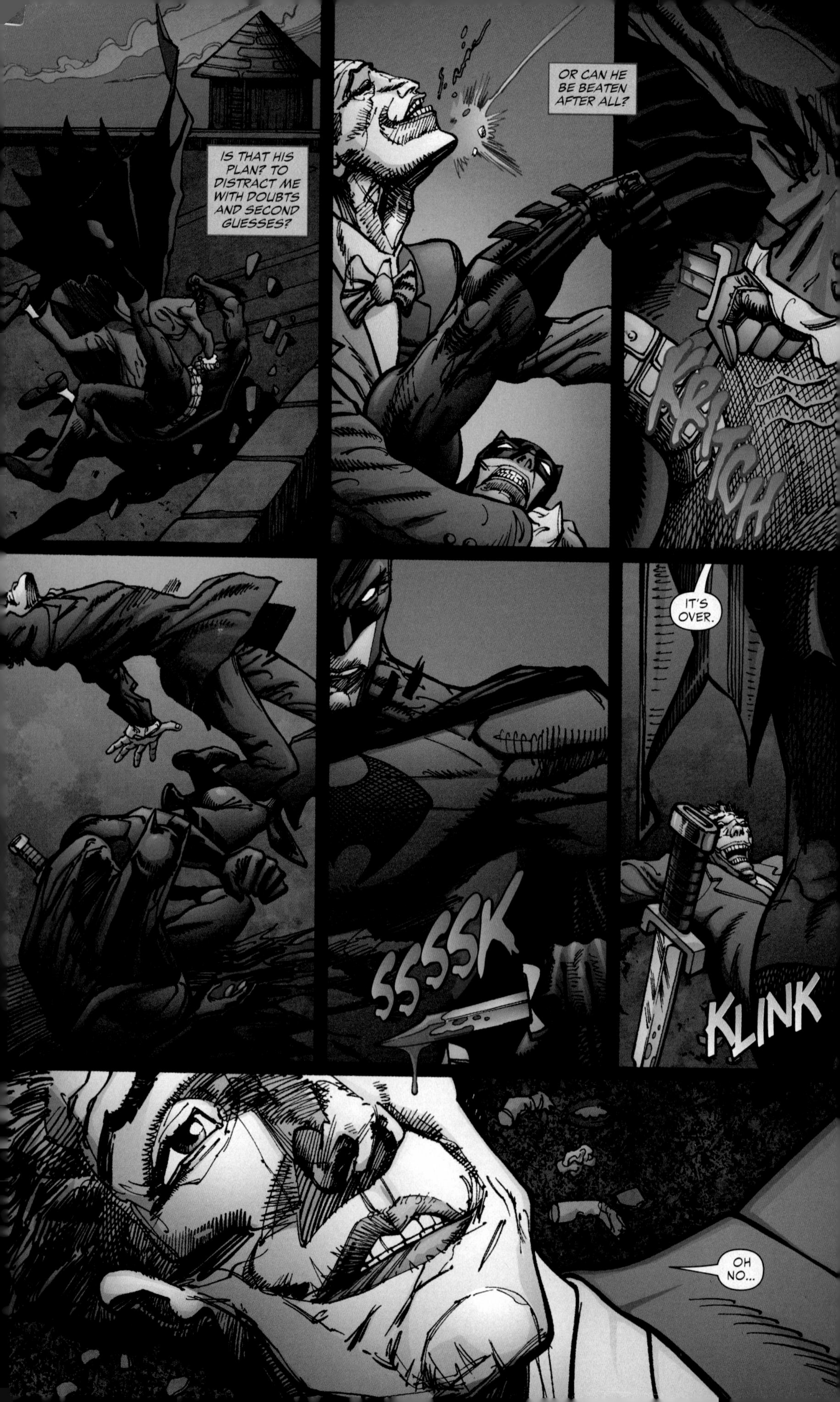

IS THAT HIS PLAN? TO DISTRACT ME WITH DOUBTS AND SECOND GUESSES?
OR CAN HE BE BEATEN AFTER ALL?
KRITCH
SSSSK
IT'S OVER.
KLINK
OH NO...

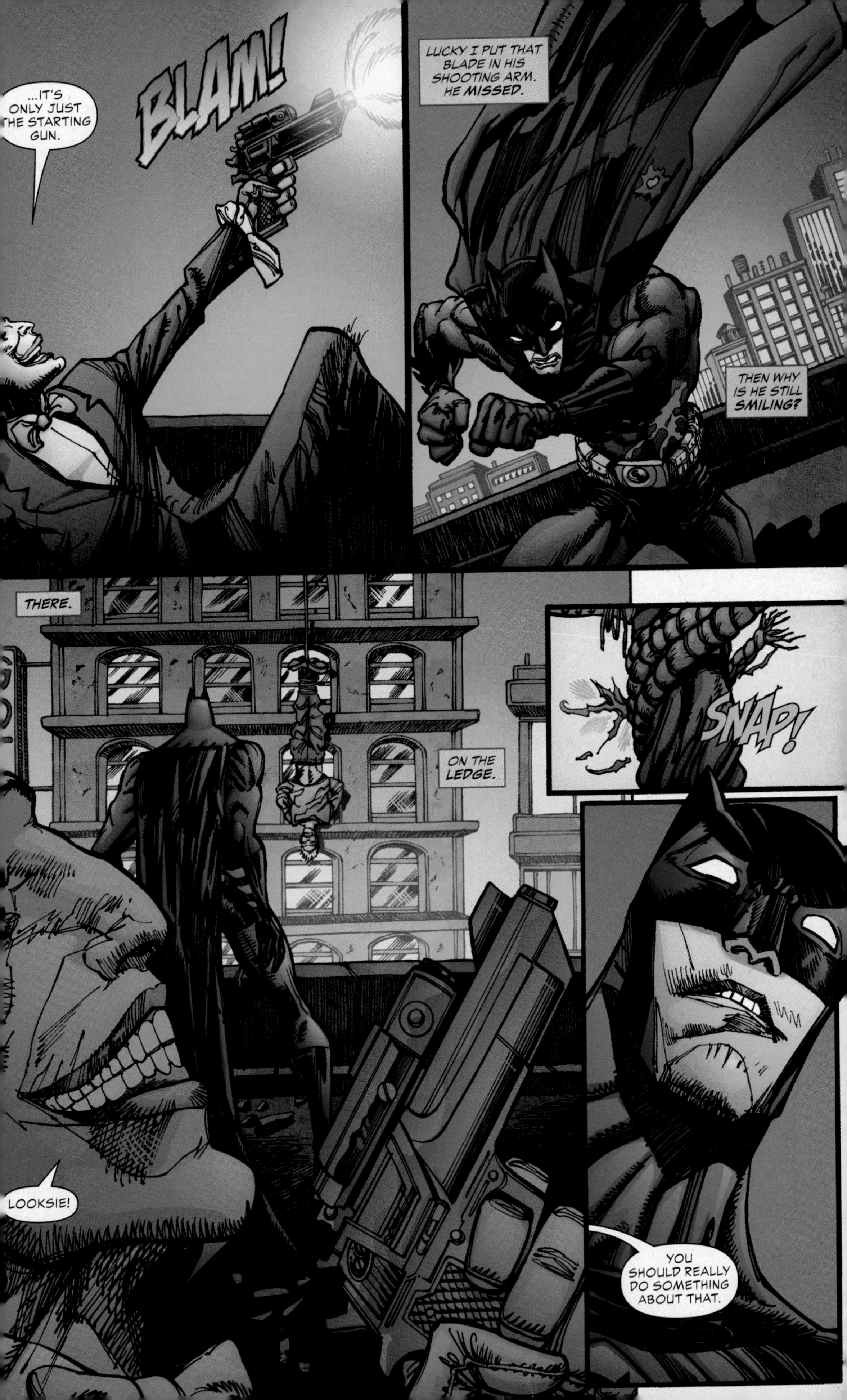

...IT'S ONLY JUST THE STARTING GUN.
BLAM!
LUCKY I PUT THAT BLADE IN HIS SHOOTING ARM. HE MISSED.
THEN WHY IS HE STILL SMILING?
THERE.
ON THE LEDGE.
SNAP!
LOOKSIE!
YOU SHOULD REALLY DO SOMETHING ABOUT THAT.

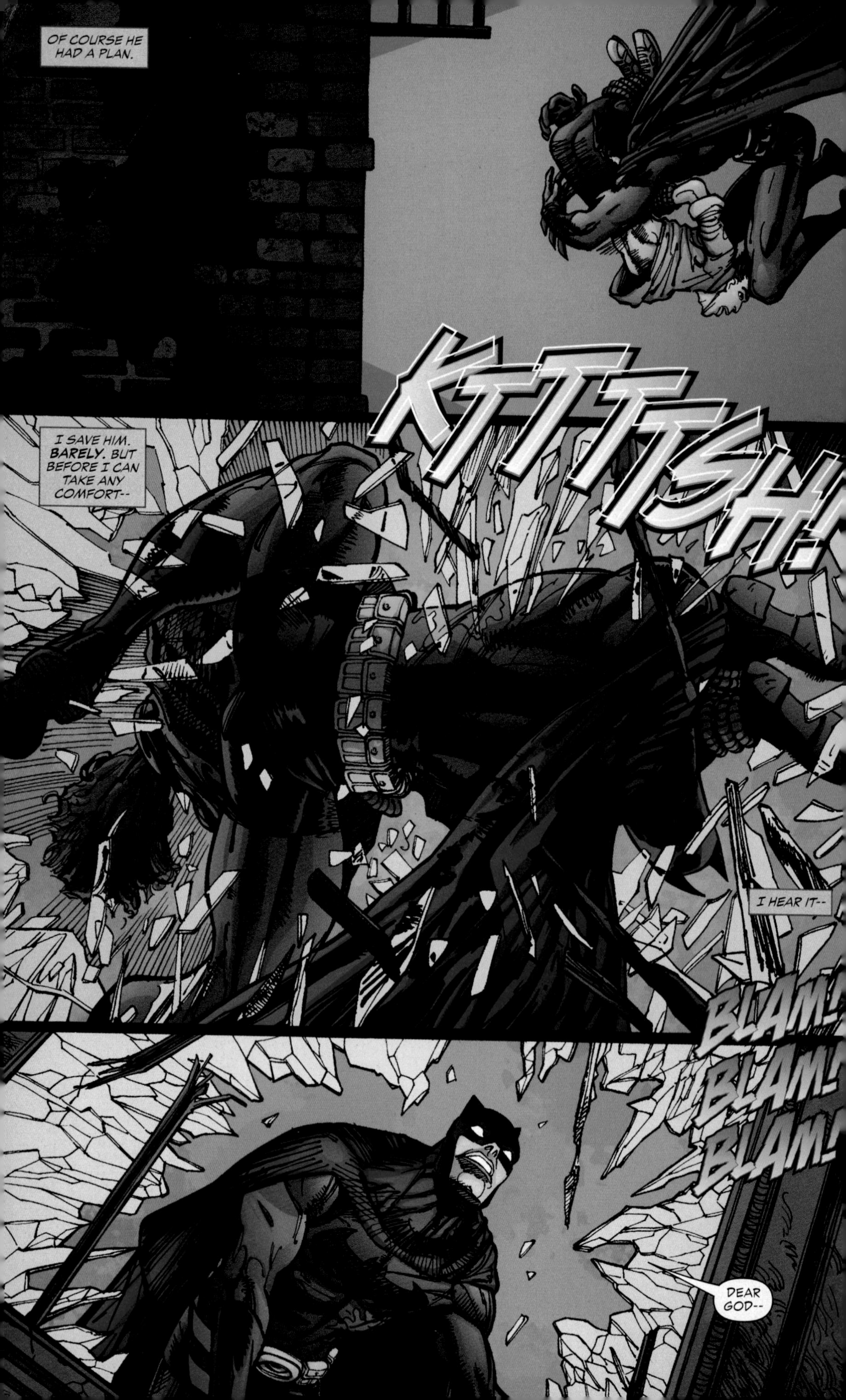
OF COURSE HE HAD A PLAN.
KTTTTSH!
I SAVE HIM. BARELY. BUT BEFORE I CAN TAKE ANY COMFORT--
I HEAR IT--
BLAM! BLAM! BLAM!
DEAR GOD--

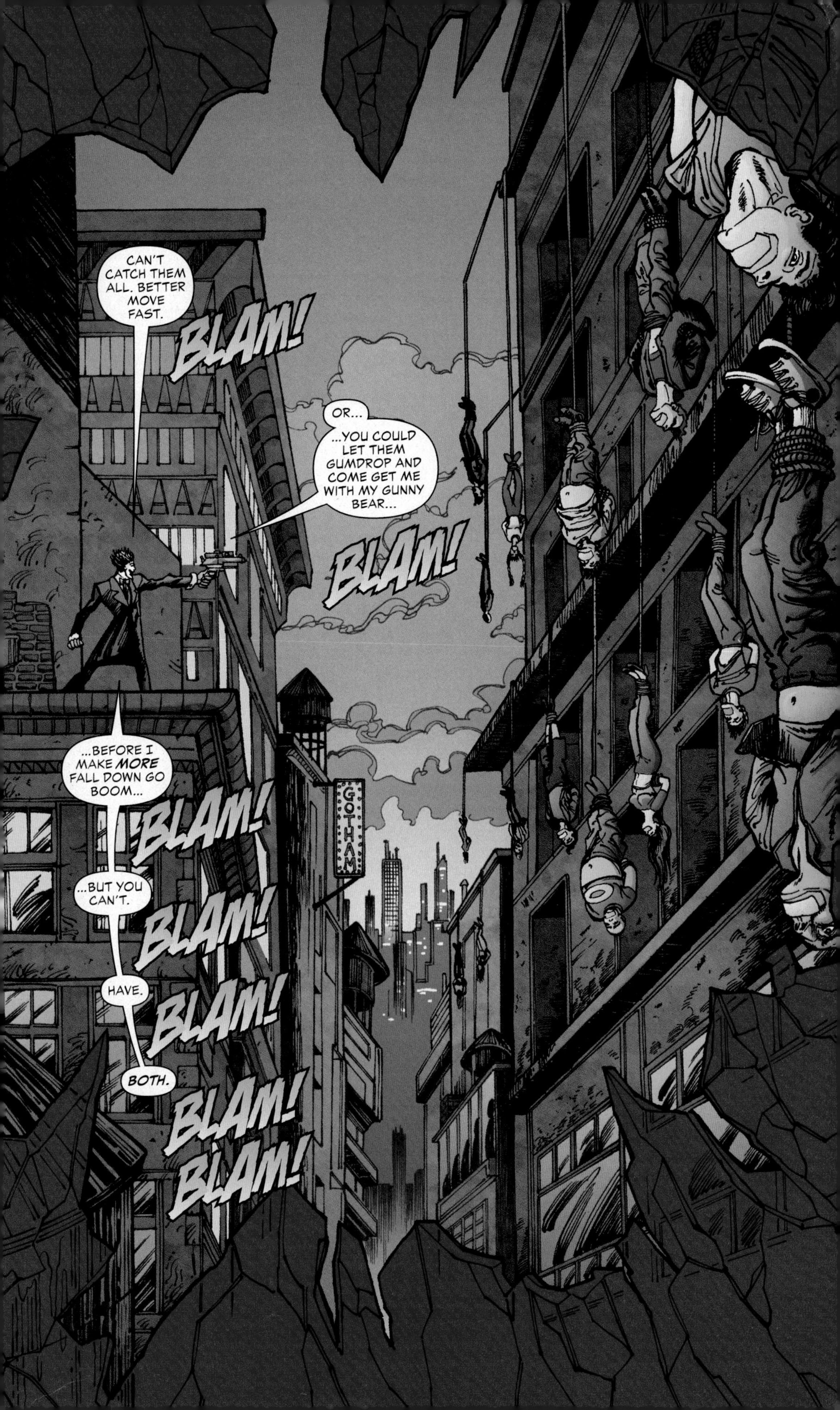

CAN'T CATCH THEM ALL. BETTER MOVE FAST.
BLAM!
OR...
...YOU COULD LET THEM GUMDROP AND COME GET ME WITH MY GUNNY BEAR...
BLAM!
...BEFORE I MAKE MORE FALL DOWN GO BOOM...
BLAM!
...BUT YOU CAN'T.
BLAM!
HAVE.
BLAM!
BOTH.
BLAM!
BLAM!
GOTHAM

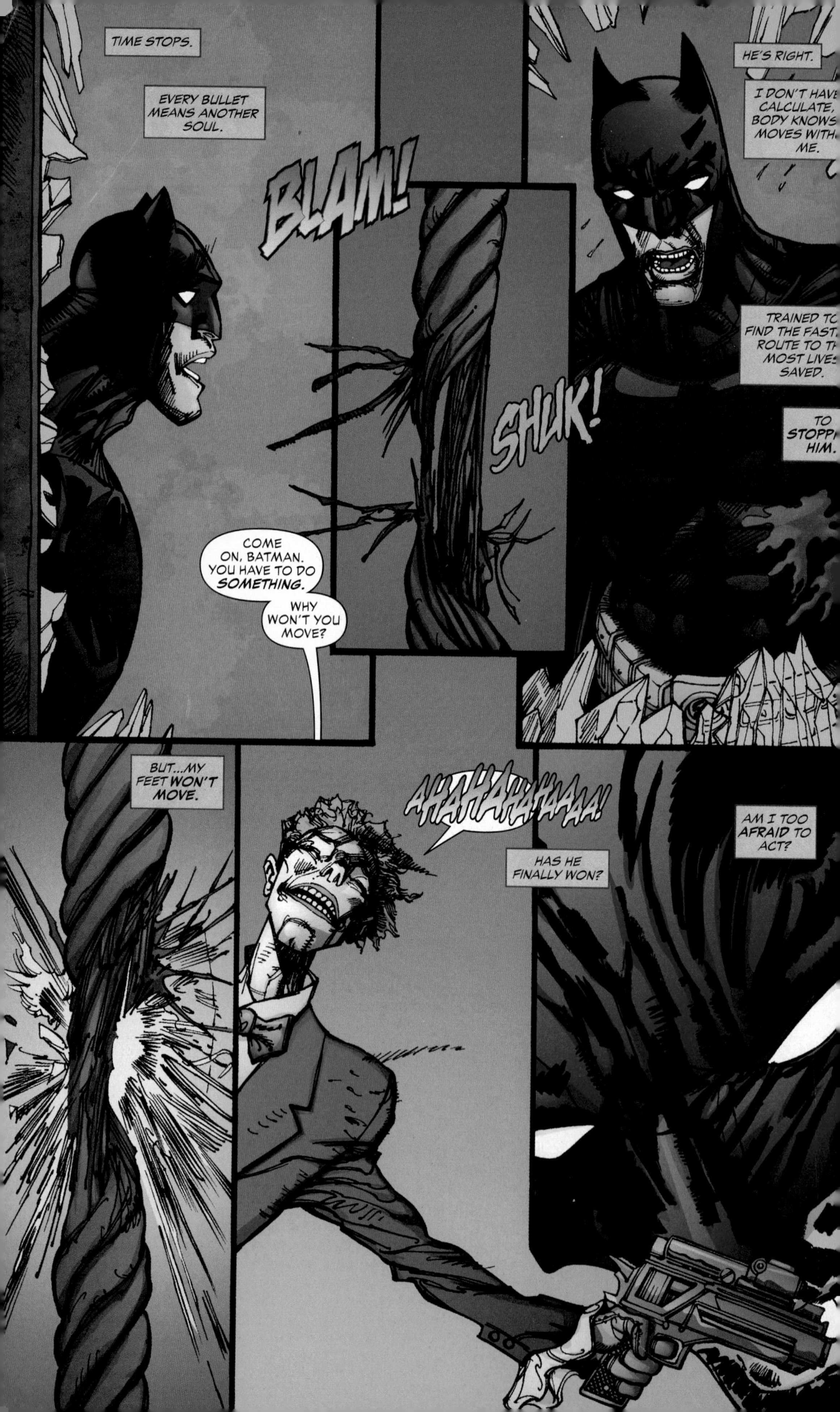
TIME STOPS.
EVERY BULLET MEANS ANOTHER SOUL.
BLAM!
COME ON, BATMAN. YOU HAVE TO DO SOMETHING.
WHY WON'T YOU MOVE?
SHUK!
HE'S RIGHT.
I DON'T HAVE CALCULATE, BODY KNOWS MOVES WITH ME.
TRAINED TO FIND THE FAST ROUTE TO T MOST LIVES SAVED.
TO STOPP HIM.
BUT...MY FEET WON'T MOVE.
AHAHAHAHAHAAAA!
HAS HE FINALLY WON?
AM I TOO AFRAID TO ACT?

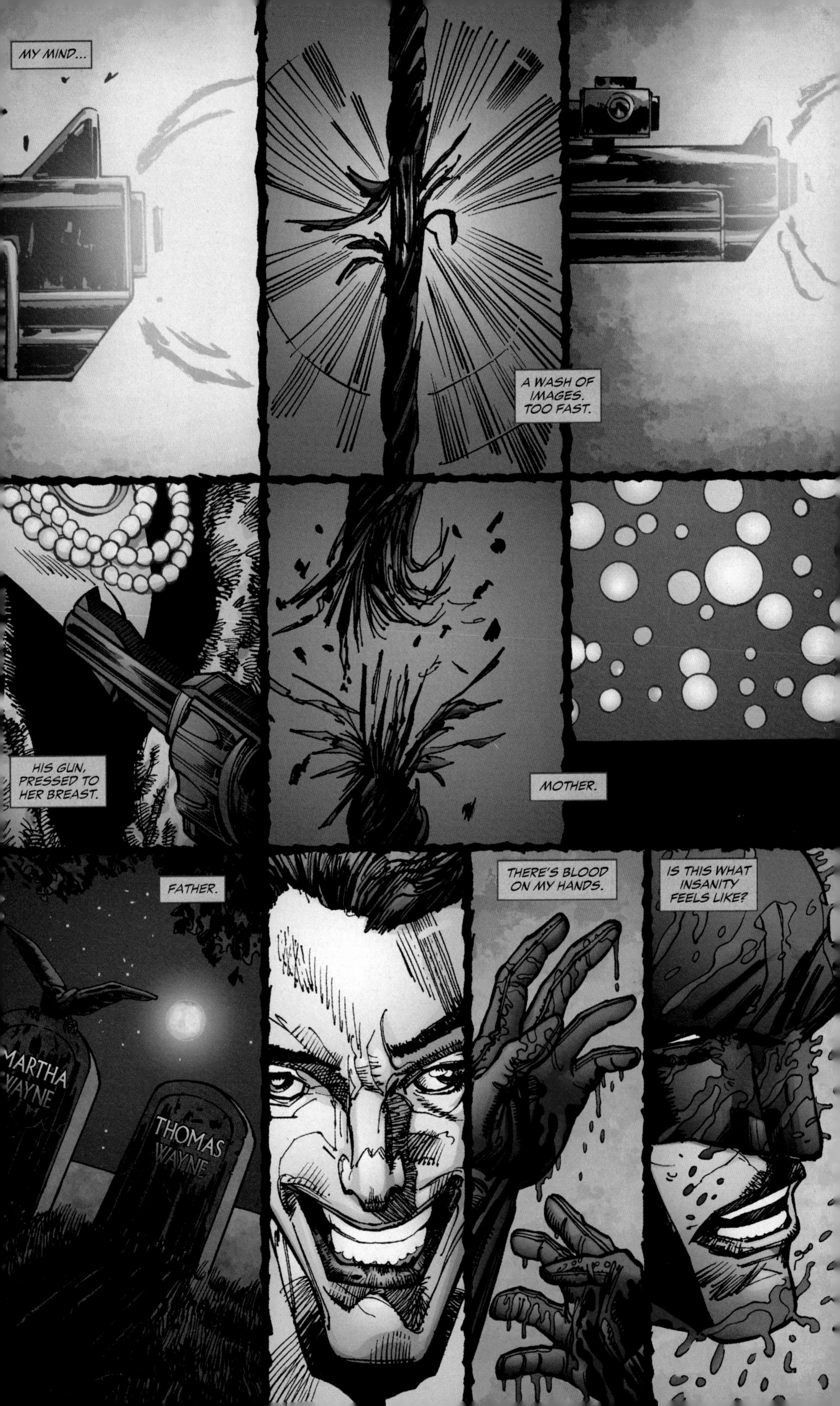
MY MIND...
A WASH OF IMAGES. TOO FAST.
HIS GUN, PRESSED TO HER BREAST.
MOTHER.
FATHER.
MARTHA WAYNE
THOMAS WAYNE
THERE'S BLOOD ON MY HANDS.
IS THIS WHAT INSANITY FEELS LIKE?

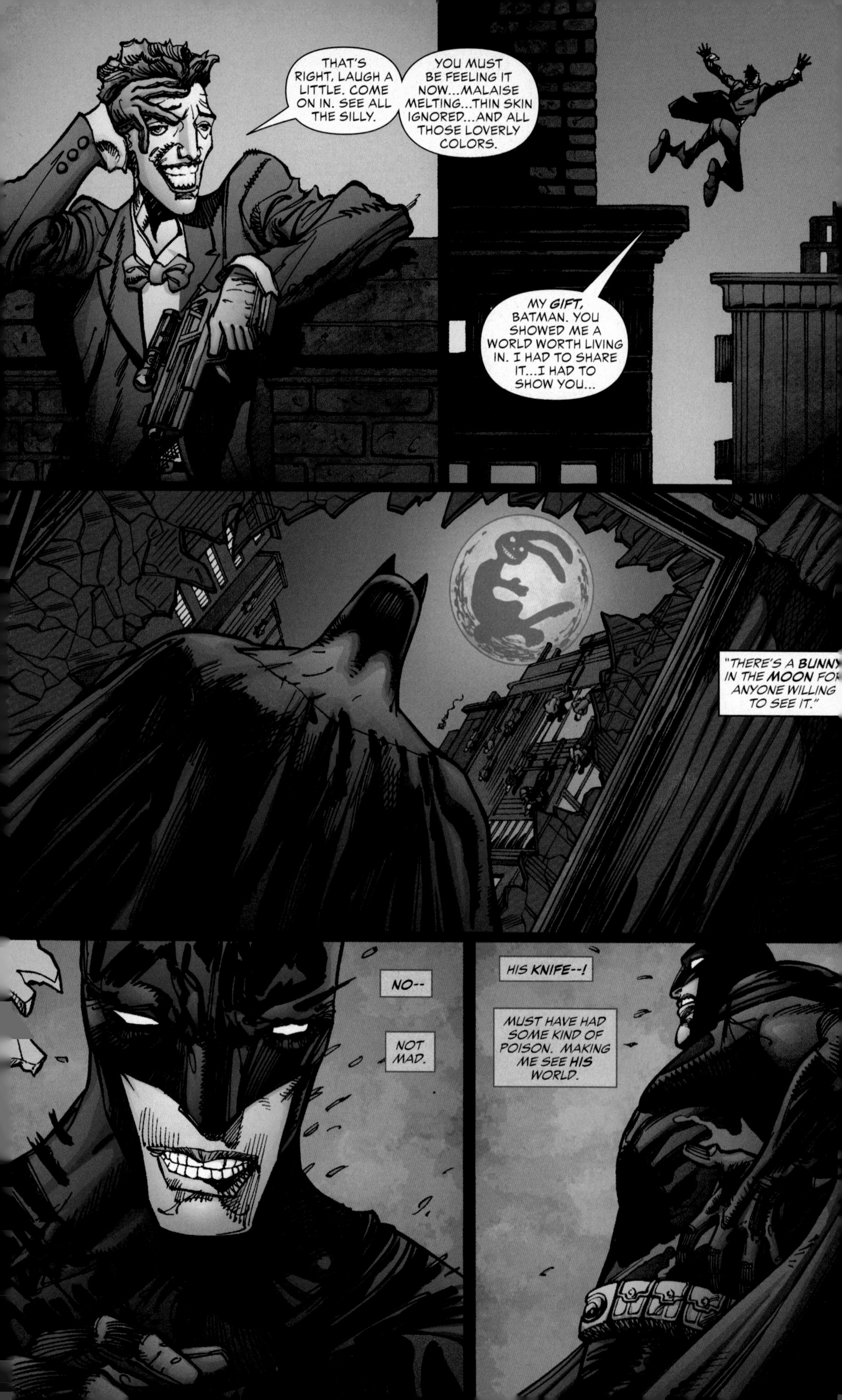

THAT'S RIGHT, LAUGH A LITTLE. COME ON IN. SEE ALL THE SILLY.
YOU MUST BE FEELING IT NOW...MALAISE MELTING...THIN SKIN IGNORED...AND ALL THOSE LOVERLY COLORS.
MY GIFT, BATMAN. YOU SHOWED ME A WORLD WORTH LIVING IN. I HAD TO SHARE IT...I HAD TO SHOW YOU...
"THERE'S A BUNNY IN THE MOON FOR ANYONE WILLING TO SEE IT."
NO--
NOT MAD.
HIS KNIFE--!
MUST HAVE HAD SOME KIND OF POISON. MAKING ME SEE HIS WORLD.

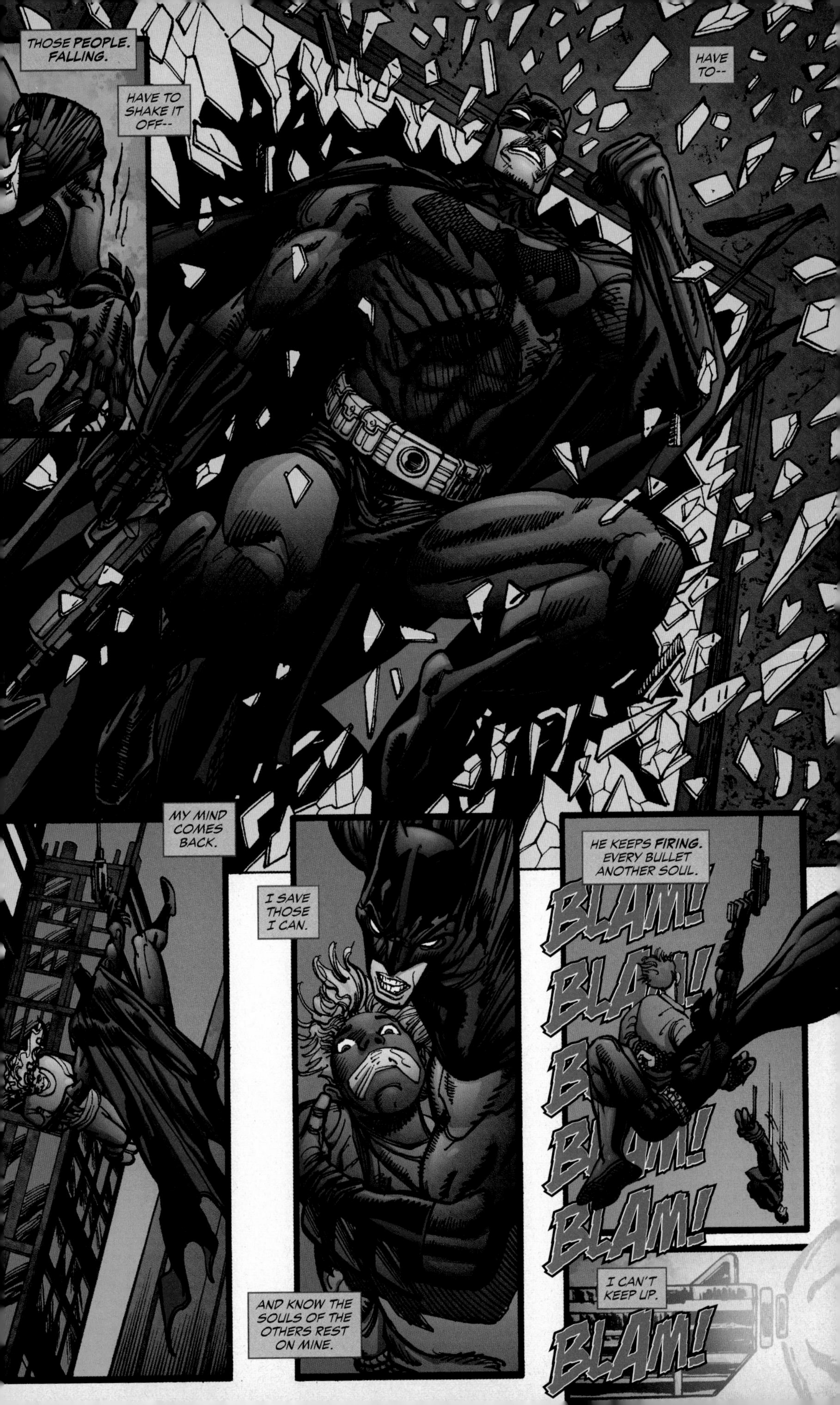

THOSE PEOPLE. FALLING.
HAVE TO SHAKE IT OFF--
HAVE TO--
MY MIND COMES BACK.
I SAVE THOSE I CAN.
AND KNOW THE SOULS OF THE OTHERS REST ON MINE.
HE KEEPS FIRING. EVERY BULLET ANOTHER SOUL.
BLAM!
BLAM!
BLAM!
BLAM!
I CAN'T KEEP UP.
BLAM!

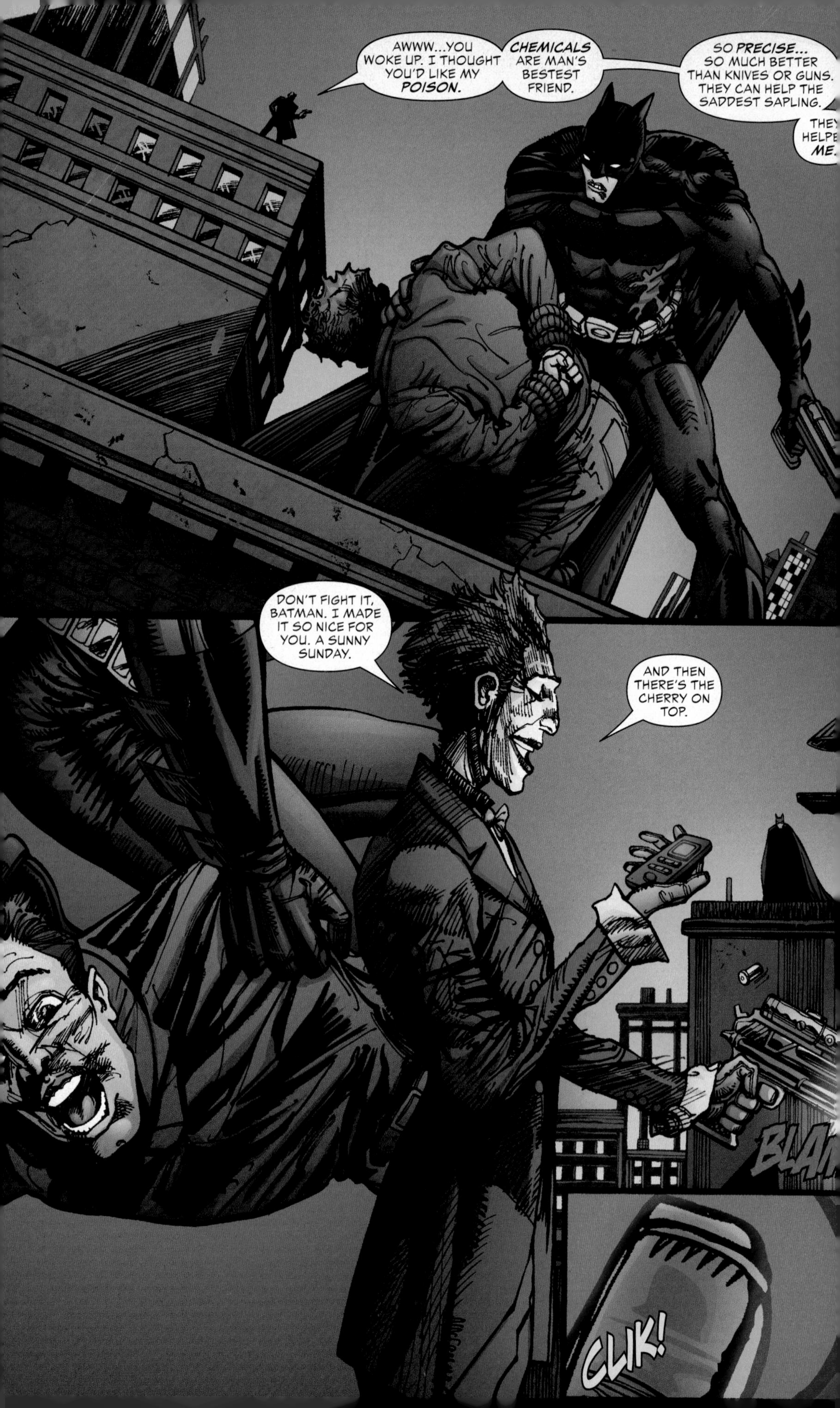

AWWW...YOU WOKE UP. I THOUGHT YOU'D LIKE MY POISON.
CHEMICALS ARE MAN'S BESTEST FRIEND.
SO PRECISE... SO MUCH BETTER THAN KNIVES OR GUNS. THEY CAN HELP THE SADDEST SAPLING.
DON'T FIGHT IT, BATMAN. I MADE IT SO NICE FOR YOU. A SUNNY SUNDAY.
AND THEN THERE'S THE CHERRY ON TOP.
CLIK!

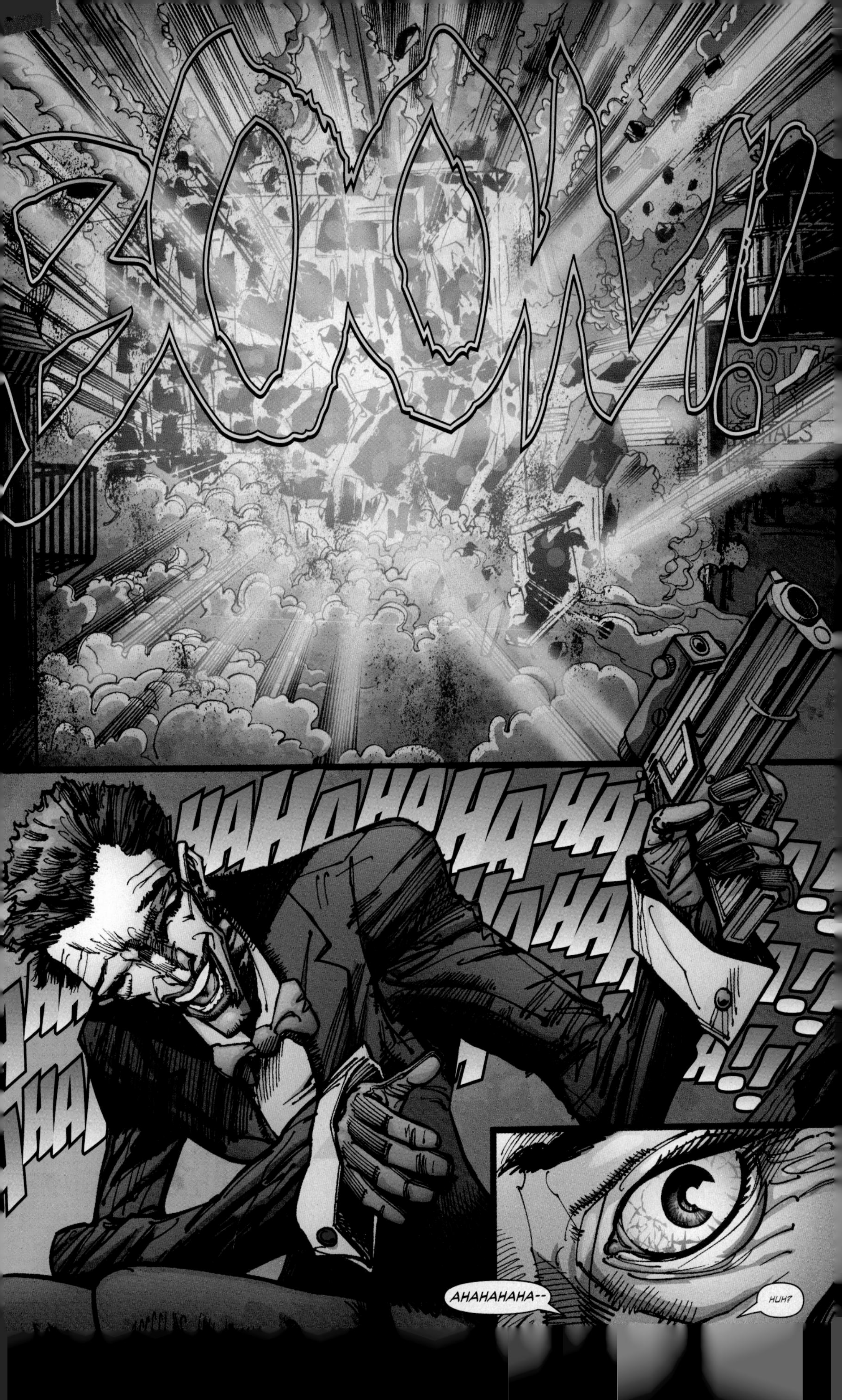

BOOOM!!
HAHAHAHAHA!!
AHAHAHAHA--
HUH?

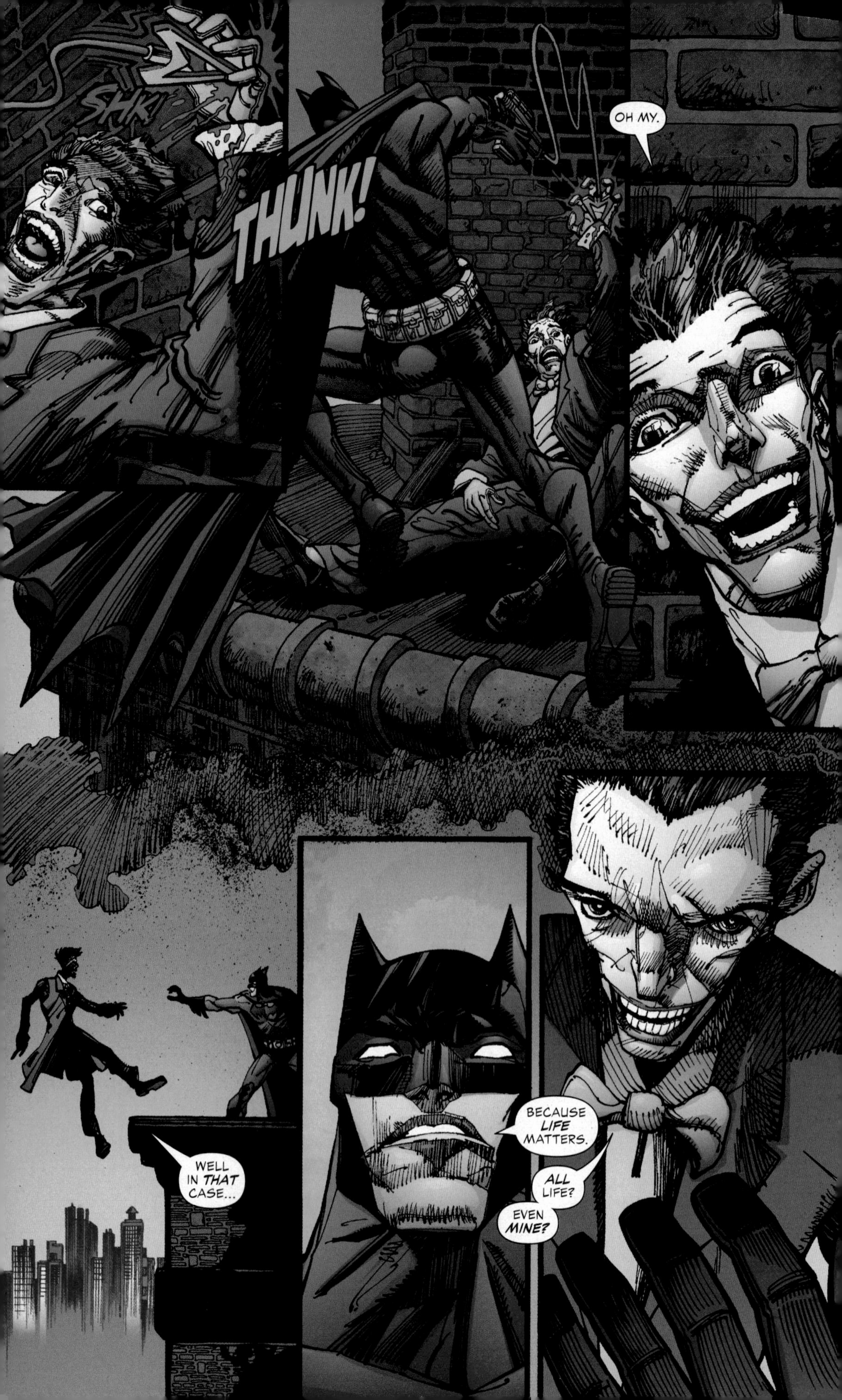
SHK!
THUNK!
OH MY.
WELL IN THAT CASE...
BECAUSE LIFE MATTERS.
ALL LIFE?
EVEN MINE?

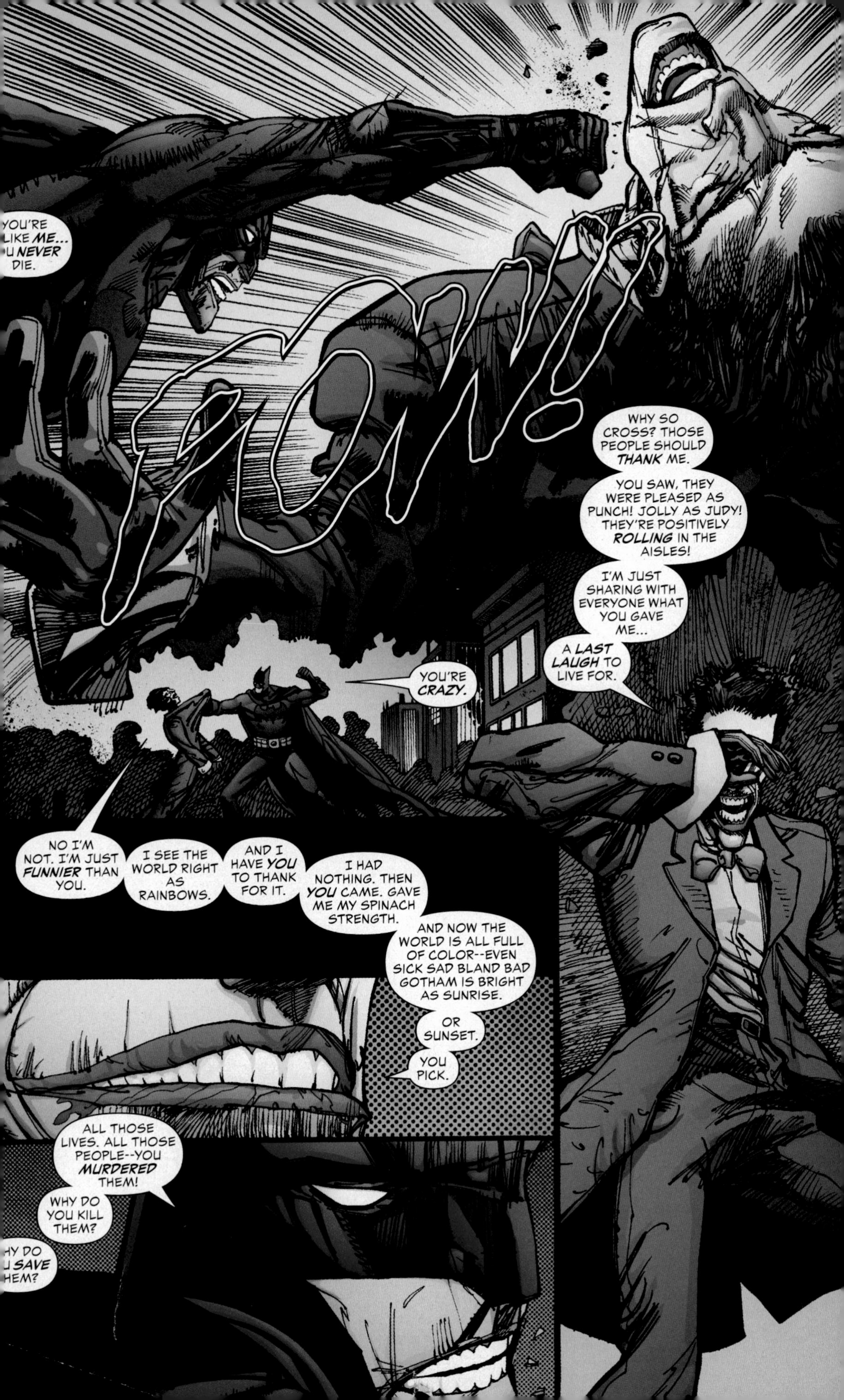
YOU'RE LIKE ME... U NEVER DIE.
POW!
WHY SO CROSS? THOSE PEOPLE SHOULD THANK ME.
YOU SAW, THEY WERE PLEASED AS PUNCH! JOLLY AS JUDY! THEY'RE POSITIVELY ROLLING IN THE AISLES!
I'M JUST SHARING WITH EVERYONE WHAT YOU GAVE ME...
A LAST LAUGH TO LIVE FOR.
YOU'RE CRAZY.
NO I'M NOT. I'M JUST FUNNIER THAN YOU.
I SEE THE WORLD RIGHT AS RAINBOWS.
AND I HAVE YOU TO THANK FOR IT.
I HAD NOTHING. THEN YOU CAME. GAVE ME MY SPINACH STRENGTH.
AND NOW THE WORLD IS ALL FULL OF COLOR--EVEN SICK SAD BLAND BAD GOTHAM IS BRIGHT AS SUNRISE.
OR SUNSET.
YOU PICK.
ALL THOSE LIVES. ALL THOSE PEOPLE--YOU MURDERED THEM!
WHY DO YOU KILL THEM?
HY DO U SAVE HEM?

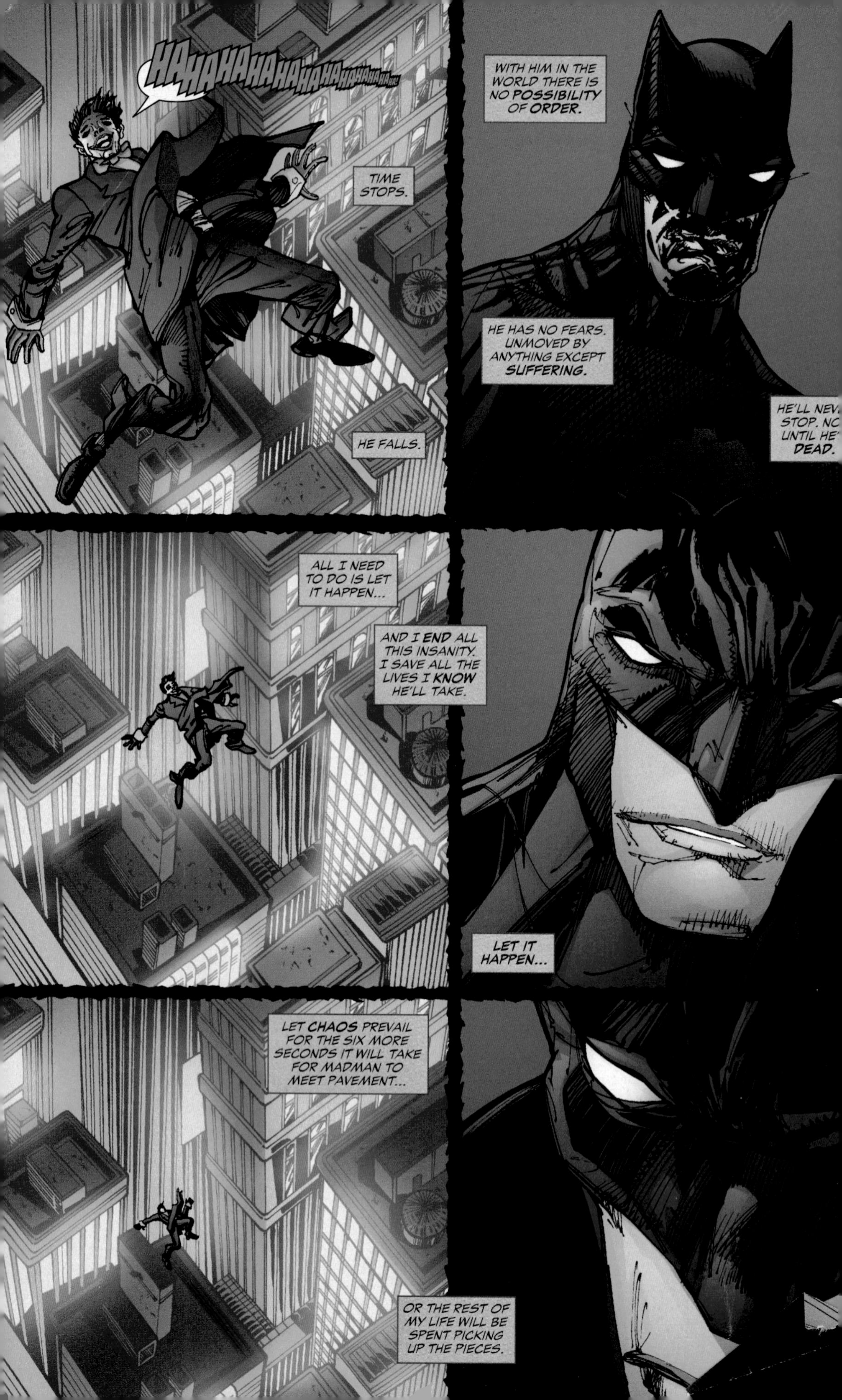

HAHAHAHAHAHAHAHAHAHAHAHAHA!
TIME STOPS.
HE FALLS.
WITH HIM IN THE WORLD THERE IS NO POSSIBILITY OF ORDER.
HE HAS NO FEARS. UNMOVED BY ANYTHING EXCEPT SUFFERING.
HE'LL NEV STOP. NC UNTIL HE' DEAD.
ALL I NEED TO DO IS LET IT HAPPEN...
AND I END ALL THIS INSANITY. I SAVE ALL THE LIVES I KNOW HE'LL TAKE.
LET IT HAPPEN...
LET CHAOS PREVAIL FOR THE SIX MORE SECONDS IT WILL TAKE FOR MADMAN TO MEET PAVEMENT...
OR THE REST OF MY LIFE WILL BE SPENT PICKING UP THE PIECES.

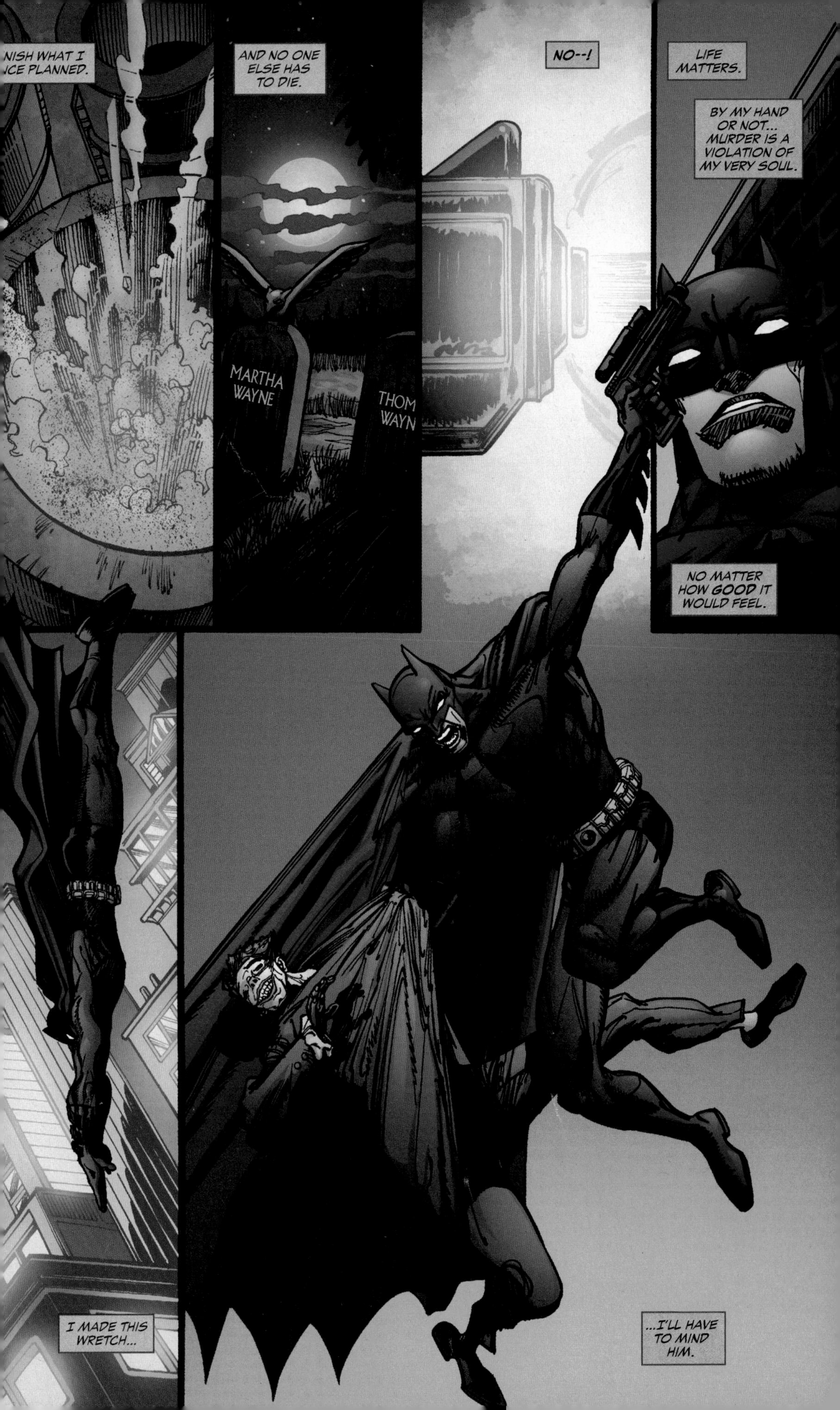
NISH WHAT I
ICE PLANNED.
AND NO ONE ELSE HAS TO DIE.
MARTHA WAYNE
THOM WAYN
NO--!
LIFE MATTERS.
BY MY HAND OR NOT... MURDER IS A VIOLATION OF MY VERY SOUL.
NO MATTER HOW GOOD IT WOULD FEEL.
I MADE THIS WRETCH...
...I'LL HAVE TO MIND HIM.

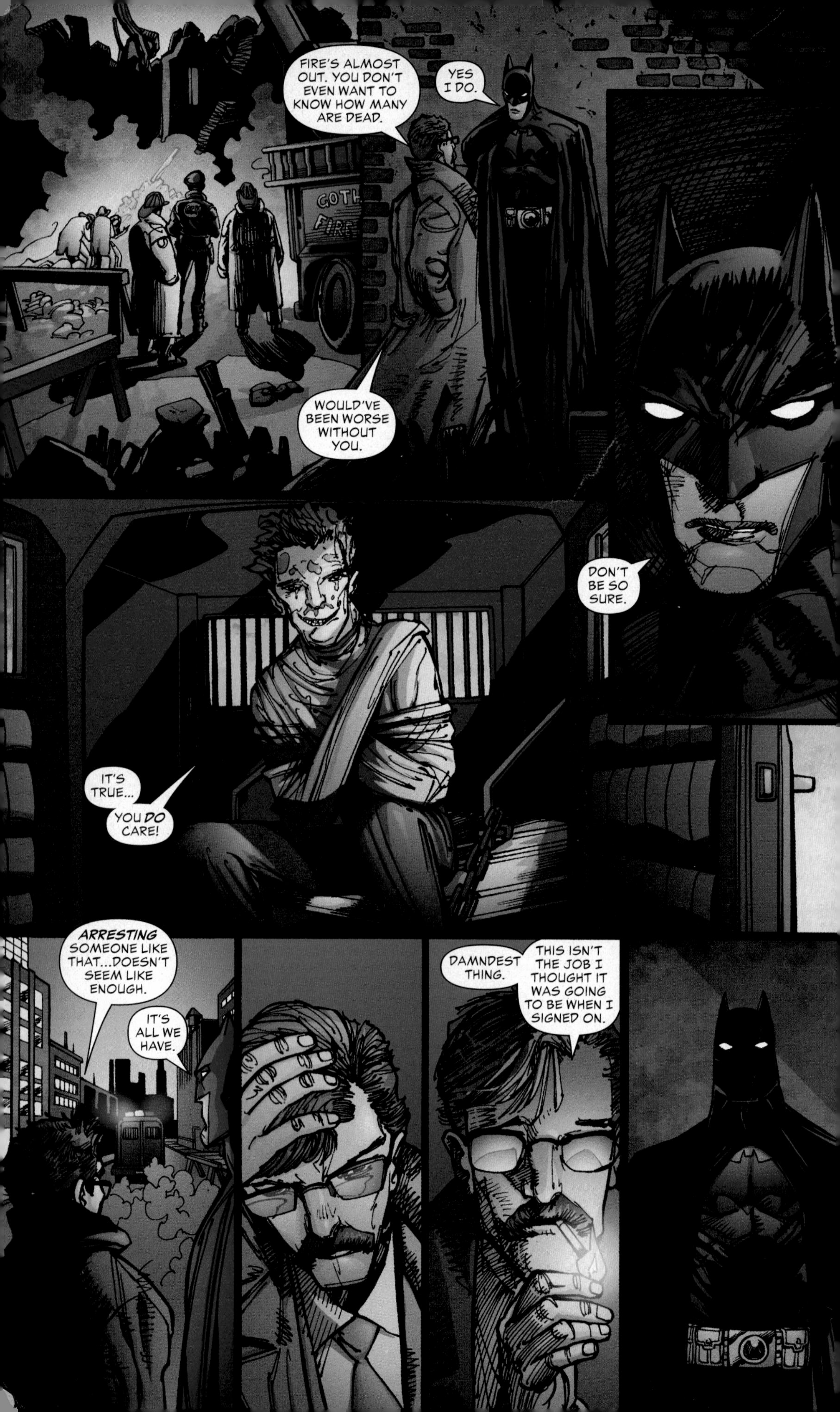
FIRE'S ALMOST OUT. YOU DON'T EVEN WANT TO KNOW HOW MANY ARE DEAD.
YES I DO.
GOTH
FIRE
WOULD'VE BEEN WORSE WITHOUT YOU.
DON'T BE SO SURE.
IT'S TRUE...
YOU DO CARE!
ARRESTING SOMEONE LIKE THAT...DOESN'T SEEM LIKE ENOUGH.
IT'S ALL WE HAVE.
DAMNDEST THING.
THIS ISN'T THE JOB I THOUGHT IT WAS GOING TO BE WHEN I SIGNED ON.

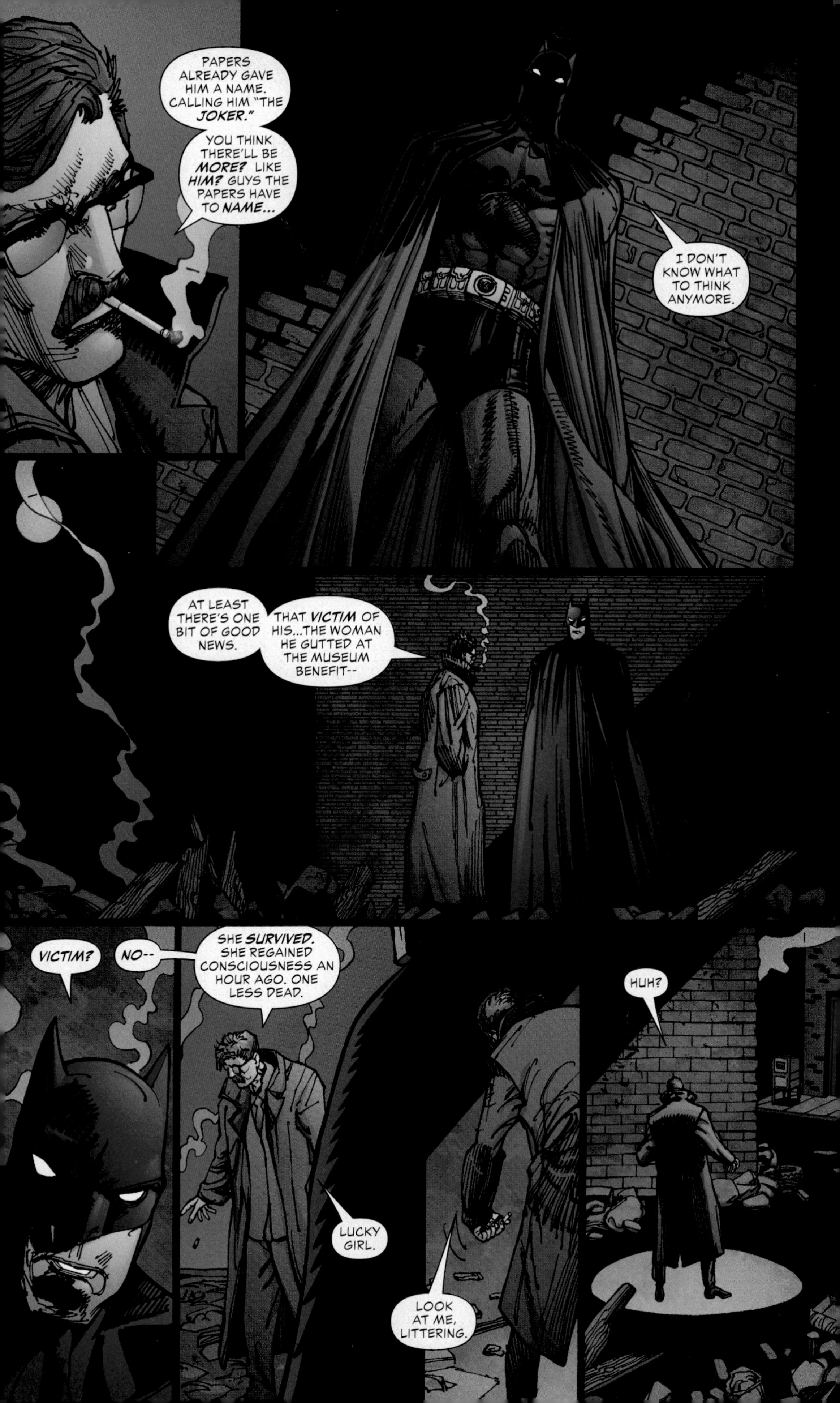
PAPERS ALREADY GAVE HIM A NAME. CALLING HIM "THE JOKER."
YOU THINK THERE'LL BE MORE? LIKE HIM? GUYS THE PAPERS HAVE TO NAME...
I DON'T KNOW WHAT TO THINK ANYMORE.
AT LEAST THERE'S ONE BIT OF GOOD NEWS.
THAT VICTIM OF HIS...THE WOMAN HE GUTTED AT THE MUSEUM BENEFIT--
VICTIM?
NO--
SHE SURVIVED. SHE REGAINED CONSCIOUSNESS AN HOUR AGO. ONE LESS DEAD.
LUCKY GIRL.
LOOK AT ME, LITTERING.
HUH?

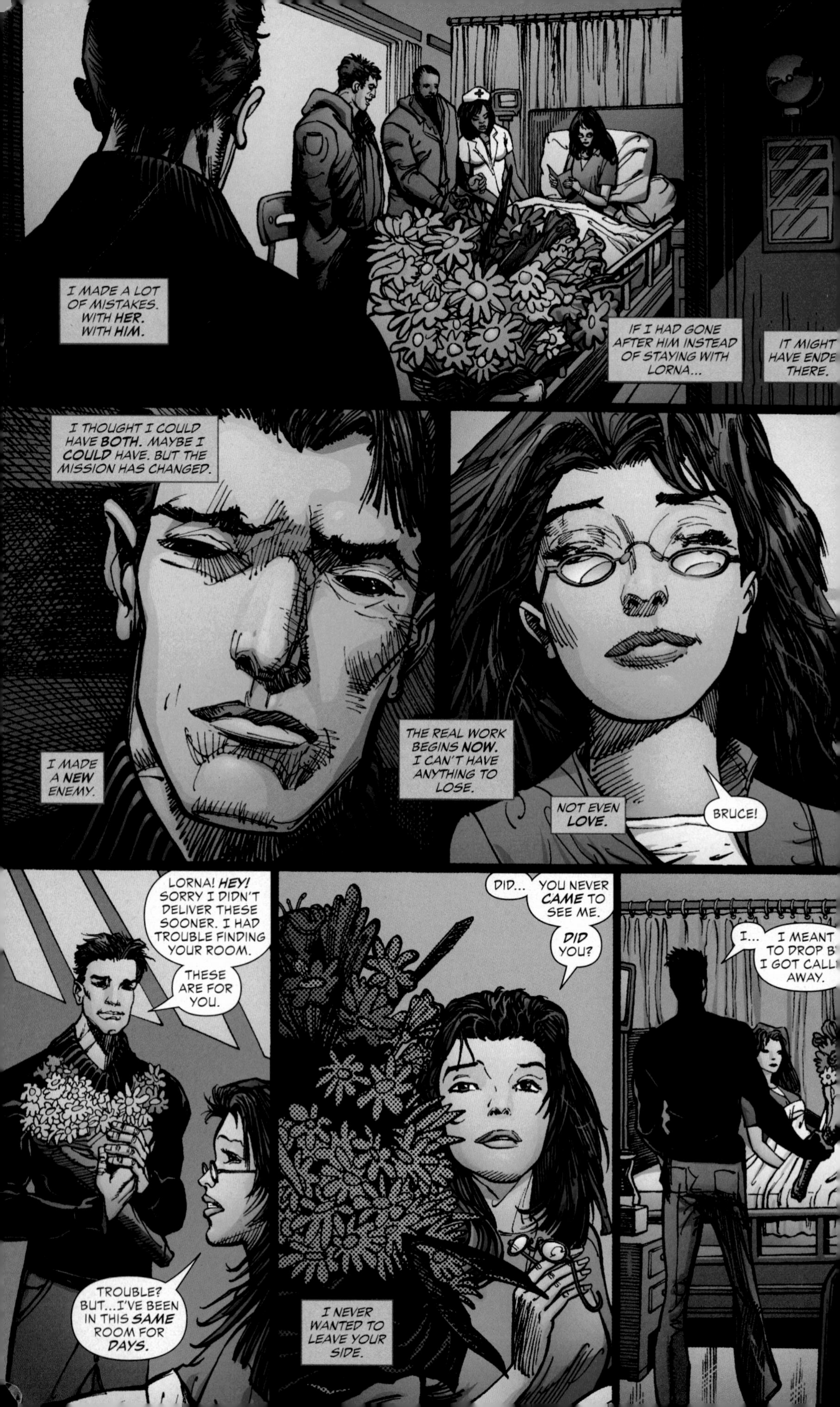

I MADE A LOT OF MISTAKES. WITH HER. WITH HIM.
IF I HAD GONE AFTER HIM INSTEAD OF STAYING WITH LORNA...
IT MIGHT HAVE ENDE THERE.
I THOUGHT I COULD HAVE BOTH. MAYBE I COULD HAVE. BUT THE MISSION HAS CHANGED.
I MADE A NEW ENEMY.
THE REAL WORK BEGINS NOW. I CAN'T HAVE ANYTHING TO LOSE.
NOT EVEN LOVE.
BRUCE!
LORNA! HEY! SORRY I DIDN'T DELIVER THESE SOONER. I HAD TROUBLE FINDING YOUR ROOM.
THESE ARE FOR YOU.
TROUBLE? BUT...I'VE BEEN IN THIS SAME ROOM FOR DAYS.
DID...
YOU NEVER CAME TO SEE ME.
DID YOU?
I NEVER WANTED TO LEAVE YOUR SIDE.
I...
I MEANT TO DROP B I GOT CALL AWAY.

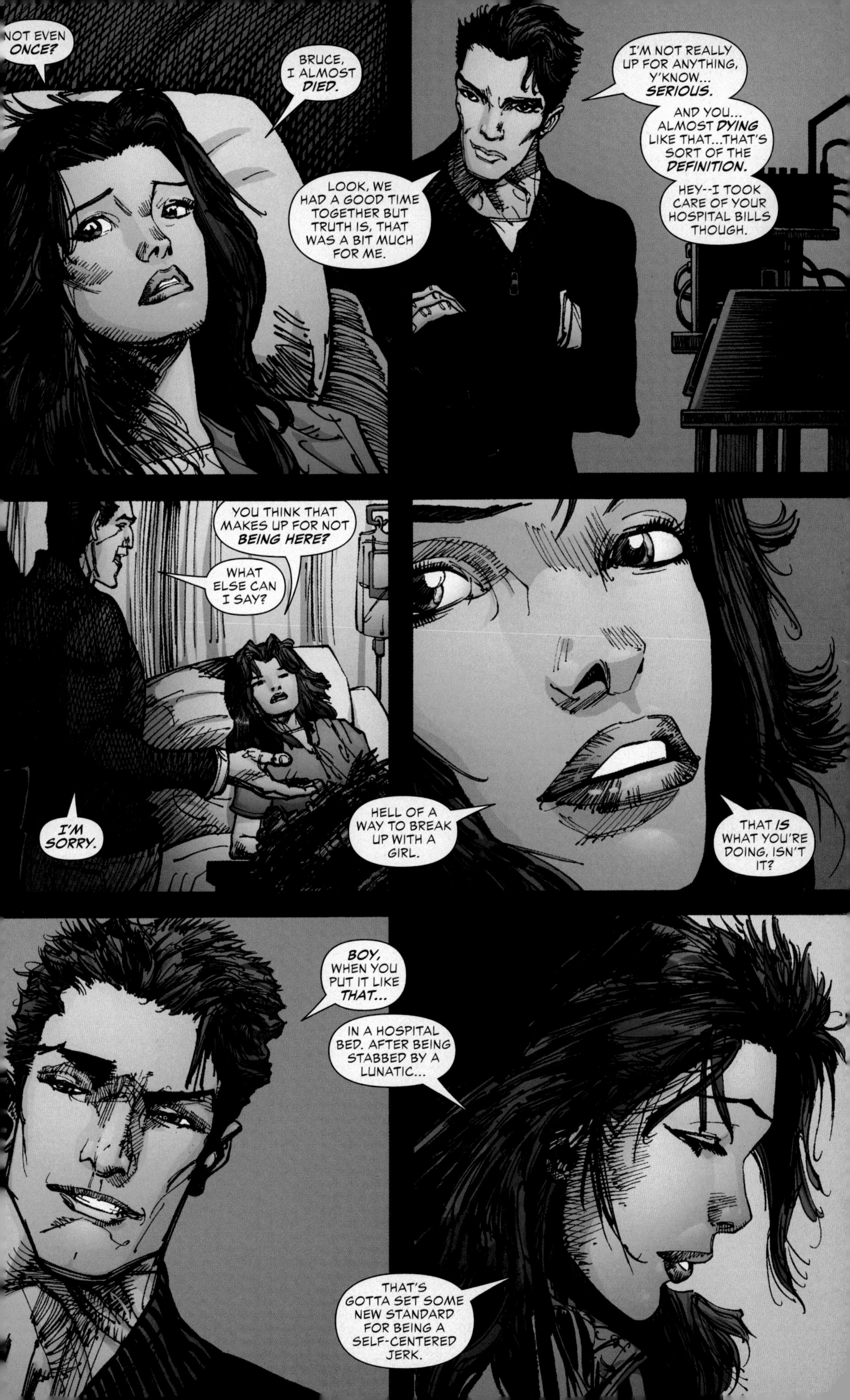
NOT EVEN ONCE?
BRUCE, I ALMOST DIED.
LOOK, WE HAD A GOOD TIME TOGETHER BUT TRUTH IS, THAT WAS A BIT MUCH FOR ME.
I'M NOT REALLY UP FOR ANYTHING, Y'KNOW... SERIOUS.
AND YOU... ALMOST DYING LIKE THAT...THAT'S SORT OF THE DEFINITION.
HEY--I TOOK CARE OF YOUR HOSPITAL BILLS THOUGH.
YOU THINK THAT MAKES UP FOR NOT BEING HERE?
WHAT ELSE CAN I SAY?
I'M SORRY.
HELL OF A WAY TO BREAK UP WITH A GIRL.
THAT IS WHAT YOU'RE DOING, ISN'T IT?
BOY, WHEN YOU PUT IT LIKE THAT...
IN A HOSPITAL BED. AFTER BEING STABBED BY A LUNATIC...
THAT'S GOTTA SET SOME NEW STANDARD FOR BEING A SELF-CENTERED JERK.

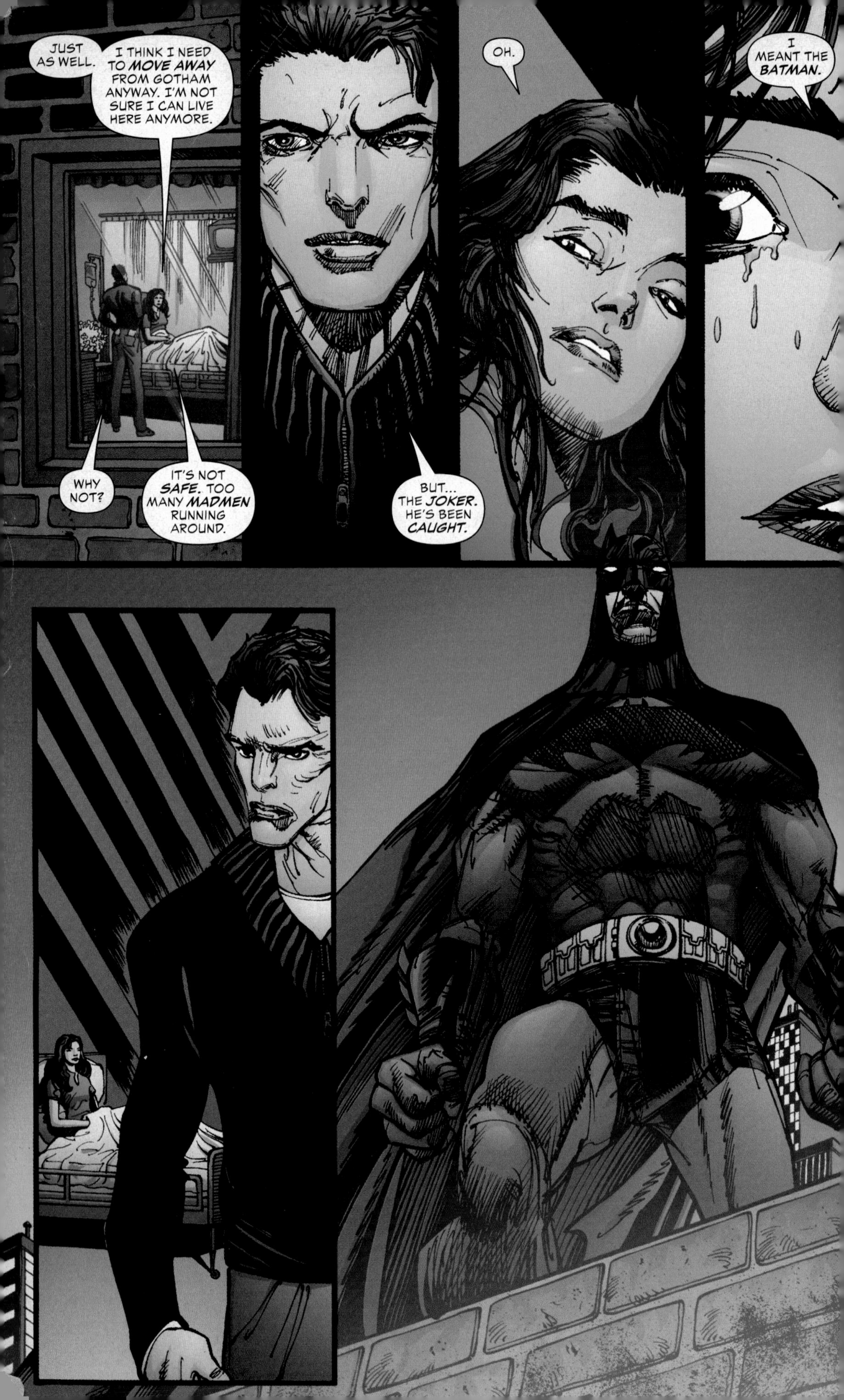
JUST AS WELL.
I THINK I NEED TO MOVE AWAY FROM GOTHAM ANYWAY. I'M NOT SURE I CAN LIVE HERE ANYMORE.
WHY NOT?
IT'S NOT SAFE. TOO MANY MADMEN RUNNING AROUND.
BUT... THE JOKER. HE'S BEEN CAUGHT.
OH.
I MEANT THE BATMAN.

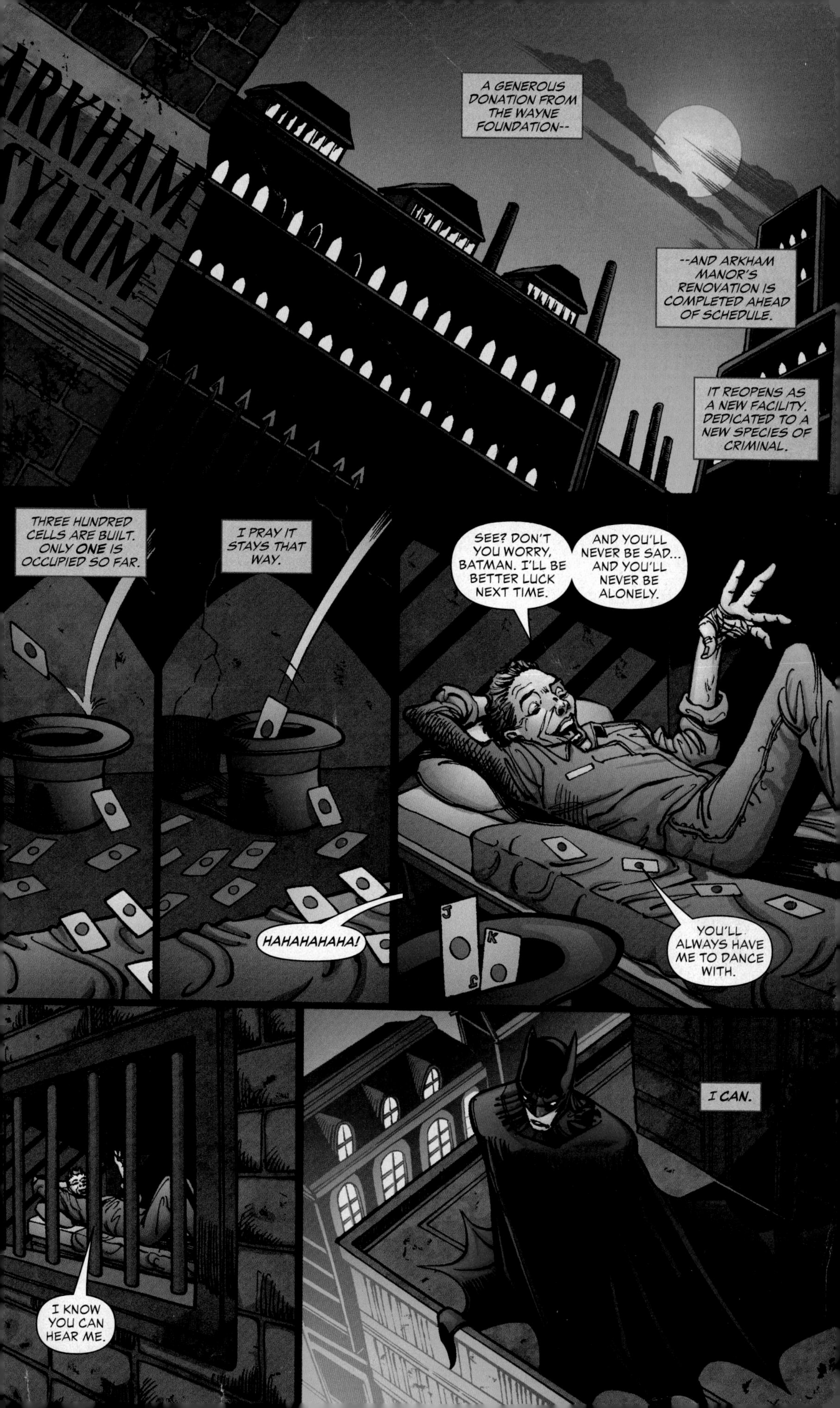
ARKHAM ASYLUM
A GENEROUS DONATION FROM THE WAYNE FOUNDATION--
--AND ARKHAM MANOR'S RENOVATION IS COMPLETED AHEAD OF SCHEDULE.
IT REOPENS AS A NEW FACILITY. DEDICATED TO A NEW SPECIES OF CRIMINAL.
THREE HUNDRED CELLS ARE BUILT. ONLY ONE IS OCCUPIED SO FAR.
I PRAY IT STAYS THAT WAY.
HAHAHAHAHA!
SEE? DON'T YOU WORRY, BATMAN. I'LL BE BETTER LUCK NEXT TIME.
AND YOU'LL NEVER BE SAD... AND YOU'LL NEVER BE ALONELY.
YOU'LL ALWAYS HAVE ME TO DANCE WITH.
I KNOW YOU CAN HEAR ME.
I CAN.

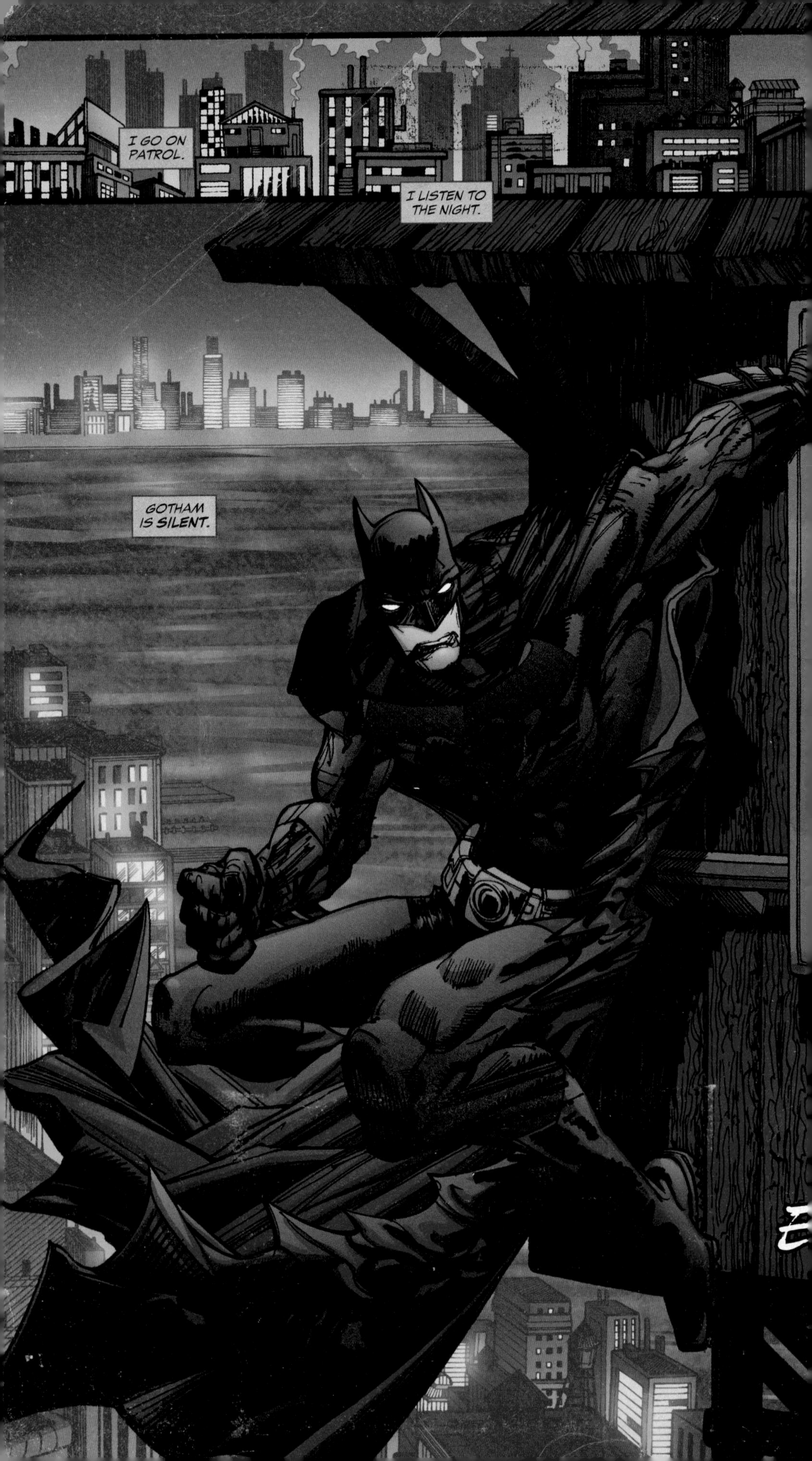
I GO ON PATROL.
I LISTEN TO THE NIGHT.
GOTHAM IS SILENT.